Tony Lopez is an English poet of international repute. He was born in Stockwell in 1950 and grew up in Brixton, South London. He began work by writing fiction for newspapers and magazines, and published five crime and science fiction novels before going to university at Essex and then Cambridge. He has received awards from the Wingate Foundation, the Society of Authors, the Arts and Humanities Research Council, and Arts Council England. His poetry is featured in *The Art of the Sonnet* (Harvard University Press), *Twentieth-Century British and Irish Poetry* (Oxford University Press), *Vanishing Points: New Modernist Poems* (Salt), *The Reality Street Book of Sonnets* (Reality Street), *Other: British and Irish Poetry since 1970* (Wesleyan University Press), and *Conductors of Chaos* (Picador). His critical writings are collected in *Meaning Performance: Essays on Poetry* (Salt) and *The Poetry of W.S. Graham* (Edinburgh University Press). He taught for many years at the University of Plymouth, where he was appointed the first Professor of Poetry. He is married with two grown up children and lives in Exmouth in Devon.

Also by Tony Lopez

False Memory (new edition), Shearsman, 2012
Darwin, Acts of Language, 2009
Poetry & Public Language (co-edited with Anthony Caleshu), Shearsman Books, 2007
Covers, Salt, 2007
Meaning Performance: Essays on Poetry, Salt, 2006
Equal Signs, Equipage, 2004
False Memory, Salt, 2003
Devolution, The Figures, 2000
Data Shadow, Reality Street, 2000
False Memory, The Figures, 1996
Negative Equity, Equipage, 1995
Stress Management, Boldface Press, 1994
A Theory of Surplus Labour, Curiously Strong, 1990
The Poetry of W.S. Graham, Edinburgh University Press, 1989
Abstract & Delicious, Secret Books, 1982
A Handbook of British Birds, Pig Press, 1982
The English Disease, Skyline Press, 1978
Change, New London Pride, 1978
Snapshots, Oasis, 1976

Only More So

Tony Lopez

Shearsman Books

First published in the United Kingdom in 2012 by
Shearsman Books
50 Westons Hill Drive
Emersons Green
Bristol
BS16 7DF

http://www.shearsman.com/

ISBN 978-1-84861-188-7

North American publication by
The University of New Orleans Publishing (UNO Press),
Isbn 978-1-60801-057-8, 2011.

The author acknowledges support from Arts Council England
for the composition of this book

LOTTERY FUNDED

Contents

Acknowledgements

My grateful thanks to the editors and publishers who have presented excerpts and earlier versions of these poems in print and web journals as follows: *Argotist Online*, Jeffrey Side; *Dispatx: Eminent Domain*, David Stent; *Ekleksographia: after Oulipo*, Philip Terry and Jesse Glass; *Practice: New Writing + Art*, Susan Tichy and Adrian Lurssen; *Salt Magazine*, John Kinsella and Chris Hamilton-Emery; *Wobbling Roof*, Paul Belbusti. Poems appeared in the anthologies *Text 2*, edited by Tony Trehy (Bury Museum and Art Gallery, 2009) and *Another Language: Poetic Experiments in Britain and North America*, edited by Kornelia Freitag and Katharina Vester (Berlin: LIT Verlag, 2009). Larry Lynch published section three as *Darwin* (Dartington: Acts of Language, 2009), a beautiful little book. I was invited to read work in progress from this project at 'Authorship and the Turn to Language', Schloss Hohentübingen, Eberhard Karls University Tübingen, Germany, December 2005 (organised by Barrett Watten and Bernd Engler); at 'Long Poems: Major Forms', University of Sussex, May 2008 (organised by Michael Kindellan, Richard Parker, Gareth Farmer and Alex Pestell); at 'PW10' Arnolfini Gallery, Bristol, May 2010 (organised by Larry Lynch and Jerome Fletcher); and at 'A Colloquy of Poets' at the University of Hull, November 2010 (organised by Martin Goodman). John Hall, Robert Hampson, Peter Manson and Rod Mengham have helped this work along. I'm delighted to have the opportunity thank these poets, artists, editors, publishers and arts entrepreneurs for their commitment and support. My grateful thanks also to Arts Council England for an award in 2010, which enabled me to travel for research and to write full time to finish this book.

for Lucy and Tom

The Hawthorne Effect

We don't live in that universe. A person without memory struggles to maintain an identity. Links to images, sounds, or other external content have been blocked. Make coffee at home. Probably that was a mistake in the penguin. Boards creaked upstairs. We worked on an exit strategy after lunch. It disappeared in the 1930s, merging with American Sign Language. Tom Stoppard charms Tracey Emin and Andrew Marr. Not worth the price of a deck chair. How many of London's urban foxes suffer from hearing problems? Repeat prescription. You begin to read detailed memories of alien abduction. White phosphorous is officially an incendiary not a chemical weapon. On Saturday, I would take my pocket money to Brixton arcade. And then, trembling before the threat of some looming catastrophe as real as anything in present time, I would freeze in fear. The additive process always makes little shifts.

My finger, bruised and deadened after being slammed in the car door, felt as if I was wearing a plaster. They could have abandoned the ruins and reconstructed the city elsewhere, they could have rebuilt it just as it was, or built it again in the same place with wide streets and open plazas. Bad theories have a short life. In the saturated markets of Western Europe, most people already have a phone. They went across the river and into the trees. Blair's pre-announced retirement was alien to our constitutional arrangements. The elements were dusty and the picture seemed to ignore our little craft. She was riding in her own train. Models of manly behaviour return to enjoy the freedom of evening. Christmas package brochures always focus on the fireplace. Seventeen road deaths a day in Italy, the victims are mostly young males. I was anxious finding my way from the frontier queue back to the hired car parked for the day. A small cottage with thick cob walls and a slate roof: an English adobe. Darwin wrote about the mystery of the "tangled bank". Patrols lasting several months are routine.

"Day and night cannot dwell together", said Chief Seattle. Intelligence is a property of living systems. Public opinion is swinging after the hurricane season. The Emperor and Empress wished their children to experience the ordinary things in life, like riding a bicycle. There were broken fragments of a house still standing in the bombsite that began close to Stockwell tube. As you move westwards in England the rocks get progressively older until you come to Wales where their age is 570 million years. Many of these languages, like the one used on Martha's Vineyard in the nineteenth century, died out before being studied. We have taken a second path that leads into the post-modern world. The sound is air-conditioned white noise. It was a device of exquisite sensitivity, which discovered pesticide residues in all living creatures, from penguins in Antarctica to nursing mothers in the USA. Two goldcrests worked their way over the golden yew trees. Soft light shined through translucent stone in the Beinecke. A gurnard for dinner. Pick up long pointed leaves under the Torbay palm, too tough for the flymo.

Woven cloth, partly covered with black coating, shiny and dull in patches, mostly worn off; and pink card showing through the weave. Although there is evidence of meaning-negotiation, very few learners take part in this process. Little slivers of zest. My mother told me she rejected thalidomide as a treatment for morning sickness. Dogs, cats and horses were used in less than 1% of last year's experimental procedures. Sugar is not a vegetable. To test the stability of this more complex model, we subjected it to periodic catastrophes. You have to approach each new thing with indifference, as if you had no aesthetic emotion. Without radar we wouldn't have made it.

When you torture people you get bad information. My present was a big yellow taxi. It was a formal decomposition: linear elements followed each other like parallels and distorted the object. More "Brainless in Brooklyn" than *Sleepless in Seattle* if you get my drift. A new juvenile body buds off and swims away. Go ahead: call it a comeback. After the Lisbon earthquake they rebuilt the city with wide streets and open plazas, using a framework of crossed wooden beams and metal tie bars to resist future shocks. An early morning drive to the East End docks. The Pope is breathing on his own but has been told not to speak. Boscastle pixie shop was washed away in the flood. The hunt rode out with a full pack of hounds. Each sentence is complete; it gives pleasure every day, every other day. In practical science, bad theories have a short life. They were magnetic, disagreeable, yet strangely sympathetic characters.

Phoenicians lived on the coast in today's Lebanon, north of Israel, and invented alphabetic writing. How are we to resist the fear-mongering rhetoric of the far right? The first man in Chicago to ride a bicycle, first to have his portrait painted by Whistler. They are jagged paths to multicultural education. Imagine a whole planet system, using the active processes of plants and animals as component parts. You recognise a total absence of good or bad taste. Animals can still be starved, slowly poisoned, burned, deliberately infected, maimed, electrocuted and brain damaged in the name of research. A toy tank transporter carried the latest and most powerful tank. A person without identity struggles to maintain a memory. Remember when domestic violence was a familiar experience. Buying land is a real statement of intent. Think of a sentence peacefully. We are creating and sustaining scarcity.

The mountains are temples of living dharma. If hot coffee (for instance) is poured into a plastic cup, animal derived chemicals come to the surface and combine with the drink. Home sign isn't handed down; it's re-invented each time it's needed. A squirrel runs across the windowsill and down the lower roof. A town in Ukraine, near the reactor, was abandoned for nearly twenty years. The head teacher took my hand at the zebra crossing on Stockwell road. A luxury cruise ship called *Spirit* is under rocket attack from pirates, one hundred miles off the coast of Somalia. Winston Churchill liked to get his decisions down on paper. The car was parked beyond the pedestrian border crossing, back in the first world.

There are sixty errors that affect the sense in each new edition. How do you feel about soft touch plastic? Google noticed the priority of links people built up and the text gathered around those links: think about it. This black British farmer never saw the countryside until he was eighteen. The air is invisible, almost intangible, unless you look at it from space. Condensation obscures the landscape. Twenty-eight thousand French cars burnt in small-scale riots. Feeling mostly content with form. Schwitters could no longer move around the column to work, it took over his living space. The moon had been made to jump over the cow in a world of superabundance and excess.

Most music critics ignore musical anxiety. She received a box from Iraq, filled with her son's belongings. Intelligent design posits that nature cannot explain life's complexity. Shoes piled under a radiator, coats hang above. Horizontal movements of the pelvis during walking are more complex than vertical movements, since they involve both rotation and tilt. I'm sweeping wet leaves when a white van stops and the driver offers tree pruning. What would happen if a machine admitted the possibility of accident or non-repetition; are these exclusively human attributes? We are looking for a middle ground between family therapy and legal bargaining.

Whalers crossing the Atlantic exploited the Gulf Stream before Benjamin Franklin mapped it in 1769. The French word means "hobby-horse" or "rocking-horse"; in German it denotes "baby-talk". Cover with foil and bake for an hour. My father holds me, wrapped up in the dark cinema, and we watch buildings burn on screen over the heads and shoulders of people in front. A starling imitates the sound of a refrigerator. Air spirals in towards the hurricane's eye, picking up energy from the warm sea. Individuals ought to have the right to manage their own memories. These strands are sometimes woven into braids and populated by strings and knots, evidence of gravitational tugs from unseen moons. The baby suffered two recent head injuries. We focus to a hand on a wrist, taking the pulse.

They no longer had access to the land. Two southward flows can be distinguished because they travel at different depths. This was a narcissistic style-centred glossy. Going to Electric Avenue for a family visit. Participants were asked to suggest adjectives and thus help to establish a common vocabulary. The end of the room was blown off: wallpaper, fireplace, windows, light fittings, broken laths and plaster, bricks, were suspended in the air. The density of dark energy should have faded faster with time. Blackbirds moved in the courtyard: running and then stopping to listen. It's your watch that says most about who you are. The grip pushes the dolly on a war movie set in 1916. We all uphold and participate in the false consciousness called "the market" and "the real world".

Mistaken for a penguin. Other companies feared being disintermediated. "Affective computing" is the attempt to design software that can recognise and align with user's emotional states. The Little Ice Age lasted sporadically from 1300 to 1850 and produced temperatures low enough to freeze the Thames in London. Who will do anything in sculpture better than a propeller? Newton spent much of his time trying to discover hidden messages in the Bible and attempting to turn lead into gold.

Carol Thatcher, queen of the jungle, wins *I'm a Celebrity*. Giving notice to his tenants in the flat above, he knocked out the ceiling, and allowed the growing column to spread along the upper floor. World War One saw a massive increase in smoking; the British Army marched on Woodbines. Previous sorties into the outbreak zone failed to find the virus source. A hundredweight of coal poured down the chute from the street. String theory has yet to make contact with the empirical universe. It was a good day when the head teacher took my hand at the crossing on the way to school. Running below the frost line on the beach. Lenin's slogan: "Education, education and education!" was implemented in Russia on a grand scale; the party employed the intelligentsia to work on Stalinist myth. Stress-induced memory boost is a mechanism evolved for survival.

Laura is a virtual fitness-trainer with carefully honed social skills. This behaviour is an emergent property of the flock. The sound was quite clear when the rat was happy and close by. A person who watches a bad thing happen and does not try to oppose it. For most workers, training is a chance to get away from the desk and eat biscuits. The North Atlantic warmed substantially during the 1990s, although that trend seems now to have halted. A driver fell asleep at the wheel of his car, which tumbled onto the track in front of a 125 express train.

They learned to keep their mouths shut. Not many guests made use of self-service parking. The Monday night soup run is on. Statements that may now appear outdated, naive or self-evident. In those days aerospace plants were moving into San Bernardino.

Loading fresh water into the ocean surface making it less dense and so preventing it from sinking. At fifteen or sixteen weeks babies' lungs lack enough surfactant to breathe unassisted. Signs were everywhere in the trenches; battalions had their own specialised sign writers. You get more false positives when searching for a common word or phrase. Space itself has inherent energy.

A painted forest scene extended all round the interior of the high tower. The idea is to use cognitive radio capable of sensing the spectral environment. We learned to keep our mouths shut and stay quiet in bed. I watched him guide his scissors neatly round the refrigerator. As they get smaller, quantum dots emit light in colours that shift towards spectrum blue. Because they are able to charge high rates throughout the country, credit card companies can afford to issue cards to those with limited ability to repay. Building blocks are not symbolic representations of quantity; they are quantity. The soup run extends into literature.

Compensation paid to thalidomide victims is currently subject to UK income tax. Pressure falls as thunderstorms grow bigger and start to merge. This process of making new pathways that override old ones is called extinction. Newly hatched butterflies are released into planted habitat with climate control, visitor walkways and carefully sited feeding tubes. Each year, corporate data storage grows by fifty percent. *Zorro* isn't going to break any new ground. There was a photo of my father in khaki uniform with his folded army beret tucked into an epaulette, and black brylcreemed hair. Without struggle there is no identity. The feel of consumer products is vital to their commercial success, and industry has long wanted to measure people's response to materials.

Schwitters was obliged to flee from the Nazi regime to Norway, where he settled for four years before moving to London. Most people believe in paranormal phenomena. Some strive to recreate the family they left and others make sure that their family will be nothing like the previous one. I heard there was a vast indigo library of dreams. Brownian motion is not completely random, as Einstein predicted, because fluid inertia makes particle trajectories more predictable than previously expected. Rain forest began to be reconstructed under glass. Air is an unstable mixture that is somehow kept constant in composition; something must be regulating it, and life at the surface is surely involved. In newly diabetic mice the results were spectacular: blood glucose fell to normal levels.

Today the House of Lords ruled that evidence gained by torture, from wherever it comes, is not admissible in British courts. We have a room full of people writing dialogue for digital agents. The job is to smile cheerily in front of the weather map predicting the future. They began to substitute the word "invest" for "spend" in statements and interviews. Still in their pyjamas and dressing gowns, passengers were instructed to assemble in the main restaurant; at least three rockets hit the ship. A particular kind of loss is involved, one caught up in the experience of humiliation and defeat.

The air we breathe, the ocean and the rocks are all either products of living organisms or else modified by their presence. "A photo portrait of John Cage, wearing denim, New York, 1991"; this is a fragment and you should consider revising it. In Hispaniola birds, which have been isolated for longer, the anti-cuckoo patterns have almost faded away. I thought I could cut out drawings of aeroplanes and get small models; I was baffled and frustrated when they did not snap into three dimensions. Building began in exhausted china clay pits near St Austell in Cornwall. You collect edges and blue bits that make the sky, you do not think about the assembled picture until you get a good chunk of it together.

The chalk cliffs of Dover are one gigantic pile of shells. The London ambulance service reported that thirty-five people were treated for knife wounds on New Year's Eve, 2005. For years before that and after, my radio was my constant companion. There must be fractures in the fabric of space-time. The coalman passes with his horse and boy. A young mother in a black dress clutches the hand of her blonde three-year-old as they stand in a field of poppies. He was a former intelligence informer. Financial deprivation is not a matter of abstract income comparisons but is directly experienced as financial anxiety. The middle of a mature living tree is dead wood with just a thin skin of living tissue around the circumference. Interfering echoes visible on a radar screen are caused by reflection from objects other than the target.

Feeling content with form, I tried extension. Belief is the most challenging of human faculties. A bad thing happened to me in the archive in 2005, now I internalise envy and hatred to give it a new shape. Each capsule contains 80 mg of the active ingredient, *propanolol hydrochloride*, in a slow release formulation. The work is fully composed out of myriad particulars into unexpected simplicity. Combining the two instruments' data will help isolate the confounding effects of atmospheric dust. Bullying and hatred is the norm in closed institutions. From these basic principles, reality unfurls.

We found large hand tools including turfing irons, trenching spades, long straw-cutters, and a fine assortment of wheeled seed drills and hoes. Periodic fires, set by electrical storms, swept through savannah. The cold war fuelled developments in artificial intelligence. For the first few months, I saw TV in vivid colour (I remember watching *Superman*) no one told me it was black and white. A long-term virtual companion will cheer you up and give support as you manage chronic disease. She was riding her own refrain. The surface is composed primarily of ejecta material from meteorite impact and volcanic debris. Kennedy, assassinated by his shadow cabinet, has lost the leadership at last. Meaning to drive or carry along with irresistible force, with a rapid continuous movement.

A sentence is quietly pleasing. A niche is the totality of factors to which a species has adapted and therefore describes its relations with other organisms. Poor diet, cramped conditions, and abnormal behaviour patterns all leave traces on the skeleton. The present state of our knowledge does not yet allow the entrance roof to be dated with certainty. The desk is in front of the window. Gas, water and electricity were cut off together and at different times because bills were unpaid. Turning from a depression into a storm and finally a hurricane as wind speeds pick up (see diagram opposite). The virus was moving into the bat population. I wrote my name on the wall in the shared bathroom on the landing downstairs from our rented rooms, my father was angry because I hadn't seen that I was sure to get caught.

Deep inferences will not often be main ideas. We no longer view attention to mechanics as interfering with higher-level processes. In early spring the oak forest bluebells and other woodland flowers bloom before the tree canopy closes and competition for sunlight reaches its peak. Opodo knows my prosody. A three-chunk inference is "The paper in front of the window". The low-skilled mother of two is assumed to have her first child at age 23, to take a nine-year employment break, and to spend twenty-one of her remaining thirty-five years employment in part-time jobs. What does this "Oh No" seem to know? The more species and interactions involved in a system, the more stable it becomes. This is an easy sentence and popular. Technical drawing.

Imagine a world with the present day arsenal of nuclear weapons but with no means of telecommunication. High productivity guarantees more biomass, not more species. Core processes become more robust and flexible over time. A female great white shark travelled 20,000 kilometres in nine months. Readings made at regular four-foot intervals showed a general but irregular fall in resistance values from east to west. People come and go like waves in the sea. Makers of fractal-shaped antennae hope to integrate wireless services into cars, cell phones and other devices. Something very threatening needs to be remembered. When radioactive rain fell on the hills and farms of the Lake District and North Wales, we decided to go home. The reader may well have been prepared to believe this without much argument. Children heard and repeated back series of sentences like the following. Oxford is a trademark of Oxford University Press.

If symptoms persist or anything unusual happens, talk to your doctor or pharmacist. Seals and pelicans are having their digital photos taken right now at La Jolla cove. The continents themselves are in motion, held at the surface by a fiery core. Although these are simulations of a lifetime they do not include the normal life-cycle elements of reproductive activity reducing full-time continuous employment, and generating spells on part-time rates of pay. The academy of the future opens its doors and current account. We are heading for the archive somewhat faster than expected.

Florida turned out to be a fine place for a terrorist to train. It has the organised, self-contained look of a live creature, full of information, marvellously skilled at handling the sun's energy. Sonar tends to cause mass strandings of whales and the northern bottlenose is a solitary animal. We flew over Dartmoor, over the Tamar, the china clay pits and tin mines of Cornwall. They hadn't really considered the power of positive thinking. I ran off with an Essex blonde, threw the TV through a window, it's all me, really. Both roofs include a superstructure employing collar beams, collar purlins, and crown posts above a cambered tie beam. A person struggles to understand: nature is complexity.

It is a ritual calendar that describes what ceremonies are to be performed on what days in honour of which divinities. I threw away the doorstop bread and dripping sandwich because I was ashamed, it wasn't like the other sandwiches. A machine may have empathy but it has no conscience. The story would be worthwhile only where there was an affect boosted high point that continued to cue retrieval without demanding sustained attention. Mechanical drawing might be pre-programmed or not. A fleshy pear shaped or oblong edible sentence with many seeds. Activation observed in the anterior / fronto-insular cortex (AI/FI) and the anterior cingulate cortex (ACC) to pain in oneself is also seen when observing pain in someone else. He threw away the doors because he was ashamed.

The authors declare no competing financial interests. Generally speaking, the "long-texts" are linguistic compositions where the creative aspect prevails; nevertheless they do often contain various repeated or stereotyped phrases. A sexual relationship lasting only one night, or a person with whom one has such a relationship. It is a type of gambling machine that is operated by a lever on one side of the machine (from the lever, and the machine's tendency to divest you of your money). A performance given only once in any particular place you care to name. Minerals normally in short supply on the high tops are being imported by relatives intent on scattering remains of their loved ones.

They comprised a distinct ethnic group in the Final Bronze Age. Three days in the Thames caused the whale to suffer dehydration.

A theory based on the fractal design of exchange surfaces and space-filling resource distribution networks, such as the animal vascular system. The limiting curves strongly deviate from the data for small arguments. Normally pollinated by insects; a means or place of entry. They planned to introduce writing into their social fabric, when they had found that by accepting a new system or convention, it was possible to join the isolated signs that had been imported from other alphabets. A statistically reliable estimate of human dispersal comprising all spatial scales does not exist. The influenza virus is unusual in that its genome is fragmented, and the mechanism that reconstitutes the genome in viral progeny is largely unknown. The form is based on an expression that can be either true or false.

A figure of speech in which an imaginary or absent person is represented as speaking or acting. This was an intentional deviation from the usual form or syntactic relation of words. The doll is on top of the desk. We are by now complicit with the silence of Marcel Duchamp. We recycle all kinds of building rubble. Cadence is the rapidity with which steps are taken. Remember the beehive hairdo. One company controls seventy percent of food traded in the world. The persistent state of disequilibrium among atmospheric gases is significant. A small patch of woodland divided into areas of closed canopy mixed with glades, where sunlight reaches the ground and where a very different plant and invertebrate community can be found.

The mid-skilled mother of two is set to have her first child at 28, and not to leave employment until her second child arrives, at age 31, and then only for two years. Why this sentence or that one, how can you tell? What happens in overload is not a dramatic breakdown in comprehension, but rather a shift to a more simple-minded interpretation of what is said. They were travelling slowly from here to eternity. Effects of a single application of human ash could be clearly seen sixteen years later. If I take the coriander from the shopping trolley before you reach the checkout. A yellow plastic toy taxi with black wheels is mine. Made or intended as a single unrepeated item or occurrence.

Observation or imagination of another person in a particular emotional state automatically activates a representation of that state in the observer. After their initial entry into the tracking system, most banknotes are reported in the vicinity of the initial entry location. New categories of articles appear and others are improved such as scythes, saws, hatchets, chisels, certainly linked to cultivation. They are a small number, men and women, outstanding in their group. We found it to be a substance unstable in theory but lasting long enough for practical purposes. There are an exceptional number of personal adornments in bronze, amber and bone. A continuous-time random walk process that incorporates scale-free jumps as well as long waiting times between displacements.

"I want to be a rider like my father", said Caspar Hauser when they found him waiting alone in the square. Writing may have come into the sphere of female competence, inasmuch as weaving was a model of the mechanism of combinations, links and sequences, and represented the earlier function of all alphabetic writing. Each budding virus particle contains a central rod of genetic material, surrounded by seven peripheral rods in a reproducible pattern. Painful stimulation was applied through electrodes to the hands of all three participants. Independent, separate, or self-contained existence is a sustainable option. The longest text of all is the *manuscript of Zagreb*, the only non-epigraphic document in the Etruscan corpus. A person without memory struggles to identify complexity.

If a body lives, the eyes will be unavoidably filled with meaning and expressiveness. Niche construction is the process by which organisms, through their own actions, modify their environment. The addition of nutrients to soils invariably leads to a loss of plant diversity. The tape shows a fox being chased by hounds, and riders going along, making no effort to stop the dogs. A house with the ground floor boards and joists pulled up and burnt in the yard, new wires threaded all through the building. Companies must pay plant workers for the time it takes to change into protective clothing and safety gear and walk to their work stations. I liked to look out from a high window far above the street. Little black ants were walking in lines, in and out of bread rolls on the table surface, and down table legs onto the floor.

We filmed image by image: it took two weeks. Fortunately, terms such as "step" and "stride" can be applied to animals with any number of legs. This confirms that Al-Sayyid Bedouin Sign Language (ABSL) is a local invention, free of outside influences. The butcherbird uses the twelve-note scale to invent melodies. It has a feeling of history and belonging, and it can locate itself both now and in the past. Small initial differences become magnified as the embryo develops and DNA is more fully expressed. A dog does this without a theory of emotion. Angry people in driving simulators had fifty percent fewer accidents when software soothed them with a calm voice.

Cloud density, if it can be linked with algal growth on the ocean surfaces, can be shown to have as large an effect on global climate as the burning of fossil fuels and the production of greenhouse gases. Composition adds one unit of processing load at the same point where it interferes with inferencing. A certain specified person needs to be remembered by another or by anyone. I know both these men personally, and I am of the opinion that this letter is an authentic document. In spite of its small size, a ghetto, placed in the middle of a metropolis, invariably created traffic problems: in Warsaw, trolley lines had to be rerouted. Writing appeared primarily in sanctuaries dedicated to female divinities.

We assess above-ground data separately to enable the inclusion of published above-ground data for an additional ten large trees. It wasn't only fear that I felt for my father. Beauty is now underfoot, wherever we take the trouble to look, this is a recent discovery. Here we report on a solid and quantitative assessment of human travelling statistics by analysing the circulation of banknotes in the United States. The piccolo, trombone and piano enter first, playing their lines in a brilliant, vulgar manner. After 1973 there were no flags to rally round. The events take place during a dinner party given by a *nouveau riche* couple. A small manufactured cheap article for personal or household adornment.

A metaphysical entity opposed to and devoid of being. What are angels doing in the human Astral body? I ran out of the cellar towards the Nevsky Prospect, it was misty on the street and beginning to get light. The cross is inscribed in the spool's terminal circle and occupies just one quadrant. Elephants got out safely, by breathing through their trunks, air close to ground level. Something offered for consideration or acceptance. The relationship between the object and person is designated by a proper name. It is a manuscript written on linen with a brush. The hormone cortisol is known to inhibit memory retrieval. Something happened in that moment which I found both incomprehensible and dreadful; my world collapsed around me. The image is surely manipulative but it is being used for charitable purposes. So far as Cage is concerned, form and content are quite separate. Google has my biography.

At one stage in the story, three young couples climb a mountain and see a glorious sunset. Humans have the capacity to empathise with the pain of others, but we don't empathise in all circumstances. The entrance often seems to be preceded by a small portico. The silver-black of the graphite is reminiscent of monochrome photography. What links the two spheres are the reference notes, which can exert their own influence over several passages. A young male, who had lived in captivity, defended the carcass of an old bull elephant against hyenas and other carrion-eaters for three days and nights. Chance followed me everywhere like a terrible nightmare. When petitioners had been dispersed, filming began. The alleged attack on Iraqi youths was confirmed in video evidence. Rolling out initially on a voluntary basis. Surrounded on all sides by enterocytes, which close over the top, sometimes creating a surface depression. The melody itself is never exposed, but is simply a frame for what must appear to be a series of improvisations.

In Warsaw the sale of armbands became a regular business. They had images that were windows into the world of spirit. This is the first empirical evidence for such an ambivalent process in nature. Stem cell clones grew in size with increasing time after heat shock and were surprisingly common. She has prepared for her big day by learning to drive, shop in a supermarket, and buy furniture from a catalogue. No one yet knows what is the optimum number for the human species. A beauty contest for HIV positive women would get coverage. Laura is strangely successful at bringing out the motivation to exercise. It is a pure non-intellectual substance heard by ear and resounding within the throat and heart.

We can dream of a return to paradise. British Gas lost two million customers in 2005. It had to be a small town in Germany. Two non-fitting gold fragments with inscriptions have come down to us. Michael's father spent a long while with his head resting against the wall, eyes closed, quietly singing a tune. The form is determined, content hit upon by accident. A life sentence. A person who is merely demonstrating, experiences an entirely different psychological state from one who performs for an audience. When they find a dead elephant, their response is shock and awe. Air cools as it spirals out of a hurricane. For the sake of uniformity, Greiser ordered that all Jews in his *Reichsgau* wear a four-inch yellow star sewed on the front and back of their clothes.

Human babies, whose mothers are given betamethazone, show signs of hyperactivity, as well as growing more slowly. My eleven-o-clock appointment is at the bank. Readers are required to keep books clean; they are not to turn down or stain the leaves, and are requested to report any damage or imperfection in the books they receive. Semicircular arches of undressed local stone frame either end of the passageway admitting both vehicles and pedestrians. When you become the victim of unprovoked violence it leaves you dispirited and angry. There have been reports of stranded northern bottlenose whales as early as 1800, before sonar and before noise pollution.

These findings suggest that plants and animals follow different metabolic scaling relations, driven by distinct mechanisms. My legs seemed to be full of ants. And besides, I had particular secret places of my own in the woods, where I used to retire by myself; and used to be from time to time much affected. This music was to me the destruction of all individuality and imagination, for the imagination can work only through memory. Images depict human bodies as fuzzy heat sources floating in an abstract clear medium onto which everything solid—walls, furniture, objects—has been melted. Each of us was craving someone left at home. Next morning before the dance, dressed in a sacred manner, I went among the people standing around that withered tree.

This strategy was achieved by a complete inversion of urban syntax. It was only later that Zimmerman equated his use of quotation with collage in art, his model being Kurt Schwitters, who assembled his works from discarded materials such as tram tickets, old shoe soles, feathers and dishcloths. The fully developed budding virion contains a set of eight rod-like structures. I was well versed in the ideas of historical materialism. We were displaced people who, in the wake of disaster, had changed language, our name made this clear. A swarm is supposed to induce simultaneous actions, but these actions are not dependent on each other. My people were butchered by those merciless heathen, standing amazed, with the blood running down to our heels.

The economy of the statement, and its tiny hint of duress, deflects questions of politics. Any list of examples will seem absurd. For Blanqui the barricade and the mouse hole were complementary elements employed for the protection of self-governing urban enclaves. This was not like my great vision, and I just went on working in the store. You might want to know who, if anyone, is speaking to whom. The wagons on the mountain pass were labelled BALKAN SOBRANIE TOBACCO. We were recording the use of the sentence in immigration. I fell back into my body, and as I did this heard voices all around and above me, and I was sitting on the ground. This is what they all do. Invisibly but unmistakably, the mask of discredit hovers over the left hand column, while the right hand column reads like a litany of all that is manifestly desirable.

It is not necessary to know them all. The fascism theorised by Nietzsche and Heidegger became a philosophical critique deployed to undermine humanism and democracy. Ocean waters boiled away and were lost to space as temperatures increased beyond those that could support life. Smaller groups appeared on the coastline or lakeshores. Being might thus be imagined with regard to others.

Darts of grass seed clung to our pullovers and socks. What happens if the meeting does not seem to be going well? My plan was to conceal myself at a friend's house, and remain there a few weeks till the search was over. You sneak into the back streets, or among bushes, to pitch coppers. They live in a kind of provisional way within their self-contained realm that can be overseen, though they do so with real intensity. It was considered to be a light sentence. "Evaluating" was called "confronting" and "timing" was known as "deciding" prior to 1982. Galileo sees a swinging church lamp. Garth Edward is a trader in carbon emissions. What comes to expression in a sense of shame? The helical field and the material it contains may expand outward, becoming a coronal mass ejection.

Once we were human, cultural history began to interact with innate ability to improve performance. Most orang-utans spend their lives without making or using tools. Only gravitons can escape the curtain into larger space, and such leakage may account for the observed weakness of gravity compared with other forces. The verb usually applies to human vocalisation. Let us read 'To Autumn' backwards. You and me were meant to be: this is us. The more connected a social network, the more likely it is that the group will retain any skill that is invented, so that in the end tolerant populations support a greater number of such behaviours. What impresses us most of all is the implicit evaluative hierarchy in the table. I was dancing with my eyes closed, just as the others did. After two to three months, banknotes should have reached an equilibrium distribution. Both men and women empathised with the pain of co-operative people, but if people were selfish, empathetic responses were absent, at least in men. It has the status of a formal mathematical statement yet to be proved. A series of towns located on high, their priority being defence. This is a prediction not easily tested. "Scenery" was invented for the theatre before it was discovered in the world at large. He was a brown spot in the midst of an expanse of olive-green gorse and nothing more. In the sum-over-histories interpretation, each path can be mapped out as a wave. As if meaning were present before being present. The star pattern outnumbers all other patterns in popularity.

We can't manage hierarchies above a certain size. Two apples for a penny: Beauty of Bath. By working together to build a robot, AI researchers would no longer be at the mercy of a single company or university. The consumptive has no choice but to gape after weather. Seven implants later, all signs are good. Impassable rivers may have halted the spread of tool use. Particles shown here are colourised and highly magnified. The poetry book arrived in the late morning post and smelt strongly of tobacco; in 1980 or in 1970 I wouldn't have noticed. Metal shelves are stacked with packets of foodstuffs and other basic products purchased in the former German Democratic Republic.

Thinking swamped by feeling. Like trees they are immobile, unable to flee. There does not appear to be any empirical or theoretical reason to suspect that the constraints working-memory puts on language processing are of any different kind or degree from the constraints they put on other kinds of intellectual performance. I was twenty-one years in that cage of obscene birds. Red apes in all locations are willing to be stung many times by honeybees to get at their honey. The landscape of family chimneys and grimy workshops pleased Satie; his home was a room in a slum tenement, which no one else had entered for 27 years. They rallied the drunken swarm, drove them backwards into open country, and set a guard over the town. Intrigued but uncertain of the reality of this detached source, we obtained a series of images from the beginning to the end of the flare, a sequence that covered about 10 minutes.

Two thirds of stellar systems are single red dwarfs. They remain over long periods of time without orientation and focus. One way to conceive of these movement traces is to imagine that the joints of the body emit vapour trails, like jets in the sky. Candidates who survive these preliminaries will be short-listed. A larger effect is to smooth out the business cycle, because migrants increase their giving during economic downturns in their homelands and scale it back during upswings. They live in huts in the bush, which are afterwards burned. There they sometimes reconfigure solar arcades, the series of arching field lines that occur back to back. The oak leaf is the favoured motif.

Bees can learn to recognise all known explosives at levels low enough to detect traces on someone's hands. I stood at the door with the others to receive the bridegroom and the bride. The microphone could easily be hidden in street signs, says the patent. From a business perspective, nuclear remains the highest-risk form of power generation. We decided on the creation of a new space in which shame could be experienced. The problem is leaving a small wake of destruction in contemporary thinking, and it is compounded by being folded back over onto the politics of Nazism. The weather was clear and sunny on 38 out of the 47 days from 7 August to 22 September 1819.

Moonlight lay upon the hills like snow. Place the labels on people, ensuring that each wearer does not see their own. In this maze there are blank areas that are impossible to enter. Meetings should start and end at the agreed time. We went to the water trough on King's Avenue, where I was to go to school. It means nothing in English, nor in the other European languages. There was an average of about ten kilometres between one house and another in the Final Bronze age. So I took my leave of them, and in coming along my heart melted into tears, more than all the while I was with them, and I was almost swallowed up with the thought that ever I should go home again. The deterioration of this sculpture over time was something that Beuys intended. Tourists are not external to the economy or ecosystem they visit.

In a world with more than three dimensions, there would be no stable orbits for electrons, no chemistry, no chemically based life forms, no us. Our dwelling is harassed by the housing shortage. Wasps clustered round the hole and tried to stick their heads through. The child is not a mere computer. It does not emit telltale radiation, like radar or laser-based devices do, so dashboard detectors cannot pick it up. The footprint is an estimate of the land used to sustain a population. Meanwhile this institution and others are working to provide good data. They are hardened through hunger, sleeping naked outdoors and undergoing various painful experiences, which they learn to suffer without complaint.

The point of our excursion was shoplifting in Woolworths. The computer doesn't know that this is the same thing. In pairs, share feelings on how meeting time is used in your team. The mist is coming home. Each chrome yellow quarter has been outlined with a saw tooth border. Square tiling generators can be used to visually represent number patterns. Biodiversity depends on a principal we might call provisional excess. As your vision recovers, you can see that the unique all-angle, real-time display could finally enable photographers to appear properly positioned and posed in timed shots of small groups, for example. Steps to record the levels of suffering in lab animals are being proposed in the UK.

The energy source for solar flares is a phenomenon called magnetic reconnection, in which the sun's magnetic field lines join and quickly reconfigure themselves. Above all, Hassan seeks to differentiate the realm of the aesthetic from other realms. I floated over the tepees and began to come down feet first at the centre of the hoop where I could see a beautiful tree all green and full of flowers. Lévy walk patterns were discovered in the foraging movements of spider monkeys. Domed terracotta ovens and hearths for cooking food, are located in small artificial caves all over the region. I heard the bell and call of the rag and bone man coming into our street. Many flowers produce fire resistant seed that germinates quickly when the rains come.

Although the languages were not given official status they were free to grow, thus ensuring maintenance. Memories, which appeared to be hard-wired, could be made pliable if they were recalled under emotive conditions produced by certain drugs. Descending warm air in the eye keeps it clear of clouds. The wing turns back into its own wake, which leads to higher lift forces than beating in still air. The Mediterranean world also underwent a series of profound shocks during the same period. The Jews took to the stars immediately. More than half the words in the document are people's names.

How is it possible to say the thing that I have just said? Various wartime insignia, brooches and medals, designed to indicate status and secret glamour, were available for sale in a shop close to school; at first I did not think about how they got to be there in the window. I collected clothes from the whole house: father's jackets, nanny's skirts and coats, gentlemen's and ladies' hats, umbrellas, galoshes—and started to improvise without any preconceived plan or aim. When they find bones they can tell either from the site or from the smell of the bones if they are related. In its wooded enclave, Little Hintock is the most secluded and unadulterated, deeply engrossed in its immediate environment. One can be sure that when any person says they were treated like an animal, the treatment was cruel. He may begin with a descriptive figure, but as often as not he will develop and transform it so that its initial identity is changed.

Giant Steps

'Blue Bird on Willow' is sourced from the Hallmark archive. Speech is slow and uncertain: considerable vagueness in the timing of whistle tones must be allowed for. A work that passes from hand to hand becomes affectively depreciated while its market value increases. In the zone there are hazards that cannot be seen, you have to follow your guide precisely and keep moving until signalled to stop. Form is an anagram. Could it be that even the structure of the thing thus envisaged is a projection of the framework of the sentence? The four kinds of discrimination are known as direct, indirect, positive and victimization. Where coloured noise techniques are used in writing, this third method may be employed to extend a phrase that would otherwise be unmanageable because of the need for somewhere to take a breath.

A camera scans the floor and finds a bed, then a pillow. A headline in the San Francisco Chronicle, 9 May 06, reads "Where have all the butterflies gone?" In *Twin Peaks*, the murderer of several women places individual letters, printed on tiny pieces of paper, underneath the fingernails of his victims. I'm at home, wearing my supermuff ear protectors, marking stories written by third-year undergraduates. The first sentence implies that a tool will be used for clearing snow, but the tool is not specified at this point. Reason produces respected public policy research on a variety of issues and publishes the critically acclaimed monthly magazine, *Reason*. All foreign fighters were told to return home to avoid the allied bombing. In the foreground is part of a car door, or just the suggestion of a car, because it's too dark to see clearly. The choice of sycamore trees seems not to be accidental. Each time you change the design of your face, have someone take a photograph of you and keep it as a record. Fidelity is slightly better with this arrangement, but hardly enough to justify the nuisance and expense of a second head joint.

Tatlin rejected the Euclidean geometricity and technological forms of such artists as Rodchenko. In the present example, almost all subjects replaced "it" with "violence", "the violent behaviour", or an equivalent. Your message dated Tuesday, 16 May 2006 08:52:47+0100 with subject "correction" has been successfully distributed to the AUTHORSHIP list (21 recipients). Omar and Asif travelled on together into the heart of the Afghanistan war. At this point a situation model is being formed, in that a link is made between two statements, and importantly, the link is not explicit but is in the mind of the reader. When Heidegger said "Our dwelling is harassed by the housing shortage" it was October 6th, 1951, he was giving a lecture at Bühlerhöhe on Hölderlin's late poem that begins "In lovely blueness blooms the steeple roof". Voluntary separation for those who ask for it is allowed for under Prison Rule 45, hence the slang use of the word "numbers".

It was a new attitude, which saw the work of art not as an organic entity based on the transformation of inspirational or emotional experience, but as an object composed of various material and conceptual elements, organised by the artist according to specific laws and techniques. Delores wraps the blue ice in a towel and places it in the bottom of the insulated bag. A screeching transient sound that is best not sustained. This block of granite, for example, is a mere thing. I walked into the clearing and was confronted directly by a coyote; we looked at each other, keeping still for a few minutes. Sorbet was developed in Florence around 1540. The phrase "I visited my teacher" will mean "I went to America". The initiative unit collects the energy of the collective, which is directed towards cognition and invention. Foraging is a tiring and risky activity. Cellular vans contain up to 12 small, individual cells "900mm high, 810mm between the forward facing plastic moulded seat and the front wall, and 650mm between the door and the side wall". We must remember that Cubism passed through a similar crisis. From the mountaintop I could see across the channel to the eastern coast of the island, the central mountains rose out of a blue haze. Blending is easier when red is applied over flesh colour. Astonishingly healthy, happy, rich and long-lived people surround Schwartz.

When the queen dies, the next-oldest female inherits the right to lay eggs. We never talked about the Taliban. Elaborative inferences are not essential for comprehension to proceed, and so the question becomes one of when readers do or do not make them. Gan stressed that the Russian Constructivists had dispensed with art and that it was the revolution which ensured that this would happen. The first models of heart function were built decades ago but they are much more sophisticated now. Merchants in Rafah's market said sales of food surged over the past four days amid a rush for flour, beans, sugar and vegetable oil. Effectuation of these matters being within the authority of the legislature, the power to achieve them through the exercise of eminent domain is established. The letters were sent in one envelope postmarked October 8th. More advanced equipment is available which can subtract head movement from eye movement, and this gives an accurate measure of eye fixations while eliminating the need for head restraint. Having invented writing, the Sumerians were able to record that the "earth turned white". From 1919 Malevich turned away from painting canvasses to design cities and individual dwelling units, creating small-scale architectural models in plaster. What if everyone was enhanced? You can tell when this happens because you will experience a tightening sensation on your face. Fair to good reliability; control rather delicate. No input signal: go to power save.

The picture hangs on the wall like a rifle or a hat. In my dream a screen was raised in front of the crowd as we walked through the gap into a high landscape of cedar woods, rocks and melting snow. It is unclear what the sand is made of or how it is formed. In 1805, Frederic Turner from Boston began to build a business selling winter ice from New England ponds. Back inside the prison, the driver placed a plastic bag on the desk, where its seal was broken and its contents tipped out by another officer. Origin here means that from which and by which something is what it is and as it is. Risk and need have to be separately assessed. The small E-flat military flute, now fairly easily obtainable from band instrument makers, sounds a minor third higher than a concert flute. Both methods start with lighter colours and then progress to darker colours. Some people are allergic to baby oil. Think, for instance, of how the words are formed in the main titles of Hitchcock's *Psycho*. Acidity of rainfall was first recorded as a problem in England in 1662; the term "acid rain" was coined there in 1872. Anaphoric referents such as these serve a number of purposes: they provide enriching information about the antecedent, but they can also inform the reader about a topic change.

Without cloud, there can be no cloud forest. The splendid and imposing gateway turned out to be a listed feature of a listed building and so could not be altered to allow easy entrance for today's vehicles. Mr Justice Sullivan said the Home Secretary had acted illegally when he used control orders to lock up Middle Eastern men for 18 hours a day in one-bedroom flats across the country after failing to bring charges under the Terrorism Act. To speak with imperfect articulation, to mispronounce, as a child learning to talk: there it is. You don't need to be afraid of sentiment. During a six-and-a-half hour spacewalk the astronauts will fill cracks in the panels using a caulk gun loaded with a gloopy sealant called Noax. We propose recovery from false rejection using statistical partial pattern trees for sentence verification. This could easily be improved by using "as I have trouble sleeping". Made from pieces of metal welded together, the internal structure of the form was revealed, incorporating space within itself. Are you an extreme dreader? Cars and sewing machines have foot-operated controls, so why not computers?

In a poplar plantation near Lakenheath, we walked through a long-established grid; golden orioles called repeatedly as they made their way in the high canopy. The complexity of the propositional text base allows us to anticipate the ease with which a passage will be read, and to predict the pattern of recall when readers attempt to describe it. Earth barricades have been hurriedly pushed across some streets in southern Gaza and towns in the north of the territory that are also considered likely targets for an Israeli assault. Please take a few minutes to read over these notices. Sunday June 4th, 2006: that sentence is lost. Your email has been received by the travel unit; where action is necessary we will process your request and respond as soon as possible. Much closer to us than sensations are things themselves. The colonial trade in slaves, sugar, rubber, cotton etc, allowed the development of a European middle class. Although the lower lip may be thick, it should not extend beyond the corners of the natural mouth. Modafinil was not developed to make people smarter. I wonder if Peter knows that Alaric died of cheese? Browse the following links to find other content related to dangling modifiers. The air bicycle will relieve the town of transport, noise and overcrowding, and will cleanse the air of petrol fumes. These questions hide a number of misconceptions.

In order to ensure that he remained in segregation, the prisoner felt compelled to commit an offence, such as assaulting an officer, every 28 days. As for the spirals, they are created by the combination of two circles revolving one above the other on different centres. I went to the visitor centre at the top of the ski lift where an audio visual following a bald eagle's flight incorporated old pioneer photos and took us back to the turn of the century. "Long-term" means lasting longer than twelve months, or for the rest of your life if this is expected to be shorter than twelve months. At the Serpentine Gallery in 1976, each performer imitated the improvised actions of the previous actor. The diagram of the flute mechanism in Appendix A was drawn by Delores Wallace. Wiping may smear colours. If the frequency of the difference tone must be found without reference to a performer, a simple formula is available. For many people the future cannot come soon enough. Mashups plot traffic camera positions, allowing users to choose a camera and take a look at the jams. This line continues down below the eye. Eventually the nano beads form a chessboard array bound together like a crystal. Popova became a member of Malevich's Suprematist circle, collaborating with him on the publication of the journal *Suprematus*, for which she did many designs. Jack completes one side before moving to the other side, as shown in figures 5–11. Therapy takes place in groups, to which one or two uniformed officers are allotted. Gradually the face becomes clearer, though still hazy and somewhat unreal: she is smiling and stepping up to meet the wild cheers of a crowd.

Thousands of half-inch woollen squares, cut from regimental uniforms, have been pieced together in a variety of configurations to make up twenty-five blocks. Spook holes literally sit beneath and above the fine domestic interior. Weapons designers are thrilled to be working on their first new warhead in two decades. I suppose that what we are looking for as readers, what we are used to, is authentic experience. In 1924 Popova died of scarlet fever. Would you rather have more pain now, or less pain within the next minute? Some studies have indicated harmful effects from prolonged breathing of talc: it is a good idea to keep this material out of your lungs. Twenty-eight institutions were, like Exeter, built in Victorian times or earlier. Key products for new consumers were clocks, watches, bicycles, sewing machines, typewriters and small arms.

A thing, as everyone thinks they know, is that around which the properties have assembled. These buildings are very small, probably used as storehouses and depositories, perhaps for sheltering single animals. It is a synthetic drug that blocks the action of adrenalin on beta-receptors in the heart. Meaning a proposal of sexual intercourse. In the experiment, droplets of sarin were put on the subject's arm. Search the document and find the phrase "a life sentence". Calls cost around eight pence per minute. The single Irish chain is a variation of the nine-patch block. We are imposing new rules of life on animals, in ways not foreseen. Between Montezuma and Cortés is complete cultural discontinuity. Seven out of twenty newsagents surveyed in the Manchester area on Tuesday June 27, 2006 were selling Cadburys chocolate bars recalled because of salmonella contamination. See if you can find and play 'January Snows' by Lúnasa. We should be suspicious when those at an advantage claim that a disadvantaged group is innately less able. Hypothetical tentacles originally reconstructed around tooth-like structures are themselves dubious, and cannot be used to refer ordontogiphes to a known lophophorate group.

Bruno's stuffed fur will be displayed at the Museum for People and Nature in Munich, and his skeleton and inner organs retained for student instruction. A particular ideology might still function after the war, but those in the know would see it not as an articulation of some truth or falsehood but as an operational device like a myth. Please move right down inside the car. A wiring system turned the performer into a human drum. The key to saving Tigers is to maintain prey density. Up went the sails, and we set out for the west with a fair following wind. Spandex is a stretchy material from which bathing suits are made. I lisped in numbers, for the numbers came. We were in Skibbereen, where they ate the donkey. The human species uses mean sea level as the base point against which heights and depths are measured. Please let us know if you encounter any data corruptions. The claim of linguistic misunderstanding is doubtful and should have attracted more scrutiny. Ideology maintains sexual inequality. The good news, he says, is that side effects might not happen after one dose of the drug. Cnidarians have genes for signalling molecules that were once thought to be exclusive to vertebrates. A rapid fear response allows the body to take evasive action. Laura helps people keep to a fitness walking plan.

We see here the rubble-strewn surface of Venus. These were the only survivors of a terrible shipwreck, known to have changed their spoken language. We used functional magnetic resonance imaging (fMRI) to investigate whether acquired liking or disliking modulated empathic responses for pain. The related notion of long distance dispersal has been established in ecology, taking into account the observation that distribution curves of a number of species show power tails owing to long-range movements. These small clusters correspond to the regenerative cells previously described. Several elements within this sequence merit our attention. Malevich's ideas received wide circulation in his Bauhaus book *The Non-Objective World*. Deep anaphors are also known as "model-interpretative anaphors" in that they require the use of knowledge that is not presented in the sentence. This train is for Edinburgh, Waverley: the next stop is Aberdour. Quantum theory predicts several phases of matter that have counter-intuitive properties. I plunged down from the bridge into the submerged cave. Contaminated waste water leaked from a pipe and dripped into the chocolate mixture. Much of Le Fanu's fiction deals with the inheritance of property and related emotional conflicts. Perhaps Jude is the character with the most highly developed sympathy for non-human creatures. The seine net was still in the water, for the boat couldn't carry it.

Written on the side in Chinese script is "Rain making rocket used for teaching". Cann quarry produced "small ladies" in the 1820s, but this was the best that Devon quarries could achieve. Tenants took care to sell their livestock or grain before it could be seized: the money raised helped runaways to emigrate. Rye and bread wheat were the most common plants, but these were not the pedigree varieties bred since the nineteenth century. Use a single asterisk * to truncate from one to five characters. Such prisoners are classified as vulnerable and kept out of sight and sound of all others as far as possible. Quiver is usually a noun. Quartertone passages should be checked with players before they are allowed to stand. Where there are no sentences there is no truth.

Materials used as ties are a reminder of the ingenuity with which local resources are exploited. It is a room or desk where visitors to or clients of an office, factory or hotel, are received on arrival. The propositions in which analysis terminates reveal the actual structure of the facts, which, if they obtain, make the propositions true. No part of the country is more than seventy miles from the sea, and temperature is almost uniform over the entire island. To repeat something from memory or read it aloud, especially before an audience. The new, reliable dates for timbers also show how woodland management improved through the late medieval period. You might need somebody too. While the damaged craft wheeled in orbit, the scientists' modes of presentation worked against a proper analysis of complex uncertainties and risks occasioned by the foam debris that struck the wing during take off. People had been dying of hunger since September and the public works failed to keep them alive. I will not offer arguments against the vocabulary I mean to replace. Miss Ireland wears Lipsy. A very shallow porch is formed by buttresses flanking the wagon doors. And is their orientation regular or haphazard?

Peggies were usually laid in conjunction with lime plaster. The continuous inscription of at least 174 letters, incised after firing and filled with white paste only in the residuous part, with rare punctuation marks, goes in a spiral and left to right from the shoulder to the middle of the body, disposed on four or five lines. A class for the youngest children in a primary school. The timbre on the sharp side of the focus is different from that on the flat. All the evidence is there. All the players are in place. Because the sequence follows the unpredictable course of the weather there is only one true position of match.

Are colours more mind dependent than weights? Neuromotor prostheses aim to replace or restore lost motor functions in paralysed humans by routing movement-related signals from the brain, around damaged parts of the nervous system, to external effectors. A chemical structure, on an enzyme for example, that provides a site of attachment. The outer edge presents a beaded knurled wire. Marked by a lack of proper caution. Fires that spread rapidly across the thatched roofs of Devon's smaller towns encouraged the use of slate roofing in the eighteenth century. The original drawings remain in Italy.

A Hawthorne effect, then, is the initial improvement in performance following a newly introduced change. We drew a racetrack in chalk all across the road and got down on hands and knees to push our toy cars. The predominance of scarlet indicates that the quilt was made after 1872, when that colour would have been plentiful, and probably before 1881 when the facing colours for infantry were limited to white, yellow, green and navy blue. Supervision takes the form of unplanned discussions and consultations on an individual or group basis. Photographs enlarged on a photocopier are useful for this type of activity. As well as representing a hopeful and romantic image, the star pattern is a needlework challenge. That amber-coloured butterfly poses the problem in miniature. From late autumn to midwinter, this tiny Austrian town, famous for its glass blowing, gets no sun at all. One woman, a pensioner, has moved back into the exclusion zone with her animals. Cells come equipped with their own built-in proofreaders and repair equipment to make sure that DNA is copied with as few mistakes as possible. The withholding of the names presents these creatures as known locally and intimately. Sentences written by the subjects were scored according to whether there was a topic shift in the sentence containing the target.

Every graph or chart embodies analytical assumptions and at a deeper level the implicit cognitive structures that shape every phase of scientific study. 181,496 lbs of oats were exported from Skibbereen to Liverpool in June 1847. For now, the Reliable Replacement Warhead remains a series of zeros and ones in the supercomputers at Los Alamos and Livermore. The tree will put on a wide ring in a year of favourable growing conditions, but a narrow ring in a poor one, such as the drought year of 1976. The receiving of a radio or television broadcast, or the quality of the signal received, is perhaps what is meant here. Paupers and little cottiers cannot keep their holdings without the potato, and for small sums of £1, £2 and £3 have given me peaceable possession in a great many cases, when the cabin is immediately levelled. The origin of the pattern name 'Dove at the Window' is unknown at present.

This painting has a mottled yellow background. People staying in the contaminated area feel they are living in another world, detached from their country. "Morf" is acronymic shorthand. Players select pieces in turn until they each have six. Bosnian Muslims who survived the war are being resettled into Serbian controlled eastern Bosnia. The pegs can be cut from dowel. It is my pleasure to write to you after much consideration since telephone communication cannot be suitable enough. What is the place of molecules in the world of consciousness? No lime mortar was mentioned. In formal terms a happening contains several actions presented sequentially, while an event contains one action (which may be repeated). This illustration shows the distraining of cattle and sheep for unpaid rent in County Galway in 1849. Their arrival may be connected with the use of gunpowder in slate quarries, allowing larger blocks to be won.

Victims said they had been threatened, their windows smashed, and their cars overturned. By marking the thematic shift with the specific referent Sally, it becomes clear that sentence 5 is telling us something new, and that this sentence does not need to be integrated with what has preceded it. Each label identified the object in question in artspeak, as if it were an exhibit in a gallery. The flexagon will open to reveal another colour. Donatello was received into the Florentine guild of St Luke as a goldsmith and stonemason. The measured signal is the arrival of photons, and the optical conductance of the interferometer is modulated by the position of the measured object. My grandmother was a world war two refugee who lived in Brixton; she never learned to speak

English. Between 1941 and 1946 Laban and Lawrence pioneered the study of industrial rhythm in a variety of factory operations. On the Antrim coverlet stitching passes through the satin top and is secured to a coarse linen lining. Words may be right-hand truncated using an asterisk. He finished his figures like this and in the last stages used his fingertips more than his brush. The value and promise of such knowledge is clear. In queenless diacamma colonies, one or a few workers restrict mating and egg laying by mutilating every other ant. Edges should be glued together using contact adhesive.

The overall impression is of a gentle dust-laden chaos. Some clinicians take issue with the use of the word "vegetative" and the unpleasant imagery it evokes. I would be insane if I thought I had a body made of glass. My late father was a limited liability cocoa and gold merchant in Sierra-Leone before his untimely death. Graphite burned for nine days, causing the main release of radioactivity into the environment. By planning the position, size and shape of the blots, the design need not be entirely a matter of chance. The pattern of burning shows up clearly on Landsat imagery. Residues 274–282, 583–600, 607–614, and 623–631 are removed for a clear view of the binding site. Substrates may freely access this space. If the curvature turns out to deviate from flatness, we would come to a conclusion unprecedented in human thought. The rivers and streams around Srebrenica flow into the green river Drina, which is dammed by a large hydroelectric plant. Protein coding regions account for only about one-third of the segments in the human genome thought to be under negative selection. But the satellite is now warmer than before, and must eventually return to equilibrium with its space surroundings by radiating the heat liberated by the resistor. There is only one basic third-order square. In 1998 an agreement with the US provided for the establishment of an international radioecology laboratory inside the exclusion zone. Deforestation is not an unstoppable or irreversible process.

This turn towards language was thought of as a progressive, naturalising move. Made from paper, cardboard and wood, these three-dimensional structures interacted with their surrounding spatial environment to differing degrees of intensity. People returned hours later with their families. A billboard located in the sea, just off the beach, with the title and release date visible above the waterline. It is intriguing to see a return to case narratives at this particular time in the history of resilience research. Even if that never happens, we have a massive problem. A gold disc filigreed and embossed on the outside with concentric motifs. Fuel elements ruptured and the resultant explosive force of steam lifted the cover plate off the reactor, releasing fission products to the atmosphere. Observations show that magnetic structures reduce or increase the local radiation flux for as long as they exist at the surface. These findings were originally obtained from calculations in which convection was approximated by turbulent diffusion. Non-human primates are still uniquely valuable in animal research because of the similarity of their brains and many of their behaviours to ours. Patients were unaware of the pain to which they had responded. Many possible universes are inhospitable to our existence.

Families returned later with their people. An entirely new way of moving domain walls, using short pulses of electrical current, could make bubble memory devices feasible at the nanoscale. The second set of magic window cards work rather differently. Grasses are better adapted to withstand fire than are woody plants. The April 1986 Chernobyl disaster, caused by a flawed reactor design and serious mistakes made by inadequately trained operational staff, was a direct consequence of cold war isolation. We can see stages in the pollution history of the earth. There were marked regional variations in the severity of both excess mortality and emigration, but their combined effect produced widespread population losses, as this map demonstrates.

The rifle hangs on the wall like a picture or a hat. We have been informed that the investigation team may require witness statements. Once you get interested in world improvement, there is no stopping. This book deals especially with Ohio mushrooms. Future experiments will measure the curvature of space with exquisite precision. Yet this primitivism is in no way faked. The main role of agriculturalists has been to simplify the world's ecosystems. Bentham enumerated "dimensions" of pleasure and pain: intensity, duration, certainty, propinquity, purity, fecundity and extent. (See also concentration camps.) The oil terminal at Whiddy Island in Bantry Bay is capable of handling the largest oil tankers afloat. As I have trouble sleeping, this could be improved by using "easily". The red makeup should be applied with a brush or cotton swab. He soon re-emerged, carrying a plastic bag bearing the prison service logo and containing a number of items that we could not make out. Mass produced steel pins and needles, fountain pens, corrugated iron, crinoline, aniline dyes, and vulcanised rubber were important early consumer products. A drug for soldiers that makes the memory of killing no more troubling than cleaning boots.

Selenium is marginal in vegan diets in Britain due to low levels in the soil. Direct parental communication was present only in the familiar form of verbal and physical abuse. Order is restored by the reappearance of the violin. It is possible to measure the tree-ring sequences from historic oak timbers in ancient roofs and match them to established tree-ring chronologies. Two pieces of stiff card and four pieces of narrow tape are required. A patient is classed as vegetative if there are no outward signs of awareness, rather than simple reflex responses to stimuli such as pain. These data suggest that the DNA damage response and tumour suppression are unlinked activities of p53, each induced by distinct signals. Americans and Canadians will buy online and enter their credit card information without ever talking to someone at the business. Everything needs to remain confidential only between both of us. Do you think I come from behind the mountain? Looking closely helps, though the paint is applied so sensually that there is the danger of falling in love. The restaurant on level 7 is open on Sunday—Thursday from 10.00 to 18.00 and on Friday and Saturday from 10.00 to 23.00. Figure 5a shows seven reconstructions of northern hemisphere temperature for the past millennium, smoothed with a 30-year low pass filter and their unweighted mean. The original message has been attached so that you can, if you wish, view it.

We refer below to the bright clumps and the magnetic network collectively as the bright component of the surface magnetic field, or magnetic brightenings. The main casualties were among the fire fighters, including those who attended the initial small fires in the roof of the turbine building. He was a finished butcher, for those brothers had a big household when they kept house together. Mr Caulfield and Mr Townshend, two Anglican clergy from Skibbereen in West Cork, travelled to London in December 1846 to meet with Charles Trevelyan at the Treasury. I took some little pieces of marble in the form of sugar cubes, a thermometer and a cuttle bone, shut them up in a bird cage, and painted the whole thing white. You must be between 21-31, healthy, with a good family medical history. The crossing between the two is utterly effortless, thus enabling the marvellous and elusive shimmer that is so characteristic of a really fine flute sound. Workers typically put on sanitary outer garments: boots, hard hats, aprons and gloves. A toxic slick is heading down the Songhua River.

So long as you have some text-based content for search engines to index you will be OK. Mergers are expected to occur every 100,000 years. But these advantages were not enough to offset the disastrous effect upon Ireland of exposure to the full impact of Britain's industrial revolution. Metalworking required enormous quantities of wood. All these changes must have left their imprint on the human genome. Those transient objects, if any existed, would not show conspicuous live features in the NB 973 waveband. This is where Bob makes his crucial mistake. The fox's earth must not be stopped or dug up and the use of terriers and guns is forbidden. It's better to be sure that no children will inherit these problems. Situated or rising only a little above the ground or some other reference point, we stay here for now.

The moon's gravitational force allows a quicker uptake of water to the fruiting body. Passages are trowelled, scraped, dripped, rubbed, brushed, blocked, knifed and elided by the mid-fifties. These are the sorts of results scientists wish for, but seldom get. Although John Coltrane has moved on to another dimension, he remains the most influential musician of our time. The student will be able to define and give examples of anti-Irish racism, and relate them to the Irish Famine experience. Nothing more than nothing can be said. Is the cat's window open? What was Dada in the 1920s is now, with the exception of Duchamp's work, just art. Let no one imagine that in owning a recording they have the music. I caught up with my backlog of podcasts and came across the extremely nice things Nicole Simon said about the show. Let's just say I don't go for that white trash trailer park look. Offset headlines and advertisements shade passages of white in *Gotham News* and *Easter Monday.* Content can do more to build your business and profits than just about any other resource or service available.

When Pharoah Sanders came to New York he had no money and slept in the subway and under stairs in tenement hallways. Your profile confidently assured me that you are a trustworthy and reliable partner after you should have assisted me to purchase a family house for my relocation. The park is often referred to as Drake's park or as the rose garden. Beam hardening effects were not significant. The picture is full of discontinuities between remembering (keeping something from the past) and forgetting (painting over it). Coltrane played alto sax in the Dizzy Gillespie big band, and sat next to Jimmy Heath, a native born Philadelphian. Everybody's dancing in the moonlight. In preparation he erases the de Kooning. Setting out one day for a birthday party, I noticed the streets were full of presents. In this way we get our navigation done for us. Contributions were invited within the general areas of instrumentation, methods and novel applications. I don't give lectures to surprise people, but out of a need for poetry. Cores came back up chock full of microbes and plant matter, along with bones from skinks, giant tortoises, parrots, owls and bats. This makes solid oxygen particularly interesting: it is considered a spin-controlled crystal that displays unusual magnetic order. As though to confirm that these seemingly random intrusions were thoroughly intended, de Kooning selected pages pertinent to the imagery of Easter for his painting *Easter Monday*. Sound as a quality for its own sake became an idea to be pursued. Static is between stations. We were expecting to stay for a while with Peggy Guggenheim and Max Ernst. The fret-saw enthusiast can use plywood. In the systemic meaning, "global" refers to the spatial scale of operation and comprises such issues as climate change brought about by atmospheric pollution. 371,000 people were eventually relocated after Chernobyl from an exclusion zone of 4,300 square kilometres. Brightening of the sun with increasing sunspot number would be difficult to explain if dark magnetic sunspots were the only structures visible on the solar disk.

H = Message –ID: Received: Date: From: Subject: To: Mime—Version: Content: Type: Content—Transfer—Encoding. We said we were looking for mushrooms. This text was written on the highways while driving from an audience in Great Barrington, Massachusetts, to one in Philadelphia, Pennsylvania. After a pause, she added, "Do they know you're a Zen Buddhist?" All exhibitors have exceptional quality handmade goods for sale. These social networks, grounded in traditionally sanctioned status, are central elements in class reproduction. Enjoy writing sessions, and free time to write or roam in the rain forest. Art David assisted Coltrane with some of the chord progressions he used on *Giant Steps* and the two men experimented frequently with modes, sounds and rhythms. Absorbed into abstraction, the subliminal anatomy accosts the viewer with a force that is at once combative and embracing.

The tardiness of music with respect to the arts just mentioned is its good fortune. High red shift galaxies can be identified using the well-established dropout technique. As the authors point out, many details about the development histories of these individuals remain unknown. There is a high probability of finding only a small but non-zero value for dark energy today, which is what we observe. A term used in the theory of speech acts to refer to the criteria which must be satisfied if the speech act is to achieve its purpose. Slates cut to inexact sizes can be holed and top-hung to produce regular course work, the irregular headers being lost from view. The reason for this change is being evaluated. It followed that tenants were entitled at least to fair rents and security of tenure. IBM currently has two research labs in India employing about 110 people. The latest brochure from Bellagio falls onto the carpet. You hear the sound of a truck driving at fifty miles per hour.

Haphazard beginnings were enlisted by de Kooning, not to avoid content but to circumvent the boundedness of intended subject matter and preconceived form. Our new colleagues at Intel really helped us, thank you very much. This is not a composition. At one time computers stored information in magnetic bubble memories defined by domain walls. The loss of lowland chalk grasslands in Dorset, southern England, is here depicted by the area remaining (Nature Conservancy Council, 1984). Instead of following a common checklist, such as those used by pilots every time they take off or land, each prison has its own programme. Any attempt to enforce such a separation is bound to lead to confusion and result in bad-sounding, unperformable nonsense. Before an invited audience, the model pressed her body, covered with blue paint, on the prepared canvas. Coloured noise can be produced in three ways. *The Great Irish Famine* was approved by the New Jersey commission on Holocaust Education on September 10th, 1996, for inclusion in the holocaust and genocide curriculum at the secondary level.

In *The Wave* (c.1942–44), organic shapes occupy a space anchored at upper right by a rectangle familiar from the paintings of figures. This guidance uses the phrase "gifted and talented" to describe all learners with gifts and talents. Later in the programme Philip Green will give a statement on Arcadia profits. The best way to guarantee safe prescription drugs is to order from licensed pharmacists that dispense only Canadian products. A clean and simple site will be good enough. Forensic evidence demonstrates that, during a period of several weeks in September and early October 1995, Serb forces dug up many of the primary mass gravesites and reburied the bodies in still more remote locations. Your program will accept starting and ending words from the input file. Whenever my parents were reading the room would fill with silence, which made me feel calm and content. It was a beautiful pink ice velour cloak with a soft white faux fur trim. I went back to Xenia and told her what had happened. The editor could not find both body tags and thus isn't able to read this page.

A Zebra head seen through gently moving Venetian blinds. Our third party developers rapidly moved their apps to universal versions to run at native speeds on the new processors: thank you very much. A coaster may not fit into the quiet, reticent, undemanding group but instead may appear lethargic, apathetic, lazy and difficult to motivate, or angry, provocative and defiant. "Pharaoh is a man of huge spiritual reservoir", said Coltrane, "he's always trying to reach out to truth". It would be good to step beyond your local Google cocoon and discover how others see things. Now, on the other hand, times have changed; music has changed, and I no longer object to the word "experimental". Ozone reduces photosynthesis and inhibits flowering and germination. Copper and bronze implements discovered in Northeast Thailand, have been tentatively dated between 7000 and 6000 years ago. A graph is not only a crucial tool in plotting data within significant parameters but it is also an integral part of the style of a presentation. 7 million people are now eligible for benefits as Chernobyl victims. Spin currents may appear wherever there are conventional charge currents. Olson refers to this process as being "ruled by information"—the inward of the shaping force. We are now approaching Kirkcaldy; alight here for the Fife coastal path. "Sentence fragment" is another term with the same meaning. In conversational speech recognition, recognizers are generally equipped with a keyword spotting capacity to accommodate a variety of speaking styles. Between 1915 and 1916, Rodchenko became acquainted with the Moscow avant-garde, including Tatlin, Popova and Malevich.

Both types of priming sentence, relative to the neutral sentence, facilitated verification times. In 1992 Letts recognized that historic straw thatch preserved under newer layers was the major surviving resource in Europe for the study of medieval plant remains. This is coach C. At his death aged thirty-seven, Raphael left a palace, two houses, vineyards and land. The galaxy described on p.186 may be, for the moment, the most distant and hence the oldest known galaxy. In 2003 another patient, Terry Wallis, stunned doctors by making a marked recovery after spending nineteen years in a minimally conscious state. He sits in a rocking chair on a veranda, looking out toward the mountains; he sees the setting sun and hears his own symphony: it's nothing but the sounds happening in the air around him.

The paintings assume a spare eloquence by 1957, their marks fewer, more decisive and broad. Children can measure the space inside a container using water or sand, counters, cubes, buttons. Customs will prepare the paperwork including determining the classification number and duty rate for your merchandise. Make your way from "Pony" to "Cart" in only five steps, changing one letter at a time to form the interim words. You are in a tough situation but I believe you must follow your heart. Does Britney have post-natal depression? I would put my head in my hands and think about numbers. Many hundreds were massacred at a football field near Nova Kasaba; the worst killing ground of the entire five-day slaughter. The word "ladder", for example is blue and shiny; "hoop" is a soft white word. The workhouse is shown to the left of the Cathedral and the tower of St Thomas' church to the far right. Bentham's idea that a fixed amount of intensity is equal in value to a fixed amount of duration rests on a false analogy with spatial measurement, where an inch is the same length in any dimension.

These pieces should not be thought of under the heading of "aesthetics" nor even under that of "philosophy of art". It is as well, before beginning, to provide the definitions of certain special terms and non-standard usages that frequently occur. With the French model, for instance, it is possible to make a glissando over a large part of the instrument's range. Of the simple diatomic molecules, oxygen is the only one to carry a magnetic moment. Dear friend, do accept my sincere apologies if my mail does not meet your personal ethics. Landlords had an almost complete control of Parliament. Swifts are massing around the building in the evening. Sometimes I pressed my fingers into my ears to get closer to the silence, which was never static, but a silky trickling motion around my head like condensation. The word ladder program is similar to a "six degrees of separation" or "oracle" game, but using words rather than people or actors. Each night my mother washed my father carefully with oil in front of the living room fire until the condition subsided.

If I noticed a smudge or error I'd rub everything out and start over. In 1849 there were still many cases of destitute roadside dead; the majority remained unidentified. Constructivism was based on three principles enunciated in the programme of the first working group of Constructivists: tectonics, *faktura*, and construction. The results suggested that by using Japanese sentences, it might be possible to examine sentence-level rather than word-level processes. The power of eminent domain is assumed to arise from natural law as an inherent power of the sovereign. An alternative hypothesis suggests that multiple connections are made, as a text is understood, including distant causal connections, even when the writing is locally coherent. Since powdering is messy, apply it outdoors if the weather permits. He misread the title on the spine as *Collecting and Polishing Stories*. It was a specific variety of Imperialism that would sacrifice the civilian populations of Hiroshima and Nagasaki in order to keep Asian markets open to American goods. Listening to other people isn't easy for me. Store all of the words from the dictionary in a HashSet. More than ninety-eight percent of the human genome is made up of non-coding DNA.

The persistence and continued spread of bracken (*pteridium aquilinium*) on heavily grazed rough pasture in Scotland is aided by the fact that it is slightly poisonous, especially to young stock. The photographic record shows that local—either Devon or Cornish—peggies continued to be used for roofing terraces of early nineteenth-century houses. Implantable neuromotor prosthetics builds on basic research into the neural basis of planning and control of movement in monkeys. Improvement works may affect your journey, particularly at weekends. A-listers were accommodated, but others watched on screens in an "overspill" marquee. I read this in the back pages of a local newspaper a couple of years ago and it formed the starting point for my film *Outlaw*. Police in Cumbria and North Yorkshire have been drawn into disputes between canoeists and anglers. The first line of the present decree (the rest is missing) is written in gold and blue with ornamental points and may have been prepared in advance. In the following decades pattern books were published in Venice, Rome and Paris and, by 1600, all over Western Europe. The memory of the famine was carried far beyond the shores of Ireland and its legacy gave rise to a new form of Irish Nationalism that looked to America for inspiration and support. Spirals round off the outline of the monogram, on a ground of triple dots and wriggling cloud-scrolls.

Stencils and designs travelled easily and far; manuscripts written in one library were often bound or rebound elsewhere at a later date. See *Parliamentary Papers*, page 55 (enclosure no. 13): no tea plants were ever received in the Botanic garden from Captain Charlton. The objects displayed were often physically unimpressive but metaphorically weighty, inspiring or humorous. Contaminated unleaded petrol has damaged oxygen sensors in thousands of cars. Anyone with any appetite for serious money knows what to do. Keith Joseph invented much of Thatcherism, but only the Iron Lady could make it real. One force has already introduced smaller pistols in its firearms unit and has ordered lighter rifles in an attempt to get more women to join. In one of the villages several people had been turned out of their houses on their refusal to work like bond slaves for nothing, others had fled. The earliest datable paper-cut by Karabacek is a mirror for princes Nasihat-i Shah Rukdar Suluk-i Muluk (Vienna Nationalbibliothek, AF112), 3 March 1411—11 August 1417 and bearing both Shah Rukh's bookplate and the seal of his library.

A young man comes to this country to engage in the business that has enriched some of his connexions. When the Prime Minister was questioned for a second time in January, a news blackout was put on the interview for similar reasons. The artists were using this symbol to make a statement about inner destruction. In 2007 we have websites rather than bricks and mortar but the intention is the same. Swinton, set somewhat apart in a large room, lay asleep in a glass case during the day for seven days. Bioactive ingredients nourish deeply from the inside with bio-marine collagen complex, pine bark anti-oxidants and blackcurrant seed extracts. This may be an overstatement, but one paradox disappears. The Keir velvet, therefore, was not a European commission and was manufactured in Persia well before 1600. In almost every country the natives have some plant they call tea. Gilbert was born in Italy in 1943, in a small village in the Dolomites. Barclays Wealth is the division of Barclays devoted to the management of wealth. Will you take the law into your own hands?

Copying is an inherent feature of the Islamic arts of the book, for patrons demanded reproductions of illustrations as well as texts, innovation is often by accident, and copyists were therefore skilled at working by means of mechanical aids. Virgil's father farmed and kept bees. We are not just stabilising memories during sleep, we're extracting the meaning. This makes emotions seem mysterious because we can't imagine what those extra features might be. Using a touch screen, the controller can circle a target vehicle or building and the pilot will see the same thing on their cockpit screen. His method was to bring back into the visual arts the rich, cultural and social heritage of Europe. Nothing may be disturbed or removed; this includes rocks, plant materials, reptiles, Indian artefacts, and fossils. Also shown was the preserved brain of Charles Babbage, inventor of the earliest computer. No one knows for sure who was giving the bride away but the smart money was on Sir Elton. At length he was led to embrace the gospel under the instruction of a pious indigo planter, and was baptized. Eclectic or hybrid arts tend to be more variable in quality because the difficulty of controlling execution is augmented by the complexity of managing the source material.

It was a photo of Marcel Broodthaers pointing at a wax figure of Jeremy Bentham. Torture victims often do not mention their traumatic experiences when they go for medical treatment. Indonesia is to resume sending samples of H5N1 flu to foreign labs following discussions with the World Health Organisation. It's not clear how you quantify the amount of carbon locked in a tree, much less guarantee that it stays there. Around Borrego Springs, tune your radio to 1610 at the end of the AM dial. Titles in bold are those known to have been given by the artist. Open access to Sky is a less compelling rallying cry than access to Open Skies. This is a good story, but is it true?

The fabric is frozen in the sense that it does not evolve: the past, the present and future are all laid out in space-time. We now have the technology to see on the ground what the pilot sees before a bomb is released. Much of today's aerodynamics research is a sunset endeavour. Gathering firewood is prohibited. Richter grasped the lessons that Abstract Expressionism had taught, the all over quality of gestural abstraction and a process-determined distribution of painterly incident. Put your forefinger against your thumb on each hand and push them together right in front of one eye, keeping the other closed, to create your own single "pinhole". Although the weapon is cheap to produce and easy to assemble, operators need skill to use it effectively. Cremation also creates problems: the fumes from vaporised dental fillings make up sixteen percent of mercury emissions. There was nothing entirely new about Tuesday's Shanghai "correction". The best teapot or cutlery is displayed to impress visitors. Government took the matter up well, and made advantageous rules for planters. But though writing was a chore, I was very good at learning the words we were given on strips of paper.

I have noticed that you write durations that are beyond the possibility of performance. On the basis of statistical dose-effect models, a total of four thousand eventual deaths from the accident are possible. My father was making dinner in the kitchen. Sleep helps us extract rules from our experience. Growing corn for ethanol simply trades one environmental crisis for another while driving up the price of an international staple. So as space-time grows, element-by-element, the quanta link together like bubbles in expanding foam. One extreme example of this social equation is *Woman with Umbrella* [*Frau mit Schirm*] 1964 (page 131). As the increase will be unrealised, valuations would be open to challenge, leading to long running legal disputes and delays. The phrase in German has the connotation of "being on the wrong track". His "vocabulary" included, as well as those objects named, coal and potato chips; kitchen, garden and builders tools. A great area for primitive camping, the roads into Blair valley are usually accessible by two-wheel drive vehicles; there are no facilities and no water is available. A deep depression is centred just west of Ireland and associated fronts will advance across the UK.

Drinks that change colour are also being developed. The walls were lined with packing cases in which the works of art had been sent around the world, marked "Picture", "With Care", "Haut", "Bas", etc, in stencilled letters. These are all factors that arise from the "Just War" tradition. A retired head teacher offered copies of all eight exam papers to a private tutor for £3000. We started with shovels and rock hammers to remove the overlying sediment, then moved on to dental picks and fine brushes to expose the bones themselves. Dark energy does more than hurry along the expansion of the universe. Banality gave him the means. From 1990–2005 there was a twenty-fold increase in illegal immigrant deaths in Pima

County, Arizona, which borders Mexico. It was a telling choice, harking back to pre-war England and traditions of vaudeville, while also identifying with the fringes of society. That huge desire to buy is driving prices up and up, beyond belief. When Richter quotes from debased sources, it is never merely for the purposes of mocking them, nor is his regard for them (no matter how they trouble or dismay him) ever contemptuous or cynical. This is a central line train to Loughton; the next station is Chancery Lane.

Darwin

There is a village under Slievemore Mountain known locally as the Deserted Village. If you think about this a little, it makes perfect sense. Producers of the US drama show *24* say they will cut the number of torture scenes. Studies on the mechanism underlying this effect should provide fundamental insights into the molecular and cellular basis of memory recall. Although each simplex is geometrically flat, they can be glued together in a variety of patterns to produce curved space times. The rings in one instance retained their luminous property nearly twenty-four hours after the insect's death. These pictures seemed to deserve to be better known. Leaving the coast for a time, we again entered the forest. The frequent occurrence of murder may be partly attributed to this habit. Time moves from left to right in the representation. Dust falls in such quantities as to dirty everything on board, and to hurt people's eyes; vessels have even run onshore owing to the obscurity of the atmosphere. One reason for choosing this species of opossum as the first marsupial genome to be sequenced is its long-standing role as a laboratory animal.

Paradise is a garden. It fits us then to be as provident as fear may teach us. What we see may be accompanied by a change in the soundtrack to what Hollywood calls exit music. Exhausted by his ordeal my father burst into tears of relief. These changes were effected in such a manner that clouds, varying in tint between a hyacinth red and chestnut brown, were continually passing over the body. In the virtual world you can look at behaviour in response to the disease. Data has come to be seen and used as a singular mass noun like information or news: the data is currently being processed. This is a forensic sentence. End credits are unusual in the gallery. An intention is embedded in its situation, in human customs and institutions. Did you see Gilbert and George on *Jonathan Ross*? Two kinds of geese frequent the Falklands.

Humans perceive the properties of a surface by interpreting visual input. On the basis of preliminary studies, we expect to identify several thousand sites of structural variation. The ending echoes the paratextual subversion of the pre-release poster, which read: "*The Birds* is coming". The village was never occupied again, except as a boley village. All the little streams are bordered by soft peat, which makes it difficult for the horses to leap them without falling. Imagine Miller's naked body laid out on the white sands of a coral beach. When a histogram is positively skewed, apparent glossiness is increased. The authors argue that over time Paul Broca's conception of the area involved in speech processing has become simplified by others. Options had to be kept open at this stage so that the mind could travel hopefully towards some eventual synthesis, which lay beyond the poem's present horizon. About a third of children with autistic disorder develop temporal lobe epilepsy by adolescence. This is a legacy website of the University of Manchester; the information it carries was frozen on 30 September 2004, and may no longer be accurate. From far off we heard the flight of the BUPA swan. When the insect was decapitated the rings remained uninterruptedly bright, but not so brilliant as before: local irritation with a needle always increased the vividness of light. Laminar flow control can be used on engines, wings, fuselage and tail.

These free-floating proteins bind to specific viral or bacterial proteins, disabling the invaders or labelling them for destruction. Pleasure is their capacity to choose well-known things. A boley village was populated in summer months by young people looking after cattle that grazed on the hillsides. Bowering impersonates Vancouver. After being imprisoned for some time in a ship, there is a charm in the unconfined feeling of walking over boundless plains of turf. In addition to gloss, perceived surface roughness and translucency also depend on image statistics. Caldeira and his colleagues reason that cooling the arctic requires much less material than cooling the planet as a whole.

The end sequences of each clone are mapped to the reference sequence. To measure the activity of individual neurons, which is crucial to the study of cognitive processes such as visual attention, electrodes must be directly inserted into a monkey's brain. She said she liked it best and did she like it best or did she change her mind upon seeing the other? Air sucked in through thousands of tiny holes near the wings eliminates turbulent flow and cuts drag. There are many physical dimensions of gloss that affect the perception of surface material. An intriguing example is lithium metal. That was my foray into neurobiology. This man had been trained into degradation lower than the slavery of the most helpless animal. I observed this phenomenon on several occasions. It takes thirty turbines to reach a kill rate of one bird a year.

Let us continue our walk by entering into the manufactory of black tea. In forests of the Western United States, about half the fires are caused by lightning. As Fries has remarked, little groups of species are generally clustered like satellites around other species. Police said the man was wearing a dark jacket, beige or golden coloured trousers and dark shoes. America is bankrolling Afghanistan. My work is now nearly finished; but as it will take me many more years to complete it, and as my health is far from strong, I have been urged to publish this abstract. These factors should be taken into account in any appraisal of the consequences of action that claims to be rational and thorough. The highest purpose is to have no purpose.

A group of animals were trained using fear conditioning. Pixels in the positive tail of luminance distribution are interpreted as highlights (mirror reflections of the illuminant) and then discounted in interpreting surface lightness. The pragmatist reminds us that a new and useful vocabulary is just that, not a sudden unmediated vision of things or texts as they are. In the house people began to stir. Not until we reach the extreme confines of life, in arctic regions or on the borders of utter desert, will competition cease. The images of children are library footage. It is not uncommon to see young men missing either hands or legs in Freetown. The Mystic Pad is now clear of writing and ready to receive fresh inscriptions. We get more done by not doing what someone else is doing. Afghan children chew on mud they scratch from the walls of their homes. The principles of selection I find distinctly given in an ancient Chinese encyclopaedia. Suppose we had a list of the books on the *Beagle*.

While working in North Africa, Cott had fake tank shadows painted on the desert surface to fool enemy reconnaissance. On Scattery Island, Kilrush, County Clare, the islanders were evacuated in 1978 but ruins of the village, known as the street, still stand. Many moths are both cryptically and disruptively patterned. A symbolic connection with the history of the city is unavoidable. We shall pick up those threads again shortly. To shift a philosophical position, it is necessary to overcome its "social inertia". Painting is the vehicle for this activity. We see beautiful co-adaptations most plainly in the woodpecker and the mistletoe; and only a little less plainly in the humblest parasite which clings to the hairs of a quadruped or feathers of a bird. To edit memory, simply enter the new value of memory into the cell and press the enter key on the keyboard. The term "intrinsic nature" is an expression that has caused more trouble than it has been worth.

Panorama did not disclose where the detector came from. Hence it is credible that the presence of a feline animal in large numbers in a district might determine, through the intervention of mice and then of bees, the frequency of certain flowers. The team is now targeting a protein called p53. Nor is there anything quite like Richter's paintings of military aircraft. Among young firs stands a pyramid, with two dates (those of the birth and death of Caspar David Friedrich). The factory contains a prison room, and is duly furnished with rattans, iron manacles, handcuffs and other requisites of Foujdaree administration. All of this detail might then be completely or partially obscured by veils of black.

Autobiography is notoriously a charter for dissemblance and rationalisation. The other argument was more muffled. Blackfriars bridge spans the river, its structure reflected in the water below. In these several senses, which pass into each other, I use for convenience the general term of Struggle for Existence. The Germans are reported to have amused themselves by dropping fake wooden bombs on Cott's non-existent tanks. Recovery was associated with rearrangements of the existing neuronal network, which may be a means of re-establishing access to long-term memories. I have sent home four bottles with animals in spirits; I have three more, but would not send them till I had a fourth. Space is emptying out, leaving our Milky Way galaxy and its neighbours on an increasingly isolated island. In this way a sentence loosens within itself. Humble bees alone visit red clover, as other bees cannot reach the nectar. A breed, like a dialect of language, can hardly be said to have a distinct origin. The tiny black mark just below the centre of Virtue's painting, which represents All Saint's Church, Exmouth, plays an important role in the creation of pictorial space and is reminiscent of Constable's similar use of distant church towers. Internet protocol was designed to route data efficiently.

When the plague spread to towns they didn't know how to stop it; even quarantine didn't work. While in the park, firearms must be unloaded, inoperative, in a case, and kept in your vehicle at all times. The authors find a slight eastward shift in the hottest spot and a slight westward shift in the coolest spot, curiously putting both spots on the same hemisphere. The bridge was hated by a good section of London artisans and tradesmen, particularly the watermen who saw in it their own impending redundancy. Please touch this screen to find a store.

Mr Daniell has observed, in his meteorological essays, that a cloud sometimes appears fixed on a mountain summit, while the wind continues to blow over it. A "holding" is an area of airspace used to delay aircraft already in flight. In 1950 Jan Hendrik Oort proposed that comets reside in a vast cloud at the outer reaches of the solar system. By systematically slowing the appreciation of the currency, the People's Bank of China is keeping their exports cheap and irresistible. Which, if any, of the three definitions of genocide applies to British rule in Ireland? Hitchcock's non-ending is more radical than the notorious "bad" conclusions of Hollywood movies from the 1970s, in which the good guys die and the bad guys win. I was much interested, on several occasions, by watching the habits of an octopus, or cuttlefish. Less frequent turns are more comfortable for passengers and crew. Although the theory has many proponents, no direct proof of Nemesis has been found. The attorney general, Lord Goldsmith, denies that he concealed secret payments to a Saudi prince. You can call up Amtrak Julie. Dickens refers to the industrial coal-produced pollution that shrouded and choked nineteenth-century London.

Using the point of a small brush, the fine architectural details that have been noted in the drawings are carefully transcribed. Dewey thought, as I do, that the vocabulary which centres around these traditional distinctions has become an obstacle to our social hopes. What level is this? The CDT universe is analogous to a coarse sweater: a large spider can crawl across the two-dimensional surface, but a tiny mite can only travel along the one-dimensional threads. Newton Abbot is the next stop; change here for services to Tor, Torquay and Paignton. This is embarrassing for Mr Blair who said on Thursday with some confidence that the US was moderating its position on climate change as the summit approached. He loves drawing in the sand and enjoys watching the waves come in and wash it away: he draws really quickly. If you don't see it you probably need a pair of glasses. *Hex* is another invention of Piet Hein. A chromatic scale of principal buzz tones gives an eleven-tone octave. The late David Wojnarowicz sewed his lips together in a silent protest against that same epidemic. If a pronoun was the target there was a topic shift on seventeen percent of occasions but when the original specific name or role was reintroduced then eighty-eight percent of sentences used a topic shift.

The tuning slide is used less as a tuning device than as a means of regulating tone quality. A non-directional beacon (NDB) is a radio broadcast station in a known location, used as an aviation or marine navigational aid. This is one of those memories formed to protect you from re-experiencing anxiety. Philosophy might be regarded as a cultural disease, which has been cured. 3.45: listen for the raisin beep. Species very closely allied to other species apparently have restricted ranges. The path between these extremes is narrow and the way is fraught with difficulties and questions. Look at how much closer the image seems: details in the cars and floors and walls are a lot sharper. In the next chapter I shall discuss the complex and little known laws of variation. Or the whole may be recorded and delivered mechanically. In 'Landscape no. 77' (Page 95), the Thames is given a greater role. This amount of sequencing is well within the capacity of the genome centres. We take up this line of critical discussion in chapter four. The victim of the attack had spent over a year building up her virtual property. For other uses, see holding (disambiguation).

The vacant binding pocket of the access protomer has a shrunken structure similar to that of the extrusion protomer. Many global companies have fallen for the area's charms including AstraZeneca and Ciba Speciality Chemicals. If you have a non-frame compliant browser, click on non-frames. The drawings attempt to encapsulate this information. When I first started to study memories I was looking at emotion and not at memory. The IAU has designated this class of objects as Centaurs. About eighteen percent of people in the sample remember where they were when they heard news of John F. Kennedy's assassination.

When I went into a coma there was only tea and vinegar in the shops, meat was rationed. Modern autopilots can be programmed to enter and fly holdings automatically. It is unlikely that the study will allay the worries of bird-lovers who look on wind farms with loathing. But on no other hypothesis can I understand their linear grouping. During the famine years they offered food and accommodation to locals willing to convert from Catholicism to the Protestant faith. If your country has poor connectivity you may find it faster to access one of the mirror sites nearer to you. Do you have a self-defining memory connected to your career decisions? Remember not to inflate your life jacket until you are outside the aircraft. I have no propositions, and therefore have no fallacy.

The plain was not quite so level as that nearer the coast, yet it betrayed no signs of any great violence. The exhibition comprised the shell of an exhibition without the normal substance—that is paintings. Her body was covered with "camouflage cream" the better to match the background. But in defining the nature of the thing, what is the use of a feeling, however certain, if thought alone has the right to speak here? Each inspection team consisted of two permanent members supplemented by a third on temporary attachment. This makes internal pickups equally difficult to use. If you could download knowledge onto a memory chip, why bother to learn anything, or value knowledge and experience? The purpose of this study was to examine whether the sentence verification decision process affected scalp recorded event-related brain potentials (ERPS). I understand the purpose of free-tagging devices like del. The accident destroyed the Chernobyl-4 reactor and killed thirty people, including twenty-eight from radiation exposure. P53 is an important mediator of DNA damage response and tumour suppression in vertebrates. If you are satisfied with this proposal, I beg you to ascend this staircase.

The best fuel is afforded by a little bush about the size of common heath, which has the useful property of burning while fresh and green. Although not valuable they were very fragile. All these sentences take shape. His pictures are executed in a modernist painterly language inherited from Abstract Expressionism. But by steps hereafter to be explained, the larger genera also tend to break up into smaller genera. All the linotype machines were destroyed. Routes shown on the map have been optimised to allow the minimum use of walkways and ensure mobility in the day during high tides up to about plus 120 cm. They had lost the emotional content of the memory. Being in a carrycot on a table in a flying boat in Africa. The question arises—and it is a serious one—whether these essays can be read in a language other than French? Works of Magritte that interested him most were those in which a written word contradicts a visual image, "to the profit", he said, "of the subject". By the time Frank Lowe was discharged from the army, Coltrane had moved on. In 1713 Spain granted England a thirty-year monopoly on the Spanish slave trade. Usable simple harmonics are shown for ready reference in Figure 2. Long before I could read words I could count numbers and when I counted, the numbers would appear as emotions or coloured shapes in my mind. It's much easier to repurpose old parts from junk DNA, than to invent new ones from scratch.

'Landscape with Three Trees' (page 75) is a tiny yet epic composition that Dutch Protestants would have interpreted as a disguised evocation of the crucifixion. Money is not a symbol, just as the existence of a use-value in the form of a commodity is no symbol. Some of the water placed in a glass was of a pale reddish tint; and, examined under a microscope, was seen to swarm with minute animalcula darting about, and often exploding. Setting off before rush hour while the streets were relatively quiet, his journey would take him down Southampton Row, along Kingsway, around Aldwych, then over Waterloo Bridge. The term *Holzwege* means more precisely a woodcutter's track, for getting access to parts of a wood and bringing down felled timber. Research is the initial step towards a successful keyword search engine optimisation campaign. Students will view anti-Irish cartoons, finding, listing and discussing racist stereotypes. The medieval artist was a craftsman with no desire for personal expression (the concept would have been meaningless), but extremely attentive to the technical excellence and durability of his product. The tessellated compositions make this clear when they are seen from a distance. Typical noontime temperatures are four degrees Celsius above absolute zero. Is there anyone in America who doesn't have a flashbulb memory of 9/11? We now count all mathematicians reachable by following links from an advisor to a student, regardless of whether the advisor is advisor one or advisor two.

The title and duties of the censors resulted from the cultural and political upheavals that are associated with Humanism. In October 1986 the work 'Fettecke' which was installed in Room 3 at the Kunstacademie, was destroyed. Brainchild of artist-critic Thomas Lawson (now Dean of the School of Art at CalArts) and writer Susan Morgan, *Real Life* was published intermittently from 1979 to 1994. She made her way to Hollywood after winning a jitterbug contest in her native Ontario. It is possible that by inducing a rewiring of the brain and increasing connectivity, memories can be retrieved again. This evidence is evident in the images he made. The king of Italy was in a villa outside Rome, ready to abdicate. Recently they've started showing *Pollock*, starring and directed by Ed Harris, on satellite TV. These results, as we shall more fully see in the next chapter, follow from the struggle for life.

They are classic peripheral artist characters who could be in any art biopic, lovable, irascible, and interchangeable, like Disney dwarves. US networks have been struggling to resurrect mainstream comedy. Do you get anxious if you can't drink your cups of tea at the same time each day? Four horses in the roundhouse provide the motive power for the threshing machine, which is being fed with sheaves pitched from a wagon. There was nowhere else to go; had they survived, they would only have come with us to Srebrenica. There is no culminating work preceded by a series of studies, just the studies. Wild strawberries grow among the tombs.

The surface near the crater is marked by high albedo ejecta. We cannot return to our village because it is not safe. What you see on the screen is determined by source code. Many animal-derived chemicals, such as fatty acids, are used in making plastic. A hunter came to find out who was playing such beautiful music. The answer depends on the nature of investment. Directives are posted. Tables and tomatoes are still tomatoes and tables. Miwa adds rough sand to local clays to give added texture, but this sometimes makes his hands bleed when he pots. The bay is full of seaweed come in on the tide. Although quite variable they were not hostile. Ministers argue that staggered opening and closing times will lead to a decrease in alcohol-fuelled town centre violence. The full text reads, "a man once travelled this mountain path" and it quotes the last two lines from a poem. In adulthood our ability to hear their cries is lost forever. The earliest successful expert systems, such as XCON, proved too expensive to maintain. We were trying to poke out a nuclear fire with scaffolding poles. The characters, however, are true to life. Two women, one of them blind, were walking the footpath on the edge of Sandy Bay Caravan Park. In these cantos, vast spaces intervene between ruler and subject, giving the relationship an almost iconic quality.

Whales have died in large numbers before. To learn from Freud you have to be critical; and psychoanalysis generally prevents this. The oval centrepiece of four ostrich feathers on a yellow ground is an example of eighteenth-century English block printing, the earliest form of textile printing. When extreme speed is required, it is necessary to face this awkwardness. The centre helps you to work through your feelings and not just treat the symptoms. Crimes against bats are rising. Serizawa was famous for developing the "stencil picture dyeing" technique. His father called him a lazy, useless son and sent him away from home.

This is the "hate system", with its "distant loop", from the far curve of which the Earth is safely lovable. A *noren* is a door curtain split vertically up the middle. The space interval now resonates strongly with potential and anxiety in regard to meaning. He often used it to dye written characters onto cotton cloth in a bold style he devised himself. Except when rising from the ground, I do not recollect ever having seen one of these birds flap its wings. But this study strongly suggests that some memories are not lost, they just cannot be accessed. Marsupials diverged from placental mammals about one hundred and eighty million years ago. The pictures, made on the north bank of the Thames, from the roof of Somerset House, are entirely different. Rory Bremner examines two types of speech technology: speaker recognition and voice verification. The total mass of comets in the Oort cloud is estimated to be forty times that of Earth. This short film shows Japanese craft artists at work making ceramic items and printed textiles; it lasts four minutes and repeats automatically. It is the experience of her floating melody that makes this possible. Leopards and bulls rest in the shade of fruit trees.

The name of the beginning was 'Only More So'. Each of these analogies suggests that fear is being deliberately generated, as a form of energy that can then be stored and directed. Engineers have established the extent of surface damage. This test would satisfy most people but not all philosophers. For fifty years we had no investment at all in the energy sector. Ian Chilvers compiled a catalogue of books in the artist Broodthaers' library, which he loved and used in his work. In 1235 Henry III received a gift of three lions from the Holy Roman Emperor, they were kept in the Tower of London.

The most productive areas are at continental margins, where sediments are stirred and their nutrients mix with the surface waters at some time during the year. Macedonia is building transmission lines to Belane and ought to be able to shelter from energy price fluctuations. All previous sets are located in memory by date order. The World Bank is bound by its founding charter not to finance nuclear power plants. Dead bats have appeared for sale on eBay. The design suggests the play of light on rippling waves, as they disappear into the distance. The reminiscence of ballad-format introduces a profound ambiguity also about voice. We cannot go back until fighting has stopped.

Most crimes against bats occur in the lofts and cellars of private homes and will never be reported. This tray might hold an ornamental burner for incense. Gertrude Stein's name was never in

Who's Who in America. If you do nothing, the system will shut down automatically in 21 seconds. About forty percent of the signs are used in conjunction with animals. We began to meet new people all the time. The word, an Arabic colloquialism, means "a man with a gun on a horse". The remaining obstacles are different for each country. There is no hippopotamus in this room at present. Atlantic and Mediterranean seashells indicate that people travelled or exchanged objects from different regions. "Resilience" is the time taken by the modified system to revert to its initial state. In 1992 Charles Pollock, studying at the Otis Art Institute, sent copies of The Dial to his teenage brother Jackson. The taxi in several photographs allows the reader to construct a narrative that may or may not be there. It was at this time that Tristan Tzara first appeared in Paris.

A regular series of lists and brochures will keep you in touch with the latest finds and best deals of the moment. He came from California and his father was an inventor. This test would satisfy most philosophers but not all people. On August 12, 1992, John Cage died. Paintings are not spread all over the entire surface of the cave walls. There is a Michelin map of the railway route at the top left, balancing the title information. I called on the secretary to show my passport. Standing alone in another cavity is an indeterminate figure that could be either an unfinished animal or human. The tubes, as I have already remarked, enter the sand nearby in a vertical direction. Plate 15 is a very similar shot to Brassaï's plate 54: trees in bloom, for example. The Turing Test was the first serious proposal in the philosophy of artificial intelligence. Skinny whales arrived in Mexico after swimming from the far reaches of the Arctic Ocean. This vase was deliberately deformed by carving and incising, giving it a rough appearance. The manifesto version is both longer (three pages opposed to two) and more typographically daring. More than 50 still visible imprints indicate that prehistoric people walked over the cave floor. This curriculum kept alive the memory of other avant-garde artists. We had never realised what mudguards were for but by the time we arrived in Nancy we knew.

Engineers have extended the surface of established damage. It is the study of the kinds of things that exist. The soprano pipistrelle weighs less than a 2p piece. Ishiguro first decided to become a ceramic artist in 1918 when he saw a beautiful tea bowl with an effect known as "oil spot" pattern in the *tenmoku* glaze. This is what close listening has to mean. At work and in closed spaces, she started to suffer extreme panic attacks. An expert system is a program that answers questions or solves problem about a specific domain of knowledge, using logical rules derived from experts. Linear signs are predominant, followed by punctuated signs, then more complex. We left for Alsace and on the road had our first and only accident. Because of the spiral binding, the book can be opened to expose front and back covers together, revealing the same image reversed, and making a converging street. The wagons were not prevented from travelling in a nearly straight line. Some figures were sketched with charcoal then covered with a liquid mixture. Reduced polar sea ice is expected to open up the Northwest Passage through the Arctic Ocean, turning it into a crowded and polluted oil tanker route for parts of the year.

The main concern of my work is to create and express shadows by manipulating the shape of the body. A bear paw-print, unique for the Palaeolithic period, has also been engraved. Fifteen motors underneath her silicon skin allow her to express a limited range of emotions, and a 400-word vocabulary enables her to hold a simple conversation. To remember, peel here. Misha Defonseca admitted that her bestseller about surviving the holocaust was a hoax. One day a spirit woman followed her inside. This sentence was made to contain a squashed frog rescued from an eco-poem. The glaze is rich with accidental effects caused by ash that has fallen onto the surface during firing. 95% of orders arrive in seven days. Only the antlers have been added. Wherever we went the Janjaweed beat us and forced us to move on.

Our emergency-landing site, stable for thousands of years, was gone. As early humans spread out from Africa, some variation arose in human DNA that remains today. What lies in wait for us at the tera scale? Perhaps the lakes are slowly leaking out of their basins, thereby supplying water to lubricate the base of the ice sheet. Cultural revolution is replaced by personal survival. Maeta specialises in white porcelain. Mr Johnson, who was appointed

Health Secretary to replace Patricia Hewitt, will have to repair damage to the morale of nurses and doctors. Forests of warmer climate wood species gradually developed, bringing with them red deer, roe deer and wild boar. Roastbeef in *Tender Buttons* is all one word. This tension is known as the hierarchy problem.

I will add some observations, which were made during this visit and on a previous occasion, when the Beagle was employed in surveying the harbour. New words were entering the language and he did not hear how they were being used. He incorporates other materials such as quail eggshells and white pearl-oyster shell. *The Blind Man* no.2 (May 1917) had on its front cover Duchamp's *Chocolate Grinder no.1* (1914), bought by Walter Arensburg and not put on public view until 1954. It is autumn; Nanjing is full of too many beautiful things. One sector was cooled, powered up and then returned to room temperature earlier in 2007. As a result, patients have difficulty controlling their movements and experience a range of cognitive and emotional problems. Their subsistence economy was based on hunting, fishing and food gathering, which explains their nomadic lifestyle. But Usami wanted to go smaller. The guiding principle of the Standard Model is that its equations are symmetrical. They glitter like stardust in the afternoon sunlight.

Population movement seems to have accelerated changes in human DNA. The style of animal painting in the deeper galleries is relatively uniform and different from the rest of the cave. What a program knows about the world in general, the facts of the specific situation in which it must act, and its goals, are all represented by sentences of some logical language. Even deeper lies the prospect of insights into the different forms of matter, the unity of outwardly distinct particle categories and the nature of space-time. It was through heightened verbal signification that music itself acquired meaning. Testing is important because a loss of vision cannot be reversed. Without a bat detector, only children and young women can hear pipistrelles' social calls. Magnetic lenses focus the electron and positron beams as they race towards one another, and detectors at the collision point analyse the particles hurtling from high-energy impacts.

Lakes appear to be triggering the flow of an ice stream within the ice sheet. But standing amid the ruins of Heraclea we find the origins of Europe. Powder chip surface is here shown at roughly 800 times its true size. Babbage never built his engine. Something so far unexplained has been cutting off much of the whales' food supply in the Arctic Circle where the ice is retreating at an unprecedented rate. Apollinaire proposed the abolition of syntax, the adjective, punctuation, typographic harmony, the tenses and persons of verbs, and verse and stanzas in poems. The collapse was in the perception of artificial intelligence by government agencies and investors. We went on, the car wandering all over the muddy road, uphill and downhill, and Gertrude Stein sticking to the wheel.

Different obstacles are for each the country remaining. Drainage has been strongly linked to the acceleration of ice movement towards the sea. All of this is normal for fictional images, and so is unconsciously accepted. The cave walls feature several hundred graffiti, the earliest of which is dated 1602. These elusive particles must have mass, which the Standard Model does not seem to explain. Hitler was a few days older than Ludwig Wittgenstein, but during the year in which they overlapped at school he was in the third class, while Ludwig was in the fifth. He already knew something about developing electronic chips.

The weak force, which is involved in radioactive beta decay, does not act on all the quarks and leptons. Today the ruins lie on the dusty outskirts of Bitola, a city little known outside the region. Being winter the tree had no leaves, but in their place numberless threads, by which various offerings, such as cigars, bread, meat, pieces of cloth etc., had been suspended. In 1978, the increase in water infiltration destroyed some paintings and altered many others. At first the extent of the problem was unknown. In several instances, they became so outraged at the inequity of outcome they heaved the cucumber slice back at the human experimenters.

Brassaï walked alone, bearing his *Voigtländer Bergheil* camera with its 10.5 Heliar lens, tripod and twenty-four plates. Walls are not spread over the entire surface of the paintings. The fake memoir is only the latest in a series of literary hoaxes perpetrated by white, middle class authors seeking to embellish their life histories in this age of autobiography. Our ability to empathize relies on neuronal systems that underpin our own bodily and emotional states. Sasaki weaves using pongee, hand-spun silk.

Answers may come in time as Voyagers continue to race through the heliosheath. We know that memory and learning occur when certain neuronal circuits connect more strongly. Single leaves were liable to become detached and lost or misplaced in subsequent bindings. She asked the media to let the family grieve in peace. Actual droplet diameters may be as small as a millionth of a metre. Poised on the rim of the tank, we talked about the breeding programme. The ubiquity of the lion is discussed below. Some of these mutations are so harmful that they are eliminated before their carriers are born.

The skin was tensioned on a frame, and a semi-circular *luna* knife was used to remove what hair and debris remained. Darwin, 57, pleaded guilty to seven charges of deception and one charge of making false statements to procure a passport. The digging would be easier if the team knew what they were looking for. NP stands for nondeterminate polynomial time. The artists did not necessarily comprehend the full significance of all that they were copying. These inky striations do not damage the picture plane. Apart from dimly glowing black holes and any artificial lighting that civilisations have rigged up, the universe goes black. This is not yet heritage territory. Virtually the entire state of Florida would be underwater. An almost exclusive feature of this chamber is the presence of angular signs on the animals, especially on bison, never on the ibex.

Some registries are a dead end. No one can tell a live male from a live female except another tuna. If you can solve a problem quickly you can verify the solution quickly. These leaves, slightly thicker than the norm, were taken from calves, which had been killed at roughly two or three months old. Long before this information limit becomes a problem, all the expanding matter in the universe will be driven outside the event horizon. These receptors come in umbrella and cone shapes: in humans the umbrella version, which is more plentiful, opens the door to serious illness. A flight of geese or an incidence of atmospheric turbulence can fool radar, and anomalous reflections of the sun can trick satellite-based infrared detectors. Artists preferred robust skins like these for pages of major decoration. Most federal workplace exposure limits are based on 1960s science. It follows that among the satellites vulnerable to such an attack are the orbital spies. This part of the brain coordinates your voluntary movements and keeps you oriented in space.

The figure was partially dismembered by a binder's knife in the nineteenth century, and the short, bifurcated flowering rod held in his right hand has been badly damaged by abrasion. No hard numbers supported the notion of collective wisdom in crowds. After 2020 the need to keep nuclear devices on standby to defend against a Near Earth Object (NEO) virtually disappears. In some cases, like folio 28, the spine of the calf can be observed running conspicuously down the middle of the page. They send out vast numbers of branches that make connections with other cells in the cerebellum. He said: "Mr Darwin has been in custody since early December and it has been an extremely difficult time for him". In September last year seven Tibetan schoolchildren were beaten and tortured in custody with electric cattle prods for writing slogans on a school wall.

The face of the angel at the top left of 29r was given no features. Studies on animals, in which brains can be physically examined, show myelin can change in response to mental experience and a creature's developmental environment. He knows that he knows all this. Teleportation is a protocol about how to send a quantum state—a wave function—from one place to another. We live in an approximately flat universe dominated by dark matter and an unidentified form of dark energy that drives cosmic acceleration. The new molecules arrange themselves at the tip of the fibril in a very organised way. There are reports of gunshots but no casualties. Darwin was pronounced dead after he disappeared during a canoe trip off Hartlepool in 2003. The distinctive handling demonstrated in landscape 769—in which the Oxo tower takes on a block-like simplicity—must stem from this experience. White matter fills nearly half the brain. These cave fish can reach about 12 centimetres in length, and skin grows over their useless eyes. The accelerating universe wipes out traces of its own origins.

Because the weather satellite was still transmitting when it was destroyed, the Chinese operators would have known its exact location at all times. The strong force is carried by eight particles known as gluons. This equivocation in the reference station is part of a sustained fiction from the very outset. When no sample is present, the light rays cancel each other out, and no light reaches the viewer. Each second, each breath, is a work which is inscribed nowhere. Stone tools were small in size, indicating that sources of new materials were not close by. In these tiny patients, memory and personality develop normally.

Bat conservationists want to persuade builders that people and bats can live together. Internet-based financial markets appear to forecast elections better than opinion polls. Where a match turns up, Bornemann tries to trace the next of kin through online databases. If the left side of the brain is taken out, most people have problems with their speech. Augustina's white dress shines out against a dark cannon and bodies. No photography is allowed in the facility, because the engineering, water processing, climate control and every other element in the design must be carefully safeguarded to prevent corporate theft. This increased the financial incentive to evict small tenants. Stepanova was a co-founder with Gan and Rodchenko of the first working group of constructivists. These access tools were created at the same time as the documents themselves.

Generations of stars have contaminated the original chemical link. By this calculation, which is necessarily imprecise, *The Book of Kells* in its original state used the skins of around 185 calves. Japanese citizens with special craft skills are designated by the Japanese government as living national treasures (*ningen kokuho*). Why do black redstarts divide up their brood in this way? The whistle tone is a rare example of an instrumental technique developed for didactic purposes and later accepted in the literature. Birmingham has adopted Winson Green, now known as the "city prison". A third class of chord, known as nearly inversionally symmetric, is scattered through the orbifold. The Skibbereen workhouse was designed to accommodate 800 persons but contained 2800 in December

1848; the local guardians provided three small timber sheds as additional room. The consistorium began in the eleventh century as an administrative body for the church, made up exclusively of cardinals.

He injected about three ounces of a strong decoction of Bohea tea into a dog, and made very little alteration in the dog. It is difficult to define the word "series" in the context of this work. Robots with artificial intelligence will be put into management positions; they will not necessarily have heads and arms. The interlinear animals mostly stand outside the programme of established symbolism and may be regarded as additions of an ornamental nature, which demonstrate the range of models available to the artists and their proximity to nature. Without performing an autopsy, the question remains open. The third pillar is the faint glow of the cosmic microwave background.

In this part of the cave we also find red painted animals: a bison or horse backbone, the forequarters of an upside down horse and a small bison surrounded by signs. Leptons, the best known of which is the electron, are immune to the strong force. Virtue worked from the riverbank when the tide was out. All four scribes were clearly products of the same scriptorium, with a few obvious differences between them in letterforms. In 1849 cholera appeared in the country. The couple were remanded in separate jails in December after Darwin returned from the dead by wandering into a London police station, saying he thought he was a missing person. We call this economy Corporation Land or Technology Land or Disney Land. There may be sheep on 50v, though it is more likely that a cat is intended. Dark energy will have an enormous impact on the future of the universe.

Yesterday charred vehicles and burnt-out rubbish littered streets close to the courthouse; French peacekeepers fired warning shots in the air. In the print made after the artist's death, the scene is plunged into a dark fog. Why should I switch to Oyster? The starfire system incorporates adaptive optics that narrow the outgoing laser beam and thus increase the density of its power. Without myelin, the signal leaks and dissipates. The arithmetic is becoming clearer. One of the proteins implicated in Huntingdon's may ironically, provide patients with subtle health benefits. Space warfare is not inevitable. Some series are composed of rather small volumes. People have two votes so their second preferences could be crucial.

In this process we often encountered a mixture of languages, unusual abbreviations, and idiosyncratic, wrong or antiquated spellings. No soft lotions supported crowd wisdom in the collective. The lack of finances and infrastructure mean that mosquitoes spread malaria unchecked. We have dispatched our armies into the land of Islam. This particular protein determines how effectively the virus can infect people. Records of the nunciative consist of the following series. Teachers are regularly sent model lesson plans, worksheets and other teaching materials by government departments, charities and private companies. Like the wolf, it is not clear why the stag is in the book. For such precision to occur, delays are necessary. This relation between distance and velocity is exactly what happens when the universe is expanding. No one disputes that the large majority of our genome has a recent African origin. When such a star finally exploded in a supernova, it would scatter these elements into space, where they would seed still-forming star systems.

On the 20th we bade farewell to the south, and with a fair wind turned the ship's head northward. Hubble determined not just the velocities of nearby galaxies but also their distances. The light was sufficient to cast on the water a long bright reflection. Painting was done with brushes of varying fineness; the most delicate are made from marten fur. This list should not be seen as definitive but rather as a convenient starting point for the elaboration of more sophisticated multilingual dictionaries of affective meaning. We did note the existence of documents generated after 1922, even though under current Vatican policy, that material remains closed to research use.

Time is measured in the number of elementary steps required by the algorithm to reach a solution. The bluefin did not become valuable as a food fish until the latter half of the twentieth century when sushi began to appear on menus around the globe. Next morning we started very early. People tend to forget that they're talking to a machine. Suppose that you are given the dimensions of various boxes and you want a way to pack them in your boot. A distinctive pattern would suggest that the Pratt and Whitney tumours were not random. He reminds his viewer that there is nothing destructive—or conspicuously radical—about this way of working. The idea of a "terrorist futures market" repulsed many in Washington. By mid-March remarkable satellite images showed that some 1300 square miles of Larsen B, a slab bigger than the state of Rhode Island, had fragmented.

This exhibition contains human remains. Some phone queries provide support centre staff with a chance to cross-sell or up sell, generating revenue from more product sales in the course of solving a service problem. The first shock was very sudden. Other characteristics less dependent on bore and ventage will be discussed later. He uses a quarter inch sable brush, applying Mehron's blue colour cup makeup. General relativity overcomes this limitation. The manuscript was inarguably at Kells from late in the eleventh century, when it was used to record property transactions.

A schooner was left in the midst of ruins, 200 yards from the beach. The Humane Association has just launched a mailing list for announcements related to emotion-oriented and affective computing. Darwin briefly squeezed his wife's hand, as they both stood in the dock at Leeds crown court yesterday, before admitting his deception. These objects will then be truly and completely invisible to us. Here we are in the depths of the mountains; no trees in the glen, only green pasturage for sheep, and here and there a plot of hay-ground, something that tells of former cultivation. Initially aimed at people who are sick, these advances move out to the needy well. Material function and form were fused, in accordance with constructivist principles. In this model, tremor might be analogous to much smaller volcanic tremor, which is thought to arise from the coupling of fluid flow to the solid earth in volcanic systems. We are now approaching Plymouth, please make sure that you take all your belongings with you and take care when leaving the train. The nature of whole landscapes has been transformed by human-induced vegetation change. Coltrane built a studio at his Long Island home and founded his own record company. The frontal lobes are the last places where myelination occurs.

Powered throughout its flight, such a missile can hug the ground to evade radar. The universe comes to resemble an inside-out black hole, with matter and radiation trapped outside the horizon rather than inside. The purpose of the scope note is to give some indication of the contents of the series. Let's get started. The vase could be transformed by a flower arrangement for a tea gathering. Alan Turing's 1950 article *Computing Machinery and Intelligence* discussed conditions for considering a machine to be intelligent. Think carefully about sentences. When Ada met Babbage.

The earthquake commenced at half-past eleven o'clock in the forenoon. She attended a private Episcopal school in north Hollywood and never did live with a foster family, become a gang member or deliver drugs. These plays provide a sort of comfort food for viewers too discerning to watch reality TV. Gentle winds blow away every unhelpful thought. Other reports said the monks were unable to leave. In citizenship, for example, what is a Lembit Öpik? There is another mechanism to regulate conflict. Heroin is now more widespread than cannabis inside prisons in England and Wales.

Darwin was living secretly next door to his wife at the seaside home in Seaton Carew for much of the time after being declared dead. At the evangelist's right foot is an inkpot, probably made from a cow's horn stuck into the earth. The largest and brightest stars will have burned up their nuclear fuel, but plenty of smaller stars will still light up the night sky. For millennia, Pacific grey whales have gathered every summer to feed in the shallow waters of the Chirikov basin, in the north Bering Sea. She made Bolade bring down food, and then ate it all up, leaving nothing for the girl who had to go hungry. Quarks have colour, and leptons do not.

Collecting & Polishing Stories

Trouble begins at the surface of the body. I'll tie my butcher's apron here. There is still more that can be done by looking closely at dust jackets. You could live in Barrow-in-Furness, never go to the theatre, and yet still collect pictures of Gertie Millar. The car either starts or it doesn't. When in an energised state, the enclosed plasma can readily radiate, absorb or reflect electromagnetic waves. The working volume of the cryostat was extremely small. The book was lost to the town in the seventeenth century. German intruders flying low over the sea would usually be able to reach the coast without detection.

The new concept of plate tectonics made everything look different. Of course we all know Anna Livia. Roses were already part of the wallpaper design, so all she had to do was copy them into a squeezed vase. You must use an email address to post a comment. Consciousness may fall through red holes into the body without skin and the mind without reason. As early as 1722, tea was being tested for ill effects by giving it to animals. For small countries with a history of instability, membership provides assurances of security and economic support. They are gears that, as they mesh, turn in opposite directions. For all these performers, acting was the family business.

This cool, clear mineral water rises in a picturesque valley in County Tipperary. No one will dispute that instincts are of the highest importance to each animal. Imagine a pear tree covered with golden fruit. I don't know how much of this is my own invention. Bats could also be a paranoid representation of the outside world regarding the human. This sentence is just as you find it. Originally the *lubok* had been a religious image, hand drawn in pencil and tinted with tempera. He was not searching for planets.

For a given string of letters, the three reading frames will give totally different proteins. Rudimentary organs plainly declare their origin and meaning in various ways. But the rough wall of wax has in every case to be finished off, by being largely gnawed away on both sides. It is good to wander along the coast, when formed of moderately hard rock, and mark the process of degradation. The frame of curtains implies a stage. Familiar points of contact enable assimilation. White and red are dialectical adjectives, the colours of the two globes, round, shiny, and fixed, which indicate alternatives of movement. From every other warm blooded animal they could feel the pulsing of The Food, or taste it on the air so rich with sweat and exhalations.

I'm not sure that Palgrave gives us the best of Herrick. Mr Swaysland, of Brighton, who during the last forty years has paid close attention to our migratory birds, informs me that he has often shot wagtails (*motacillae*), wheatears, and whinchats (*saxicolae*), on their first arrival to our shores, before they alighted; and he has several times noticed little cakes of earth attached to their feet. Fear, Morecambe always insisted, was what motivated their act. One model was Ponge's *Notebook of the Pine Woods*, a journal of the author's stay in hiding from the Nazis.

Manski went back to Hayek's original work to examine the quantitative underpinnings of his ideas. Developing advanced anti-satellite weapons will trigger a new international arms race. Described as "Special Tangiers Edition" the cover has a full page drawing of Burroughs wearing a fez. The difficulty in finding the split in the curtains, the belated appearances, the eavesdropping, and the mime of the mad throttler—each of these makes the viewer comprehend the curtains. Only the mechanic himself is present, pretending to be a houseplant. This elective mutism should be questioned. It doesn't hurt a bit, and it can't be poison ivy.

Early peoples supposedly thought of their feelings and actions as the result of possession by some external spirit or deity and did not fully demarcate their own bodies from the environment. Hence the saving of wax by largely saving honey and the time consumed in collecting pollen must be an important element of success to any family of bees. In the full extent of the series, every element undergoes a gradual but ceaseless qualification. The response is sudden because it has to wait until the next concept emerges. Synthetic viruses might help to elucidate in detail the pathways by which cells become malignant. Reality transcends whatever a model can grasp, or whatever a model can represent to our understanding.

The war did cause patterns of infection to change. And even in cases that are definitely pictographic, the iconicity is fugitive. At the end of lunch there were no more questions.

US researchers are not allowed to pay women for their eggs. Enquirers at Nottingham Tourist information centres were given a free Robin Hood postcard when they bought a stamp. Interlace, which in the *Book of Kells* reached a high order of ingenuity, developed from the art of antiquity. Crucially, an unexpected sense of compassion could creep into sketches. Such parts, however modified, unless their common origin became wholly obscured, would be serially homologous. Because "e" is the most frequently used letter in both English and French, the constraint is constantly felt. Outward travel must not be in the past. So the Bundesbank pitched the Lombard rate at 9.75 per cent, but still Bonn would not come to order.

Near perfect light absorbers are needed for detectors called bolometers, which sense photons by converting their energy to heat. No one expected the vaccine to make some participants more susceptible to infection. Some sound absorbing material was removed and small increases in volume were made. Those receiving the brochure spent £35.5 million on accommodation short breaks in the UK. The narrow beam would give them protection against jamming and good performance against low flying aircraft. It is tempting to prolong the swordplay. The inscriptions on the wall are Roman translations of the original German captions. This question of mutism should be elective. I would just like a glass of water.

The craft era of computer manufacture is now coming to an end. Could making food tastier encourage people to eat less? On windy days, when the prison would in any case get some air, it worked perfectly. The increase in wires resulted in a stronger, less coarse-looking paper. Through a discussion of the objects he has collected, King portrays what it is to be human, to be confused, to be lonely, to make mistakes, and to try to fix them. Why would you take the crisp, sharply separated input and blur it out, make it noisier? Honda's Asimo robot has been given software that understands three people shouting at once.

Collecting makes us think about how categories of value are formed and reformed. The idea is not to go it alone without pharmaceutical companies. Among the beaches and fish restaurants of Southern California, the refugee intellectuals, in Claussen's memorable phrase, had been "expelled into paradise". Scientists use the primates because their brains are closer to the human brain than any other species. The community is not in any obvious sense a state. This is simply a strip of paper, normally between one and three inches deep, wrapped around the jacket in exactly the same way as the jacket itself is wrapped around the book.

With tone indication the meanings are clearly distinguished. So far, the argument follows so-called classical mechanics. None of these films has the intensity or the authority of the extraordinary *Pickpocket* (1959), but they are all recognisably made by the same director. The cell reads the letters three at a time to translate them into a protein molecule. Hence a new relationship between architecture and moral behaviour was made possible. The entire line was then cast as one slug of metal, the matrices returning to the magazine. That is not what privatisation meant in France. Clients are guided in the forest by resident biologists whose primary function is long-term research into the ecology of the region. The profile of respondents is shown in table 4.5.

These teeth bear claw like protrusions that the nestlings use to tear away the outer layer of their mother's skin. One button always provided a small payout; the other supplied a larger one but much less often. Perverse market signals are channelling most of the pharmaceutical industry's research skills into areas that only marginally improve health. A monkey model of Huntingdon's disease created by gene transfer is only a work in progress.

On 22 May, a severed right foot washed up on Kirkland Island near Vancouver. These vicissitudes are not accidental. One in every five of the planet's citizens is Chinese. Externalities, though integrated into cost-benefit analysis techniques, are always in practice experts' estimates. Model prisons proliferated. Honeybees can't count, but if you give them a high concentration of sugar, they remember. It is difficult to make a strong case for the unreality of a virus. The movement of the end-words is a retrograde loop, somewhat simpler than the retrograde cross of the sestina.

If the tools are bad, nature's voice is muffled. This resembles a figure in folio 86r line 2, forming the *T* of *Tunc*, and the tiny detail of a man, upside down, clasping his knees at the top of the shaft of the first *I* of the *Initium* page (folio 130r). The central idea is to include our own human existence as a part of our understanding of the universe. Draft a letter for visitors from a remote traditional culture, explaining to them how to behave as tourists in your locality.

Where were prey animals yesterday? The object had been to suppress the meaning in sounds. This is why any organisation of suspense would be trivial. In the boreal zone, shrubs and trees create a dark surface above snow in winter. The emulsion remained sensitive over long periods of time, whereas the cloud chamber was reactive only for a fraction of a second. As a result the guillemot chicks were getting more fish but fewer calories. Pages 863 and 921 detail progress towards a transgenic monkey model for Huntingdon's disease. Few studies have quantified the Japanese drug lag. We take out of the park all plastic, glass and aluminium. The function of inspection was greatly enhanced by the use of these materials.

Debate centred on thought experiments, a favourite technique of Bohr and Einstein. Cold came on, and each more southern zone became fitted for the inhabitants of the north. The commutation of lines in the pantoum demands a molecular autonomy. Dark hawks hear us. Consideration of these various facts impresses the mind almost in the same manner, as does the vain endeavour to grapple with the idea of eternity. As a way of making sense of the world, teleology has always been attractive, and the expulsion of God from the usual forms of scientific explanation has really only changed the idiom. INSIDE FRONT COVER: A lone Gentoo penguin (*pygoscelis papua*), adrift on a blue iceberg in the Gerlache Passage, Antarctic Peninsula, Southern Ocean, Antarctica.

People talk in detail about what they ate, bought, read and watched on television, and often do so passionately. To persist or to return they need human protection, not only physical but also legal and taxonomic. Unfortunately, none of these techniques is much use when a body is recovered from the ocean. For each region there are clear and much needed maps of language families. By tinkering with local neurons, they hope to learn how to change the volume of the noise. Fossil hunters on the Antarctic mainland are limited to a few exposed sites. If you like hybrids, you'll love our new separator films.

Once a body refloats, it only takes the night current or tide to wash it ashore. The west must get on with it. Gene therapy helped some children who were born without a working immune system. Their first priority was to minimize shouting by guests: service standards had recently been poor. Swiss law requires that the social benefit must be weighed against the burden to animals before any animal experiment can take place. This relationship, published in 1900 and now known as the Sabine equation is still the basis of room acoustic design.

Adorno's *Habilitation* thesis on Kierkegaard was accepted the day Hitler came to power. If the polarisations do not match, someone is listening in. Neurons are a good example of a non-linear system, firing only when the electrical potential across their membrane reaches a critical threshold. His voice is soft and hoarse from having a tube down his throat, his hands shake and he has a tendency to ramble. Rodchenko did not actually pick up a camera until the early 1920s. The function of the treadwheel was to aggravate toil, measure it and equalise its distribution amongst prisoners. Then there was no consistent conceptual framework into which moving continents could fit.

When they try to forecast the future, experts are normally wrong. The three ways of reading are called reading frames. If in many various experiments the natural object behaves like the model, one is happy and thinks that the image fits the reality in essential features. The plant is set to begin producing bioethanol later this year. How far should we go in allowing bubbles to run their course? The turn angles vary and appear random to the naked eye. Noise has a strict mathematical definition and what looks like noise in a complex biological system usually turns out to be a signal leaking from elsewhere.

Suppose that the neo-classical account of market economies is mistaken, or seriously flawed. So far, the features of Yang and colleagues' transgenic primates do not favour any one hypothesis. And their family romance exerts its own fascination, replete with enough complexes and psychosexual secrets to keep an army of analysts occupied for years. The adult does not cover itself with dust, but is dark brown and fully winged. Modern mapping devices count atoms as they move under gravity.

But the mechanism of inhibition is unknown, hindering the development of clinically useful drugs. That very capacity is part of the crisis. Tourists tend to cluster in specific zones of the destination area. A host of lobbyists, pressure groups and corporate consultants hover round. The basic "atoms" of these structures are C-shaped split rings made from patterned metal films on circuit boards. Affordances vary with season and weather, and the age and current needs of individuals.

The phantom triangle is constructed in a different way, and in a different area of the brain, from the "real" one. What other reasons might there be for the end of nature? The survival value of emotions should not surprise us. The fourth floor has been moved to the ninth floor. As propositions they form a system of related symbol-meanings that may be considered and developed as such. First, the brain has to recognise that what is coming in is language. In trip to spleen is Hardwick. It is tempting to dismiss the wordplay.

Often the falsehoods are quite banal and their very pointlessness underlines the teller's clear belief that they are true. Fire suppression kills off native fire-dependent species and creates shrubby undergrowth in place of open forest. The demon may also be useful in quantum computing, where it is important to isolate individual atoms so their properties can be measured. In her first experiment she sank six pigs in water 7 to 15 metres deep. This description of the Nazis' adoption of homeopathy is particularly compelling and sobering. In the case of tourism purchases, the trial stage of decision-making has received less attention from theorists.

All there was underneath was the word "failed" and an "OK" button. The peoples living in the park are autonomous, and continue with their traditional means of food production, medicine and social custom. We cannot know the world by inserting objects into our brains. The first question required the participants to have insight into the burglar's mind, while the second required only general knowledge. You will not find in semantics any remedy for decayed teeth or illusions of grandeur or class conflicts. Truth is not a question of any superficial logical surface structure. In some people, it seems, the anterior cingulate cortex lights up as soon as the heart is short of oxygen. Yet they can repeat words and finish well-known phrases.

You have at the same time a food crisis, an oil crisis and a financial crisis. Where are the safe hiding places that I may need to use in an emergency? Turning again to theoretical descriptions to validate their results, the authors modelled the quantum tunnelling process. We cannot always tell whether references to nature are meant to include or exclude people. But if inferences made and conclusions reached are to be valid, the subject matter dealt with and the operations employed must be such as to yield identical results for all who infer and reason. "It is me", she explained, "split and divided". In type 1 diabetes, the beta cells are destroyed by the body's own immune system.

It starts as a cultural history of sunshine, but veers off into other directions—sun worship in literature, TV weather persons, health implications, and so on. Hales discovered many varieties of air in his experiments. Nineteenth century part-issues were normally distributed in twenty parts with the nineteenth and twentieth issued as one number. Virologists are working close to nature. I then put into the hive, instead of a thick rectangular piece of wax, a thin and narrow knife-edged ridge, coloured with vermilion. We may imagine regular playgoers picking up echoes from one performance to another.

At first sight roses mean purple love. The Objectivist is an Apex Tech repairman, not afraid to get his hands dirty. Imagine a tree fruit golden with covered paper. This process is called long-term potentiation. When she finally encountered spoken words her brain processed them in the area normally reserved for environmental noises. How does a carefree child, when it has grown up, become a parent? Images are not stored as facsimile pictures of things, events, words or sentences. For most people, aesthetics is superfluous.

Government's role in the privatised economy is confined to elementary regulation, the preservation of stable money, and the rule of law.

They started by devising a series of experimental scenarios that manipulate the clarity of reward cues, then ran them in both honeybees and humans. A major obstacle was that atoms in the vapour tended to diffuse, blurring the recovered image. The risks of that practice are not known with precision. Procedural memories, like riding a bike, are stored here. There is no known mechanism by which purposeless functions come to evolve. The non-temporal phase of propositions receives attention later. Sometimes the memories are fragmented, and sometimes they are precise replays of some traumatic event. Any sense may be affected by Agnosia. In a typical concert hall, only the audience and the seating absorb sound as a black surface absorbs light. During the convalescence of animals, great benefit is derived from almost any change in their habits of life. This bird never leaves the quiet inland sounds.

The main foundry building stands back from the road. Meaning begins to develop. You can't make wilderness any more by drawing a line on a map. Physics ought to describe only the correlation of observations. The craft of writing software will not become obsolete. A pear can be grafted far more readily on a quince, which is ranked as a distant genus, than on the apple, which is a member of the same genus. Historians could navigate among electronic sources and break down conceptual boundaries. The twelfth picture shows the execution. It was crushed by watermill and used for porcelain. The fabric was painted with glue and sprinkled with emery powder.

Finding aids usually list places alphabetically with reference to the reel or fiche number. Conceptions of space and time arise not through intuition but because of their utility in reducing complexity of phenomena to a manageable order. In subsequent trials, the activity phase becomes shorter, the movements less random. John gave the boy the dog bit a bandage. Why do senior Communist officials dye their hair black? The written versions of sentences contained no morpheme boundaries. At the moment these brain movies are jerky, like early films. You can measure our impact already, in drought, flood and melt.

This type "H" hangar was a large lightweight timber frame construction covered with heavy canvas. In the short term, however, citizens were proud of having a camp in town. Obviously A cannot be the cause of B if A does not exist. So the mixture has a higher entropy. Like the cat, we begin in the middle of things. The dislocated element "John" in 38, on the other hand, does not have operator-like properties. Most Devon wills were destroyed during the Second World War. Each spot exhibits a greyish, radiating crystal pattern. There is no formal contradiction in any of this. The press greeted the foundation of the camp as "bringing new hope for the Dachau Business World".

At the heart of the pragmatic theory we are using is the notion of relevance, defined in terms of contextual effects and processing effort. Experience in itself is not primarily cognitive. Every social policy, in particular, has a reflexive effect on those who carry it forward. As I gazed out at my class, their names hovering in the air above their heads, they seemed expectant. Either form of ink is then applied by brush to the already crazed surface. So far I have discussed only the abject aspects of social difference. The end of a copper bar is heated in the kiln and, when hot, is dipped into salt water. Some control towers were also provided with an exterior iron stairway. This enabled the striking part to be changed for the different tools that had to be forged.

Where sentences occur in pairs they were presented in the order given. This is not an autobiography. C's responses seemed random, and it was clear that he had no idea what was going on. Feelings of discomfort produced by an irritating stimulus tend to spread until activity succeeds in overcoming it. Keeping these reservations in mind, we none the less assume that such constructions are part of the grammar of English and that their status is fully grammatical. Tiny white flecks dot this sample of reduced, dark red contiguous to a greenish white oxidised area. The Wayback machine identified several of the sites in our sample as unavailable because of robots. txt. Plate glass became cheaper than brick. Readers who have used the Internet already know that web links die. But we can create further problems by putting more characters and reports in the story. Memories are groups of neurons that fire together in the same pattern each time they are activated. At that moment she suddenly felt exhausted and frozen, and lay down on the bed.

Lateral inhibition causes light-receiving cells in the retina to shut down when the light-receiving cells around them are activated. The sentence printed in this paper on page 52, column B, II. 28-29 is not true. Reconciliation ecology is an applied science that assists us in designing habitats we can share with other species. We graphed the data and performed a regression analysis to look for trends over time. Exterior surfaces were treated as planes skimming the steel skeleton rather than as a mass joined to it. This was the first time that radio-controlled flights had been made from the landing grounds.

A dense network of flues can be seen buried in the walls. They have a digital display that shows their current coordinates. In the batch recipe, a small amount of iron oxide is also added. Among reclaimed mine soils, dispersion variance increased with the amount of time since reclamation. The basin was part of the Cherokee Indian Nation until the Nation was moved in 1837. Investment depends on the answer of nature. If the poles were so warm, what were the tropics like? In abandoned terrace fields overlying pumice tuffs, soil degradation processes determine dominant plant life forms. Paper had a number of virtues. All gold and silver firing was formerly done with pine wood fuel. The tracking was easy to transport, lay and repair, and provided a robust non-skid surface that could quickly be camouflaged.

Variegated dots range from blue and grey to green and brown and are interspersed with entrapped bubbles that fortify the overall blue. We wanted to know if link decay increased with time, so we used Microsoft Excel to calculate the linear regression that best followed the overall trend. The Acclimatisation Society released a hundred starlings in New York City's Central Park in 1890 and 1891. Soils are deep sandy loams and are underlain by folded schist and gneiss. Diameter class of cut stumps was recorded for trees harvested during the 1919–1923 logging operations. A third option would be to democratise the concept of the public good. Defunct industrial buildings have been gutted and converted into museums or tourist attractions: the *Canterbury Tales* is a themed attraction housed in a deconsecrated church.

The mouthparts of true bugs consist of a tube-like instrument, the rostrum, which is one of the features that distinguish them from beetles. But robustness of abstraction has cloaked imprecision and ambiguity on the level of application or reference. This survey provides a basis for reconstructing the forest structure, composition, and diversity prior to the chestnut blight in the Southern Appalachians. Private companies turned out to be the largest exploiters of concentration camp prisoners, and the process began by using them in construction work. The list of outputs produced by each possible input is the function of the node. If an attractor has so many steps that it cannot be repeated by a cell before it dies, then it is not an example of order at all. The volume of space in the universe appears to be growing without limit.

Many small stems were present at that time, and this suggests that the forest was then in the initiation stage of stand development. Given enough time, every deterministic Boolean network will fall into a repeating pattern of activity. Each of the cognitive radio devices tries to identify a slice of pristine airwave space where a wireless device could operate without blocking other signals. At cone 9 or slightly less, the patterns are smaller-spaced and less boldly stained. The compiler relied on records from contributing libraries, which were not always accurate. We continued with matching cards, but showing him one side only, before interrogating him as in 23.

The children saw themselves washing. Self-consciousness may well be inferential; hence there is no need to postulate an intuitive self.

The canopy dominant *castanea dentata*, was replaced by more than one species across the environmental gradient. Nugget variance values were lower than 65 per cent of their corresponding total sill values. European settlers continued the practice of light semi-annual burning and grazing. Celadon glazes are usually uniform in colour and rely on the white purity of the porcelain body. In articles published seven years earlier, 38 per cent of web citations were dead. People with mania often talk too much. At Coweeta the above site variables modify the local environment. This was put into action by a primitive form of clutch. Often the patient's feet are cold.

John and Peter waited for 15 minutes and then they started walking towards the theatre. Ideals may fascinate the imagination but they are not focused enough to be used as instruments of reconstruction. Neither side can decide which is in control, so the two both try to produce words, with disastrous results. It probably cannot register a fly in a distant corner, only a fly within tongue's reach. You as can see. The bad side is loneliness and existential dread. So far the word "relation" has been rather indiscriminately employed.

Hamada travelled to England where he worked for four years at Bernard Leach's pottery. The manuscript was displayed in the long room of the college library, and gradually assumed a new role as an art object. Several times the novel allows the narrative to enter bat consciousness and show us what it is like to be a vampire bat. The flyleaf should have carried the inscription 14, 28, 32, 42. There is such a thing as too much information. If he breaks this beam, he knows it will set off an alarm.

A delicate modelling of piers and arches gave the prison courts a palatial, Jacobean appearance. Imagine that you are pouring milk into your coffee. On either side of the kiln chamber there is a door, which is closed with brick during firing. Ian from Braintree slipped over the edge. All four sites were drastically disturbed and coal was removed from the underlying layers followed by reclamation with topsoil application. Consider the first two rows of the function shown in figure 8. We heard an explosion, the dust covered us, and then we saw dead bodies everywhere. The photograph showed a small room in the stable block containing a pile of hay and discarded items.

Rationality has nothing to do with it. Honey in the cake was indispensable but in degenerate times treacle became the substitute. The sawmill, which occupied the space between the foundry and the grinding house, has now gone. Many movements are based on sounds of speech or elements of music. We cannot tell by intuitive inspection if we have such a starting point. Is this a serious story or a joke? The heritage minister handed in his resignation, saying his position was no longer sustainable. Nor is the concept of cost to be taken in a purely technical or material sense. Proprioception involves so many different brain areas that it is very rare for it to be altogether lost.

The tap was cased in a metal box to prevent vandalisation. I will here only allude to what may be called correlated variation. California passed a bill eliminating the indeterminate sentence. Julie saved the railroad more than 13 million dollars that it would have cost for humans to handle calls. Only by assimilation into an undifferentiated mood of synoptic "melancholy" could these sounds be made part of a georgic perspective. Quarks, which make up protons and neutrons, generate and feel all three forces. The frame of a looking glass was blackened, and the gilding must have been volatilised, for a smelling-bottle, which stood on the chimneypiece, was coated with bright metallic particles, which adhered as firmly as if they had been enamelled.

People who lose the ability to structure sentences through brain injury tend to have lesions towards the front of the language cortex. A second firing makes it even more receptive. Theolonius Monk wrote 'Bemsha Swing' not 'Beshma Swing' (Corrections and clarifications, page 36, July 18, 2008). I have lost my belief in the effectiveness and humanity of social work. At the turn of the century, Bury was the largest paper making area in the world. "Voices come, but not words", said one patient. 42 per cent of second homes on Skye are used less than five weeks each year. Each such response is specific: it has no sign-function; it does not represent anything else to which it is linked.

This test consisted of the twenty-five items in 1 below. Handles were made there and fitted to the tools. Best blue colorations are achieved in the middle levels of the kiln with full reduction at cone 10. Pathogens were unlikely to kill seedlings because pathogens are rare in the crater basin of Mount Usu (Yoshida, 1989). Writing about space is difficult. You must be a British citizen to apply. In the middle of a downturn, and without surplus cash, the least-bad option is for the chancellor to borrow more. Suppose that Sally is honest and reliable, that her perceptual capacities are not impaired and that Harry knows all this and so is inclined to trust her report.

She is writing a cultural history of American hotels. As electricity became more affordable the transparent skin lost its economic advantage. We call this kind of movie "Oscar bait". All the wheels on the shaft were fixed in position and their wedges removed. This is a discontinuous picture of habit reorganisation and depends on the release of impulse from prior habits. Attempts to prevent bubbles seem to be largely fruitless. Texas is not unique. The shape as depicted defines a region within which the electron will be present 90 per cent of the time. We then keyed in the amount of space between each word.

The physical sound or mark gets its meaning in and by a conjoint community of functional use, not by any explicit convening in a "convention" or by passing resolutions that a certain sound or mark shall have a specified meaning. The couple did not look at each other as they shared the dock, separated by a security guard. It was only after he had mastered these normal regularities of the language that we gradually introduced impossible constructions. This was one of the earliest applications of dither, or the deliberate addition of noise. Many mothers suffered unnecessarily, believing that they had caused their children's disorders. Not everyone was happy.

The flock of subjects take commands and fulfil them in the world of things. As Fannie and Freddie show, regulators are easily captured and outwitted. This could be the day. The influenza vaccine failed this winter. Heidegger consumes Nietzsche and his works under a singular name. The material culture and development of certain peoples are greatly influenced by the animals found in their districts. Drops in temperature would be countered by a reduction in the haze. A gap in data transmission during this time meant that its detailed structure could not be determined. Soldiers woke regularly with a rash of highly irritating bites they called Baghdad boils. Cuddly animals don't persuade poor people to back conservation. They salute and insult their audience good-naturedly; they end with a song and take a curtain call. This double parallelism is by no means an accident or an illusion. But that is not all Bresson means. In Britain privatisation meant selling state utilities to their existing managements, turning them into joint-stock companies owned by pension funds and insurance companies, and breaking the power of Trade unions. The technique relied on a retrovirus to shuttle a functional copy of IL2RG into the patient's bone marrow stem cells, from which immune cells are generated. The Herdwick's special claim to consideration was their connection to their native ground, itself a kind of national sacred space.

"I got the wheel of a wheelbarrow!" one happy villager told me; "and my neighbour got the rest of it". Meanings that are formed on this basis are sure to exclude much that is required for intelligent control of activity. According to this view, nature itself is infected with an objective indeterminacy; there is an element of absolute chance in the world. Peirce had an attic study accessible only by ladder, and there he retreated by drawing up the ladder behind him. When working normally it would probably have generated about 12 horse power. Most recent scholarship tends to consider Ko a crackled variety of Kuan.

By the time of the 1934 survey, the forest had only 10 years to recover from logging before the chestnut blight induced mortality of virtually all remaining chestnut trees. Ice sheets continually adjust to the amount of meltwater, keeping overall velocities more or less constant. No family is to have any article of clothing from the society unless the members of it attend some place of worship. The University of Sussex is not offering the UK's first beekeeping BSc. Now, with troops in Iraq and Afghanistan, scientists are turning their attention to the little-understood plague of sandflies.

We mounted a sprayer and global positioning system on an expensive toy helicopter. Chimpanzees don't get sick from the human malaria parasite, *Plasmodium falciparum*. If there is more methane than carbon dioxide in the atmosphere, methane's interaction with ultraviolet light produces photochemical "soot". Rats were tested for cue-induced cocaine-seeking after 1 and 45 days of withdrawal. Modern cells require sophisticated protein channels and pumps to mediate the exchange of molecules with their environment. Abduction is the process of forming an explanatory hypothesis. Unruly visitations of threatening ecology appear not only in films that take place in and around Los Angeles. They say it is not possible to test pupil attainment, teacher effectiveness and school accountability through one device.

What we have here, then, are two different kinds of not seeing. We all know, from Nietzsche, about animal happiness. Losses in North Sea gas production are no longer separately identified in the Simplified Petroleum Product Reporting System, which was introduced in January 2001. Regular users of services, especially those who commute to work by train, have had to adjust their lives to accommodate delays. They possess rich clothing, valuable beads, and beautiful feathers. This trip takes 12½ minutes at an average speed of 32 miles per hour. By impersonating the animal he wished to kill, a hunter could come very close to a herd without being observed.

Finally the driver seeks to find meaning in what he sees: to relate the visible objects to the stock of ideas in his mind. Schedule 8 is the name for the section of the contract that covers track access charges and that provides a comprehensive performance regime for the timing of trains over the network. The tension of the warp can be adjusted by tightening or loosening this rope. Because they lived in the midst of wooded mountains, great herds of deer and elk came to the edge of their villages. At the intersection between man's animal body and thinking, Heidegger and Nietzsche differ decidedly.

Before the Spaniards came, the men's dress consisted of soft-tanned deerskin or woven cloth. The attribution of reactionary delays will always be attributed to the original delay. The result simulates embroidery, but the method is weaving. Recorded losses increased by 3 percent between 2005 and 2006, and are now at their highest level since 2000. Fifty wild horses stared at me. But Wood's use of semiotics addresses the question of determinations with more fluidity. It is only the bewitchment of abstract codes—whether in words or money—and our belief in them, which allows us to escape from the earth.

The number of adults emerging at the end of the 35-day life cycle was recorded for each container. Charring sugar yields a high-performance catalyst of amorphous carbon, which can be shaped into graphene sheets just one or two nanometers thick. One challenge is not to saturate the uniform so heavily with insecticide that it becomes toxic to the wearer. Surrounded by strangers in white coats, she is played short pairs of synthesized chord sequences and asked whether the two sequences are identical or not. Acidification was easy to comprehend, sounded alarming, and drove home the idea that carbon dioxide was a pollutant.

The harbour now reaches up the Mystic River, while the Charles River has been dammed to make an ornamental basin. Animal impersonators probably preceded all other impersonations. The apparent motion of the visual field is shown by small arrow symbols, directly alongside or on top of the self-motion band. The main library is at the heart of the main campus and has room for over 540 readers in modern air-conditioned surroundings. The many small holes and domes that form in the ice when it starts to melt become temporary habitats for organisms to escape predation. These are events that simply happen, out of nowhere. For a "standard" shock, the downstream flow would be subsonic, but Voyager 2 found it to be cooler than expected and supersonic.

The Spanish parliament's environment committee last week approved resolutions for chimpanzees, gorillas and orang-utans to gain some statutory rights currently applicable only to humans. Hallucination, panic attacks or other disordered behaviours are consequences far downstream of faulty genes. The pressure of the extrusion and manipulation of the silk by the spider's legs transforms liquid silk into a flexible thread. Mirror-neuron activity is thought to generate a more-or-less explicit simulation of others' actions in the observer's brain.

By inducing memory in one yeast and seeing speedy GAL2 expression in the other, they show that memory of galactose is transferable through cytoplasm. It was assumed that insects would sense ambient temperature via their antennae. The structure reveals a "candy-floss" coating of disordered protein and carbohydrate. Is a late arrival of volatiles also possible for the moon? The solar wind blows outward from the sun and forms a bubble of solar material in the interstellar medium. With the drier weather and the relaxation of speed restrictions in summer 2001, passengers expected a speedy return to a service that was reliable and punctual. It should not be necessary to spend much time on instrumental value.

Diagrams would be supplemented by a conventional map. Animal horns are pierced and fastened to the top of the mask, or imitation horns of mountain sheep are ingeniously moulded from deerskin. This is a simplified situation, but not an unusual one. Only members of the family might enter these chambers. There is no medical need to clone a human. Reprogramming shatters the long-standing concept that the identity of differentiated adult cells is indelible. By the above singular manner of building, strength is continually given to the comb, with the utmost ultimate economy of wax. Shoes are about sex.

By the time that Darwin's younger son, Anthony, 29, gave evidence, Anne Darwin was composed again. The harm was twofold; people fell ill and their trust in the vaccine system was undermined. For more than a century, fishing boats—particularly Dutch beam trawlers, whose nets scrape the seabed—have been scooping prehistoric material out of the North Sea. They watched as beads clumped into larger structures, creating a glass-like gel. If "action understanding" is to occur by internal simulation, the process must enlist both motor and sensory systems in the brain. Eradication now seems impossible, and the task of containing the virus has become chronic and costly.

You set the helicopter's flight pattern with a computer mouse. The laws will ban potentially harmful research, ape trading, profiting from apes, and using apes in performances. Lumpers dominate physics. They have subconsciously internalised the rules of musical grammar. An experimental subject lies with her head clamped inside a functional magnetic resonance imaging chamber. The Hopi dolls are squat and stolid with characteristic garments carved into the wood. Photochromic materials are used in light-sensitive lenses and data-storage devices. Honeybee queens emit a pheromone to switch off the ovaries of female worker bees. Before they are measured, atoms and subatomic particles exist in a "superposition" in which they have many mutually contradictory properties.

Music originally written as a profound statement of religious belief can be used as a background for domestic chores, or as a stimulus for a laboratory experiment. Incidents will only be attributed to the neutral zone provided that all other causes of delay have been investigated, considered and exhausted. To the Pueblo people all animals are living spirits and their right to exist is unquestioned. During our investigations, we made all trips in the daytime, in the presence of normal city traffic, but not at rush hours.

While offshore companies report live crude at field, the disposals from oil terminals and offshore loading fields are reported as stabilised crude oil. Torn jeans in my grandmother's time and brass bedsteads in my mother's meant poverty. Sensors that fly beneath balloons can be used again and again, although getting them back from wind-blown landing sites can be a trial. Animal headdresses and costumes were used as magic and decoy. These localised events induce a non-local, long-ranged, relaxation of stress over the system.

As the shepherd of being gathers his flock, he omits the unsightliness of consumption. Peasant uprisings have little chance of success when the governing elites are unified and the state is strong. In the early Mesolithic period, this area would have been tidal wetlands. The ghosts of the dead are called *anitu* and *bombo*. Because this "memory" requires certain chromatin regulators, it provides evidence for a heritable chromatin state. This light-induced colour change can happen whether the molecule is a solid or in a solution. Much less information is available for eastern Scotland. Larger polychrome doors like this one are found on rice granaries and noble houses.

The peaceful lake became a fast flowing estuary into which only the most foolhardy fisherman dared to launch his canoe. Everyone was not happy. It's a stripped-down, tiny machine of just seven genes, with all sorts of structural tricks to replicate itself while evading the immune system. Ramps should be carefully connected to the visual destination they are leading to; the transition must be prepared for, and perhaps prolonged. Coloured designs are incorporated in sash ends through the brocade weave. Sundays and public holidays are excluded.

Warm water is known to be entering the Arctic Ocean through the Fram Strait and that warmer and denser Atlantic water is thought to accumulate at the bottom of the arctic basin. The contours are sharply outlined in black. The first stochastic models showed that populations could become extinct even if deterministic models concluded they would persist indefinitely. One example of chromatin inheritance comes from yeast, which seems to "remember" prior growth conditions. Wooden stencils were sometimes used for the application of paintings on bark cloth. Two more substantial Bellman hangars were also provided.

Peirce set himself to criticize the doctrine of intuition or immediate knowledge. The trap involved a bamboo spear cocked on a rattan spring, which was triggered by a wire. This reaction was consistent across languages, indicating that it reflects a general conceptual deficit rather than some idiosyncratic linguistic defect. We considered at some length the ethical problem of deceiving him about the status of Epun, and concluded that our actions were justifiable. Most wartime airfields appear on Ordnance Survey Landranger maps that are generally available for reference in public libraries. These patches develop beneath forest canopies that are structurally heterogeneous in space and time.

When two fields such as these come together, lowering standards is not an option. A bamboo tube is inserted into the tree trunk and the cylinder, so that the fluids from the corpse can be drained and gathered in a pot. Decoherence theory suggests that collapse does not occur instantaneously. The human body does not welcome an injection of horse serum. The termination shock is a weak, quasi-perpendicular shock that heats the thermal plasma very little. All these body paints are made up of earth pigments and plant stains which do not require the use of glue to make them adhere. We also detected a strong increase in the expression of stress-induced and anti-proliferative genes.

Sooty skies and a methane-dependent climate were maintained by feedback within the biosphere. Geneticists know nothing about psychiatric disease and have no frame of reference for thinking about the brain. Day by day, some individuals succeed and others fail to locate packets. The process, which led up to the release of the Judge's verdict, was followed in real time. Living on a very rich protein diet, they have to drink large amounts of water to prevent urea excess, and the use of small melted icebergs as drinking water could dangerously increase their salt intake.

The submerged landscape of Doggerland could throw light on how burial practices diverged as rising seas isolated Britain. This is a soft stone statue of uncertain function. At Vedbaek Bogebakken, one woman has a projectile point embedded in her spine. Despite their dark skin and low sunlight exposure, these populations avoid rickets by the intake of fresh fish liver. After the tape has been rolling for a while, a woman in a gorilla suit walks onto the screen, faces the camera, beats her chest with her fists, and then leaves. The live tortoise is afterward carried in the dance. By the 1950s, some unused masks were still kept in the communal house. Pennies in a field of sufficient dollars will be ignored whatever their numbers.

As described in Chapter 3, the principles of virtual ethnography did not exist fully formed at the outset. The Strategic Rail Authority's Officer responsible for Great Western indicated that he believes the company to be franchise compliant. At first glance a snake looks like a long tail with a head at one end. We might ask, for instance, is this house constructed or real? Job seekers have weeded out prospective employers for the same reason.

Death is announced by the beating of gongs and drums. A specialist carves these figures from Jackfruit wood; when polished with coconut oil, they acquire skin tones and later take on a greyish patina from the rain. How much the whales will be affected by ice loss is hard to foresee. On this pattern of circulation is now being imposed still another element, the new expressway system.

Experimental Subjects

People go to work in the fields at mid-morning when their blood begins to flow and strength returns. Nearly all show profuse crackle, often made more conspicuous by the greyish stain resulting from burial. Thus the marginal value of the current patch is compared to the average value of moving on. The string used to tie the amulet serves as a means of measuring child growth. When determining priority need, the applicant's rent arrears were a wholly irrelevant consideration. In October 1987 we had what you might call a bit of a practice run. The formulaic linguistic units are usually on the level of sentence or phrase, seldom more than one sentence. Authorities should not claim that there is no risk of violence just because an injunction could be granted. He set out strings to show where the paving should go. The bodies are dark and the glaze an opaque and heavily crackled greyish white or brown. In the encounter-contingent model, a searching forager randomly comes upon edible resources. This impressive image is fastened to the decorated house-front (figure 90). The main shape of the northern gardens is now set. No time is wasted on cultures that do not mature. It was the search for "officer material" that led to the development of IQ testing in World War I. The liquid in the tubes should be colourless and pure.

Below is a list of ten enigmas of memory. The monkey replaces the object to obtain the food reward. So it is to the beautiful Franca that we owe the concept of "overdetermination". Dementia and normal brain aging erode the self, and prevent it being unitary and unchanging. Argentina conducted parabolic flights from 1952–54 using South American water turtles as test subjects. The source of disease is somewhere further upstream. Kirchner's most famous painting is simply entitled *Berlin Street Scene* (1913). The Ludlow, about waist-high, requires only a minimum of floor space.

Who sold you that Jackalantern's tale? Frame by frame the restiveness of his speech is captured, as the light slowly changes to morning. We demonstrated that seedling colonisation was mostly determined by the intensity of land degradation with narrow scale, in particular, by physical changes in microtopography derived from melting snow. In these fish, even when fully adult, the migrating eye never gets further than the dorsal midline. Doggerland may have been a sort of paradise for Mesolithic people. For a solar mission, Ulysses never really got that close. The interstellar medium is represented by a uniform, soft flow of soapy water in from the left.

Errors may also occur when non-standard conditions are used to meter the oil flow. Ramadan began. Extremities of the body feel less defined and there is a sense of merging with the empty space around. In the last frame of the page, she watches from a window as he runs across the snow, his woollen hat falling off disregarded behind him. He placed pieces of gold on the visual cortex of the monkey. The problem lies in the time-scale: complexity is the end point of a long trajectory. Since their country was subdued by the Dutch, at the beginning of the twentieth century, the culture of the Kondo Sapata people has changed.

A thick sooty patina indicates that these pieces have been stored in the attic. Material accumulation is unattractive to those who must move frequently and carry their property with them. In arctic environments, Inuit have a remarkable sensitivity to salt, which is traditionally considered to be dangerous. Although part of this inner ring has now been constructed, the location of other parts is controversial. However, 52, 53 and 54 were included within longer passages that were presented for correction. Do we use this knowledge to modify the climate locally? Only about ten thousand years have elapsed since the first appearance of agriculture in the fossil record.

Changes in the animals' physical circumstances were complicated by changes in the way they were perceived. The noise-benefit relationship is shaped like an inverted "U". The next two questions can be skipped since they refer specifically to closed endings. The Standard Medical Emergency Field Triage tag (MT-137) is a simplified model used extensively by US military units, schools, colleges and fire departments, as well as a large number of state and local response agencies in America and the United Kingdom. The average wounded man reacted well to Pentothal, and there were few exceptions. All these issues resurface in the renewed attempts to identify engrams by means of functional neuro-imaging.

A locking screw on the stick permits quick setting to any desired measure. These people cut me up like a chicken on the dinner table. Once, during the time we were banned, I saw my father in Cannes. They started travelling this morning, but still have not arrived.

Spirits are limited in number and recycle over time. The image may be scaled down and subject to copyright. All environments contain more species that are edible to humans than can be effectively harvested. It is an injection that makes the community strong. The etymological roots of the term "engram" are Greek, it means "something converted into writing". The fossil record recapitulates all these problems. Object oriented databases retain this characteristic: the user is shielded from the structure of the data. The colours are muted, the painting is nervy, the atmosphere lewd.

Transfer patterns are consistent with reciprocity and risk-minimisation. Put your leaderboard banner here! The name of the artist is given on the two seals at the left side. You should perform necessary immediate care. The first systematic investigation of skill learning involved a skill that is now obsolete. I have given this very cursory overview in order to make two points. While earth gongs and cymbals must vibrate around a fixed point, there is no such restriction in zero gravity. Both sending and recipient governments should expect this presence to last for around a decade, and must commit to it.

She was a labourer's daughter who left school at thirteen to work in a post office. If you do nothing, the system will shut down automatically in one minute fifty six seconds. Spaces and quads are not inserted until the entire line is set, the stick's gauge indicating which spaces are necessary to fill out the line. In front of us loomed a baby the size of a double-decker bus. To tamp down his delusions, he was given Haloperidol an antipsychotic medication that blocks the manufacture of dopamine in the brain, thereby accelerating cognitive decline. This was the fatal confusion that Tithonus made.

Skill is not subserved by the same brain circuits that subserve declarative memory. Some people feel guilty at the sight of a blue light. You could breathe fresh air deep into your lungs and feel your soul reviving. In some instances, primarily the written versions of the novel, Wu Song cannot see clearly and hits an old tree instead of the tiger. In Sidhu, the applicant was living in a women's refuge. A recipient of a *hxaro* gift often alters it, gives it a personal touch, before passing it on. Non-egalitarian practices merely converted the white man into a more tangible symbol of what Crees were not.

While costly signalling generates net benefits for the signaller; it does not require reciprocity. The applicant was not considered to be intentionally homeless. Some performers describe Wu Song as having a staff, which the tiger grasps with its mouth and breaks. Markings on the wall showed the line of the roof it had once supported. The audience remained silent, unsure of the speaker's point. These two photographs of a girl with bomb-blast injuries were taken one year apart. At the limit of the texts we examine, every process repeats every other—and there is no need for direct memory to work in the past, since the past is always eternally present.

Most of Davidson's own collection, the Sektor Library, passed after his son's death to the Plymouth Athenaeum where it was destroyed in the blitz in 1942. When the correct identity is discovered, the child will thenceforth bear the name of that spirit as its personal name. The duty is to take reasonable steps to prevent loss or to prevent or mitigate damage to the property. They were conventional flowers on a yellow ground. Some instances of the tiger tale show close linguistic relationship, pointing to mutual textual borrowing or borrowing from a "master text", whether oral or written.

The original grindstones came from the Sheriff Hill quarries at Gateshead-on-Tyne, and would have been brought by sea to Exeter. The next morning some of our closest friends were literally trapped in their houses by fallen trees. In this exhibit vacuum processes have been used to replace body fluids with various plastics that decay extremely slowly. The term "mental skill" should be avoided, as all skills are mental. The monkey is placed in a Wisconsin General

Testing Apparatus. It is recognised that those seeking help may well be under considerable strain, may be confused, and may not find it easy to explain their position clearly and logically. A decision to allow the child to live must be made prior to its fourth day of life.

The damage spreads over a significant area of the brain before the patient actually notices that anything is wrong. So long as he holds his map the wrong way up he will never find the house. Once, tall pines and cypresses sheltered this graveyard. A goat called Esmeralda had the run of the villa; it lived upstairs with us. The story brilliantly recalls how, with heavy snow, the world is made quiet. "I am standing in front of a poster of a beautiful baby boy", announced Dave, "one of the most precious things in the world". The booklets are printed on low quality fragile paper, with animal glue binding.

Please do not tell anyone about your application. It was on these shears that the shield-shaped Cornish shovels were trimmed. By the time Hélène got married, the Nazis had killed all her closest friends. No study has yet tested whether trust varies by subjects' knowledge or familiarity with the target. The expansion is suggestive of an infectious disease. The repeat may well be deliberate. There were three long frame-bases of decreasing sizes. Everyone had left the garden in the middle of a working day, intending to come back.

Unlike other systems, which only show patient deterioration, the cruciform disaster tag is flexible and allows for the priority to be upgraded or downgraded. We find coral red bats flying in blue clouds, a blue formal band on the rim, neck and near the base. The Ealing decision was applied in Camden. If shorter men feed more children, a spread of genes conferring short stature can be expected. Every realm has its own deities: very important ones live in the sky, those on earth live in the forests, the trees, the waters, the stones and caves.

This specimen shows a piece of the gut infected by typhus. Magill designed the forceps and the semi closed anaesthetic circuit. He deliberately blurred the final edge of the figure as he teased out a series of thin layers. The first test subject for zero gravity was a monkey at White Sands Testing area. The problem is that the authorial function was never meant to apply to human actions. In 2000 he apparently seriously considered resigning the papacy due to failing health. Next to that is uncoated black, with his glaze layer fluorescing blue.

There must be some type of engram to ensure the persistence of memory. But the change could be minute, distributed, and alternate over time from one side to another. A vaccinator, who is a member of one's kin network, or an in-law, will not usually ask for payment. Agency and power align. Blood stealing anxieties were expressed forcefully in some of the narrative accounts that mothers gave as part of the survey. At that time the northern barbarians invaded the Empire. The "interim" housing consisted of a caravan, parked on land belonging to a county council.

Sometimes the statue stands on the neck of a buffalo. The small game animal, clutch of eggs, or large melon found by an individual are examples of packets. Thus if the child picks up a hazardous object, parents generally leave it to explore the dangers on its own. When the Sung court fled southward from the invading Tartars and established a new capital at Hang Chou, pottery kilns were set up in the vicinity of the palace under the direction of an official named Shao. Notes to this chapter begin on page 239.

Liu Shi and her maid prepared a bun filled with strong poison. The kiwi was not dead. Sensitization is a lingering manifestation of arousal. A rich example comes from the Lukasa memory device (Roberts et al, 1996), which contains topographical, historical, property, and political relations in a single, hand held board (figure 5.5). The new generation created the decentralised network of firms that characterised the valley. In idle moments I summarised forty chapters of *Oliver Twist* for the use of my upstairs neighbour.

Ludlow cases, of small double cap design, slide into cabinets on a slant. We are receiving a free subsidy from nature. Lines up to 120 picas long are set in a Long Stick as a unit with a single justification. The monkey survived the flight unharmed but died on impact when the parachutes failed to open. In the past, uniforms were made of wool or cotton, with simple but durable weaves saturated in an insecticide such as Permethrin. The growth form has changed from a dominant tree to a small sprouting sapling, and the number of sapling sprouts has declined over time.

It is likely that simple systems may come to include bionic hybrids of neural tissue and printed circuits. These photographs illustrate the system of grading applied to military recruits during World War I. Informed consent required a mother's signature, after discussing a take-home information sheet with others. The latter is not concerned with illness, but with sub normality or severe sub normality. The obligation to house passes to the notified authority when the conditions for referral are fulfilled. There is space under your seats for small soft bags.

When a line has more than seven characters, these are either shrunk so that three characters occupy the space of two "normal" characters, or two small characters are placed side by side in the line. The Maasai need honey but the Okiek do not need any Maasai product to the same extent. However, I had a stroke of luck when a bat flew into the meeting and, amazingly, I caught it in my hand. The screen on the right follows the helicopter journey of the Medical Emergency Response Team, as they bring the casualty to the hospital. Pursuing the found item precludes seeking and obtaining something else.

As the ice melts, a plume of fresh water forms right beneath it. Females also live at depth. We followed the development of some animals with straight shells over the course of several days. The film contains very little data. Bees leaving home to find food followed the anise odour whether or not the pheromone was present in the nest. Sooty or not, it is almost inevitable that a climate based on methane would be Gaian, in the loose sense of the word. Eventually human subjects subjected to free-floating weightlessness in a specially designed cargo aircraft, such as the KC-135.

Other sounds appeared more rapid and loud. I thought, for a moment, he might cry, for he must have been a bit hormonal. Candidates in North Korean parliamentary elections are hand picked by the ruling party and Kim. But creating leeway to survive uncertainty is only half the struggle. Each of the other known death receptors functions through subtle permutations of this process (different ligands, adapters and points of entry into the caspase cascade). Replication failure was not a problem. The military establishments in both the United States and Russia track objects in orbit.

Individuals never tested Alex on the labels they taught. The prognosis is gloomy. This includes not only lessened ability to fend when homeless, but also being less able to fend for oneself in finding and keeping accommodation. In the end good characters prevail against the odds, and the villains are punished without mercy. Transfusions establish blood as a potential commodity. The tacit knowledge they shared created a marked competitive advantage for Valley firms. The method exploits the fact that brain process speed is strongly temperature dependent. Why does the sense of belatedness make one particularly vulnerable to conspiracy theories?

Some hunters produce and give more to food transfer networks than they receive in return. These objects each enfold an organizational history and subtend a particular temporality or spatiality. What the statistics don't tell us is why. Quantum information is usually sent by entangled light. In many cases, imaging is done afterwards to monitor the progress of recovery. Surrogate endpoints might allow clinical trials to be shorter and cheaper. Until now, research has focused on momentum and energy. It is surprising that undisturbed tropical forests currently do not seem to be at equilibrium.

Passive diffusion through this lined passageway is hindered in a size dependent manner. Village authorities are often anxious to ensure that mobile vaccination teams at least stay and eat in the community, even if they cannot be persuaded to stay overnight. This is a proper point to digress briefly into a conceptual issue. Gamo Anyo may have been a real person, and her legend possibly dates to somewhere in the Ming dynasty. This book is meant to be reassuring. Increased CO2 in the atmosphere could fertilise extra growth in mature forests.

Now a new broadly applicable technique has been used to localize the clock circuitry that underlines the timing of birdsong. Holidays are public and Sundays excluded. This inhibition is greatly enhanced when transport factor is present. Embryos of both species were fixed as previously described. The components of such a system can range from metallic nanoparticles to biopolymers and macroscopic objects. A small herd, perhaps thirty in number, was still roaming Yellowstone National Park.

Hunters can find that the bush is tied. This document contains detailed reports of the results of exposure to radiation. And the shiny floor didn't even look very shiny. A small study within this work will evaluate run-off water quality, especially for artificial pitches. Thus, when the magnetic field is turned off and the structures are dried, they don't fall apart and can be studied individually. Succession involves not only initial growth to full canopy height, but also subsequent gradual shifts in species composition.

Some fifteen groups visited the Baptist Hospital, curious about its efforts to meet this medical need. Detailed controls were included against inadvertent cueing during thirty years' study of the cognitive and communicative abilities of Alex, the African grey parrot. *Memory* publishes high quality papers in all areas of memory research. The globe was positioned in the void normally occupied by the cosmonaut. A single roof-truss hung crazily in mid-air, held in position by the undergrowth. Thus Wang Wen was invited over to the west wing of the mansion to feel the ailing Mistress Liu's pulse.

In 1965 the Mattel Company released Astronaut Barbie, a ten-inch plastic doll dressed in a silver space suit. At my first Goth party, I encountered couples attached by leashes and collars. Men are assembled into the nation metonymically. Strong cycles of boom and bust tend to reveal incompetence and fraud. Each player has a network of contacts in the arena. Commoners and titleholders could be attracted to and join houses that were wealthier than their own. The Archaics could only live in Europe if they solved the problems of a seasonal environment.

Flight grade equipment had to be installed and tested, together with specially designed seats for the audience, capable of sustaining accelerations of up to 10g over a period of 20 seconds (ten times the force of gravity). Life with Althusser was never easy. The new generation of databases, as yet scarcely represented in the biodiversity world, are object-relational or object-oriented. I had no friends in the city as yet. Tumour blood vessels in mutant mice were not leaky like those in normal mice. Iridium, which operates a constellation of 66 low Earth orbit satellites providing satellite-phone services, says that it regularly monitors data about space debris but had no prior warning of the collision.

Polar emissions vary with time, and seem not to be linked with strong magnetospherical compressions. There are many females in these flocks, since the males often stay in Germany or Scandinavia. When he left, he thanked me again for trusting him to come into my house. Most scoopophobics enter intermittent frenetic states, in which they increase their publication output to a level that precludes even themselves from reading all the papers they publish. Each is constantly faced with irruptions from other objects, which cut across their time lines, spatial units, or chunking of matter.

Trees across the tropics are getting bigger and offering help in the fight against climate change. A corporal is about to order them onto lorries and despatch them to base. In text C we do not find such repeated phrases and sentences. The children have yellow jackets with biscuit faces. Part III makes provision for local housing to take steps to protect the property of homeless people. Inuit store food and are logistically organised, although most are not territorial or hierarchical. Reconstruction of activity areas within sites can be achieved by wear analysis. Surplus is now used in competitive feasts to create contractual debt involving interest payments. Failure is possible.

Faced with such figures, slow trackers must explain why hunter-gatherer populations increase only very slowly. Even so, the network is its own explanation of motive. Stone labrets are important evidence for status differences on the coast because wearing them leaves indelible evidence on the teeth. The struggle for blood is evident, for instance, in women's reproductive lives. This holds true even for novels, which do not rely upon the depiction of actual historical personages. Decoration, blue on white, conventional landscape, with mountains, valleys, boats; all painted in fine varying shades of blue.

In Ealing, two applicants had been found intentionally homeless by Slough. Maize is the main food for mourners; their food taboo is important because rice is the staple. The one song with stage directions is entitled "Mistress Wang gets her jar mended". Before long it dawned on us that we had a problem. The trees were now mature and the wall behind was bowing under the pressure. Some subjects became quite ill; others, especially experienced test pilots, showed no adverse effects from prolonged weightlessness.

To four responses these are least possible questions. I went to the window and saw my car on fire. Equivalence is the frame and cohesion the indicator. What will happen when Kyoko and Sekkō meet? Where a word is explained clearly in the text it is not included in the glossary. Pine martens were being skinned and there was beaver. Mao attended the village school for five years, working part time on the family farm. This is a five-move problem. Changes in brain volume are believed to correlate well with memory performance.

They sent entangled light pulses through a simulated atmosphere, finding that when the pulse's amplitude fell within a certain range it remained entangled. The appropriate temporality for any of these partial objects in space is singular. The camellia's waxy, deep green leaves and pink flowers frame a simple granite war memorial. In many cases, forager groups have been geographically isolated, receiving no gene flow. Chaffinches coming to bird tables in winter are sometimes seen to have a kind of tumour on one of their feet. They were totally rotten, but held in place by their own weight, and remarkably the glass was still intact. Before all that, let's take a look ahead to tomorrow morning.

A forager will nearly always depart a patch before it has been fully depleted of resources. We have shown that the brain changes sensory input. A cell's size is conceptual, not merely a fact. People must have transported animals by sea. A common manifestation of culture is collective memory. Everybody checks his or her car before getting in. Later specimens show an improvement in the glaze colour, which is often pale green though still sometimes tinged with olive. When Mao met Nixon in February 1972, it was noted that a nurse stood by to steady him.

Lives which are continually being reproduced in thinking, behaviour, material culture and communal order, change continuously because of interpretation. There was a shift from enmer wheat to spelt in later prehistory, and from these to bread wheat in the Roman period. Crystal growers are being forced to scatter. In some cases the users are volunteers who agree to be studied. Each coloured fringe corresponds to 28 millimetres of ground motion, and shows that the ground east of the fault has risen while the basin containing L'Aquila has sunk.

Two iron rails are placed across the top of the installation. They reduce consumption variance by pooling and distributing the catch, a form of risk minimisation. The impetus for Althusser's memoir came from an article in *Le Monde* about Issei Sagawa, a Japanese citizen who, while living in Paris, killed and ate a young Dutch woman. The uprising was not spontaneous. There was no enclosure of the land that was subject to flooding. Filled with joy, Sekkō is riding on a train to meet Kokichi. Non-redundant contacts are connected by a structural hole. Motions of the stylus made the tiny triangular indentations of cuneiform characters in the clay.

We primarily use non-invasive procedures on monkeys—about 90% are behaviour and genetics studies. Observations in the upper left corner are a severe test of the argument. Limited liability results in many behavioural changes, not all of which are desirable. By taking action to guard or promote the nation, every citizen comes to embody it. Many companies would relocate offshore and investors follow them with their funds. The middens are underlain by blown sand, a deposit made up of tiny marine shells, flora minifera and other calcareous matter blown onto the land. Mole Council should have found these couples were homeless.

Flies under red light showed no response. Biological processes can be self-referential too. Is there an alternative to the retrograde fascism of the family? People describe vaccines as "chasing out" illness. This situation is addressed by models of patch choice and patch residence time. The peptide chain that connects their extracellular and intracellular parts snakes through the membrane only once. Storing information on comparatively bulky tablets encouraged neat writing. Each monkey was shown a series of dot patterns on a computer screen, and had to decide whether the centre of a circular pattern was protruding or receding.

Larger-scale experiments are also starting to emerge. Regulatory agencies need to be more proactive in preparing for avant-garde products. Asteroids appear much "redder" than the meteorites derived from them. The structural hole argument has four signature qualities. Imagine you are walking in thick fog, looking for a friend wearing a green leather jacket. Why is the child afraid of the bear? Mao was the principal author of the Great Leap and its main producer. People in early twentieth-century costume sit in rowing boats at Golden Lane swimming pool to watch a high-definition screening of *Titanic* to celebrate the 2009 Oscars. The first stars may have been born rapidly rotating, however, and rotation can entirely modify these results.

Ionized bubbles are shown in blue, and regions of high molecule abundance in green. I give off a small glow that illuminates my surroundings. The aetiology of the syndrome is composite. Eventually vegetation built up and covered these remains with peat. No one wants to be ugly. Information does not spread evenly across the competitive arena. Sekkō's departure from home recasts the viewer-landscape relationship established through the opening credits. New valley firms created the next generation of semiconductor devices, such as memory circuits and microprocessors. In this context, language is increasingly understood not just as a material but also as a kind of "site". Ch'in coins were round with square holes in the middle, suitable for stringing on cords.

Each type of dementia targets a different neural network. Hollowing out a vault is the work of experts. These factors are carefully appraised in reaching a decision like that implied by the encounter-contingent model. Star clusters are expected to lie at the centre of gas voids. For a short period at the end of mining, trees returned to their previous densities. Here we present a method of analyzing large numbers of Google search queries to track influenza-like illness in a population. The first emperor died in 210 BC while on a tour of the eastern provinces.

Making avoidance easier is a matter of data and resources. If the dark matter is warm, having substantial velocity dispersion, density perturbations on small length scales are smoothed. This feature may allow the virus to deliver its genome into host cells. These systems use sequential time-steps to sort out the order of events. The centre would then reconstruct the image and transmit it back to the phone. But Diane was strong, glorying in her peak-time moment, and Tarrant failed to dominate. Animal bones, too, are consistent with the idea of a trading station.

It is possible to rent rather than own everything from web-hosting resources to lab space and equipment. The people affected gradually lose their memory, their logic and eventually their ability to speak and move. Turtle-meat transfers have certain features consistent with the costly-signalling hypothesis. But when the kiln is swept out with fresh air at the end of firing, the aerial oxygen reacts on the hot exposed body where it is not protected by glaze and converts the iron to reddish ferric oxide. This image, amongst millions of others, has infiltrated language.

These bison have some cattle genes, but they also have institutional memory. Many settlements emerged as consumers and very few as producers. Cranial deformation for high status and free individuals continued on the southern coast until the contact period. In her distress she attempts to get rid of the dangerous witness, her maid, but when Diao Nanlou returns home unexpectedly, he tragically eats the poisoned bun and dies. The first High Court decision on priority need was *Islam*, not cross-appealed by the authority on this point. Where do they come from, what kind of ship do they have?

Love resides as an image in the memory. Kriwet's *Text-Signs*, 1968, a set of which are shown in the ICA's Lower Gallery, are made from stamped aluminium. They have been cut off with a knife and they are irregular both in their spacing and in the depth that they have been cut into the bone. Pfizer, based in New York, has a smaller market presence, but owns a healthier pipeline of candidate HIV drugs. Archetti finds that domesticated apples rarely have red leaves in autumn. Pottery styles may be some sort of clue to the nature of social identity. Kafka's three sisters died in Nazi concentration camps.

Words are built of RGB pixels projected directly onto the retina for hours each day. The occupation has always been unpopular in

Iraq. If the power in the primordial density spectrum is reduced on small scales, the first stars will form much later than in the standard CDM-based scenario. The aim has been to reprogram cells without pushing genes into the genome, where they risk causing damage. Using phone data, Eagle's team was able to differentiate students studying business from those studying other subject with 96% accuracy.

When a non-uniform electrical field is applied to a non-conducting material, that material experiences a force. The fight against cyber attacks can never be won. Increases in diffuse radiation enhanced the terrestrial carbon sink by about 25%. But the area around the well had been kept clean. All this supports the central provisioning of the settlement for its subsistence needs by a controlling authority. *Song of the White Orchid*, however, avoids acknowledging these two political movements. Rubbing was common, with meaning being about movement across boundaries, access and expression.

Overleaf is an artist's impression of the figures near the infantry general in the second pit. Water accumulated in small hollows created by animals, around stones and at the base of trees where roots grew over each other. Students of Confucius were not chosen on grounds of birth. He saw a mess of clumped proteins in the form of plaques, and tangles of fibrils like snarled up thread. Many questions remain. Mice stored at -20°C for 16 years have been cloned, raising the possibility that extinct animals could be "resurrected" from frozen tissue samples.

Optical manipulation of electron spin produces much faster operations and has the added advantage that it allows for an optical interface. Due to demographic increase, Pygmies will either be dominated by Bantu societies, through food dependency, or will have to abandon their way of life and become farmers. As Acconci cut, spliced, moved and displaced words, he performed many of the principal actions of the new sculpture. This terminal is back online. Earth belongs to the living.

One arm is outstretched to collect honey from a hive and is surrounded by swarming bees while the other holds a collecting jar. This chapter contains the core argument of the book. When she works at the farm with Kōkichi and Norio, dust gets into her eyes. Tours is intact, except for some old damage from 1940. Nested networks appear to occur in many biological and social contexts, suggesting that the results are relevant in a wide range of fields—from biology to banking. On Islay, flint beach pebbles, especially on the west coast, were the main source of stone for tools.

Big pharmaceutical companies should be on the lookout. Major works on the politics of environmental discourse do not mention environmental informatics at any point: they write as if there is no layer at all between science and politics. I decided to explore the church itself. Two large panels have pictures of, on one side, a romantic scene, and on the other an audience of military officials; also four fan-shaped panels of flowers, trees etc, all in brilliant enamels of the highest quality. The secretary of state will be under a duty to inform the authority if the applicant is an asylum seeker, if requested to do so.

Risky or hot decisions involve an evaluation of reward and punishment, with emotional significance attached to both outcomes. Many species are edging northwards in response to climate change, among them the UK-resident butterflies marbled white (*melanargia galathea*) and small skipper (*thymelicus sylvestris*). Most of the characters in *Casablanca* are trapped. The art zone grew out of a factory complex, abandoned in the late 1980s. To further investigate the predictability of the 3D folding, we assembled an open DNA box in which the sample strands closing lid D were omitted.

There was no Rolleiflex stock, but plenty of Leica film and all sorts of accessories. There were also a few human bones, especially of hands and feet. We designed an automated method of selecting influenza-like-illness search queries, requiring no previous knowledge of influenza. The various pigment and media respond differently when viewed under ultraviolet light, each emitting a characteristic coloured fluorescence that enhances our ability to see different layers.

This simulator uses a surrounding magnetic field to track surgical instruments, and creates a virtual "instant replay" of the procedure's critical stages. Many modern novels use this approach with varying degrees of distance and intimacy. We now have a large body of evidence documenting fine-grained behavioural variability. The big cylinder coffin is put on a scaffold, or placed in a house-like structure. These data do not suggest a population crash or a negative association with the Japanese white-eye. Rechavi adds that the boy's disease, which affects the immune system, may have made it easier for the tumour to grow.

He further augmented his income by trading grain. Static magnetic field slowed the flies' circadian clocks, but only in the presence of blue light. In *The Sinking Giant*, an enormous, rusty ship's bow tilts upwards from a sea of broken blocks of ice. Homer was Pound's father. He was carrying a machine gun and I thought it was a German. The surgical tent had a white floor and white walls, and white mosquito netting shut off the vestibule from the operating tables. If a flat structure is selected, there is a choice about how contacts are to be connected within the network.

Competitor complaints are generally a sign of a weak case. Store in a cool dry place out of direct sunlight away from household chemicals. Talks on defining the satellite began in 2002, with a tentative launch date set for 2012. The special relationship with Stanford University was also a factor in the Valley's evolution. One day I got a pair of white espadrilles, I was so happy, they looked so cute; I'd wanted them so much. Neurofibrillary tangles, inside neurons, are now known to be made of an insoluble protein called tau. These cities were small and enclosed by rammed-earth walls, sometimes faced with stone.

Woodland life should not be undervalued. The film narrative does not clearly indicate whether or not she is actually illiterate. The dense network is a virtually worthless monitoring device. A large metal barrow blocked the narrow street, which was still burning. Chevalier looked just like Chevalier. Self-consciousness comes about through memory, understanding and will. Blood was being slowly transfused into his left arm. The scale of a letter in a word changes one's visual perception of the word. System intrusion detected. Cones were placed on the revolving record turntables.

When the stone came from earlier settlements, it embodied nature and ancestry and engendered permanence of memory. We measured the flux of proteins across membranes when both a transport factor and a control protein were present at the same time. Chirality in snails is determined by a still uncharacterised maternal factor, but once chirality is established, *nodal* and *pitx* are expressed on one side of the embryo. *The Primary Assembly File* (1995) offers regular mailings of new material to its subscribers to meet their quantitative needs.

Among these bones are many thousand flakes and pebble tools. Outside the smoky rush of Birmingham, Boulton's strongest friendship was still with Darwin. Another crab appears from among the waves behind him. Each expression has a unique interpretation or function depending upon the arrangement of the elements. As the gas radiates but does not cool, there must be a compensating energy-injection mechanism. The works were created on an electric typewriter, using red, black and green inks, and the pieces exhibited here were made in 1980 on scrolls of rice paper.

Both the fine teeth of the comb, and its riveting system, distinguish it from other double-sided composites from Middle Saxon London. These patterns belong to a class of self-organising, self-repairing reaction-diffusion systems that were originally discovered by the mathematician Alan Turing. Facing anthropogenic change, the network can work against us. Only seven or eight such species are predicted to lose all suitable climate from the network. The strategy yields many false positives and further diminishes the correlation between findings in animal models and humans.

There is simply no experience that informs the child about the iterative and limitless power of list building. Two more fallen Samurai can be glimpsed in the middle distance. Darwin and his companions descended ever deeper, squeezing through narrow passages, hearing only their own breath and the constant rush of water through hidden channels. The air was thick with the smell of decomposing horseflesh. Samples were obtained from the CESAR-6 core using a sediment slab cutter to extract slabs of the still-wet diatom ooze.

Tests for each chemical require an average of 3200 animals for a single two-generation test—a total of 17.6 million animals for 5500 substances. As training progresses a force is applied to the arms that the children must correct for. The boy at the phone said, "They hear airplanes". Vaccination programmes will provide a unique opportunity to identify any extremely rare side effects. But many human thoughts are abstract, with no explicit or even necessary sensory connection. In printing types, soldered on the head of the lead coffin, is the name: "John Baskerville".

These are domestic pictures, with no worries about keeping children away from disturbing experiments or costly apparatus. When a piston was fitted into the loop of the cylinder, the ordinary air pressure on its surface would drive it down into this vacuum. I always like to fold a little mayonnaise and black pepper into the brown meat. Some impressions have heavier blue waves extending higher in the composition and sometimes printed over a pale blue background filling the entire sheet. There was a new American grave by the roadside. Private security companies will lose legal immunity.

The temperature and density of the remaining ground-state atoms were measured by absorption imaging. Each of those subunits is a tangle of many proteins and RNA. The functionalized DNA box was assembled, purified and subjected to ensemble FRET measurements. In *Nation-building Strategy*, the hollow corpses of four water buffaloes, each cut in half horizontally, rest on bamboo mats. A range of transcription factors are involved in setting a maturing white blood cell on the right path. Investors have since filed several class-action lawsuits against the company. Please ensure that you are travelling in the correct part of the train.

We stopped for a few moments chat and a glass of Calvados at the evacuation hospital. Man cannot do without the experience and knowledge of the rice priests, who have to pay honour to and attract the *To Tiboyong*, the Rice Spirits. Some questions can be answered even more briefly. An innovative cooling device chills a brain circuit and slows birdsong. These are the solid, dotted and thin line contacts in the pie chart. When Deter died in 1906, Alzheimer scrutinized her brain using a staining technique developed by his colleague Franz Nissl. Have your data met with excitement or skepticism?

This non-linguistic, set-based system is present in human development but it then transformed as a result of an interface with the abstract properties of human syntax. The cards cannot be factored into a product state as before, because they no longer share the same suits. Crack open each of the three claw sections with a short sharp chop from the thickest part of your knife blade. Workmen stub their spades on lead and hastily cover it up. Critics of Mao Zedong often have compared the Chairman with the first Emperor.

Zhou says that he intends to use the KBBF laser to take arsenic oxide studies even further. The only way round these problems, everyone agrees, is to develop reliable biomarkers to help follow the progress of disease and treatment. However, if you do not change the names, the naming system loses its connection to theory and becomes an arbitrary mapping of the world. The display shows Met Tag Disaster Triage Tags with Ties. Replanting shelterbelts had to be our primary concern. No other print in the series so strongly suggests the influence of photographs.

Brush the mullet with a little olive oil and sprinkle lightly with ordinary salt. Some ware may require several such treatments before sufficient crazing takes place. Since 2000 the number of UK animal experiments has increased by one third. It was not until the release of detailed mortality statistics in the 1980s that it became generally known that between 20 and 30 million people had perished, primarily in the years 1959–61. Little iron has been recovered from the pits. The dense network contains only one non-redundant contact. General Motors was granted eminent domain powers.

Three of the patients were conscious. We had easy chairs. Only the shopkeeper's wife in the congregation is commended for being "generous, spiritual, and possessed of an unswerving instinct for what is right". The third issue is the testing of multiple end points, which also contributes to false positive results. So are there musical forms that cannot be perceived and therefore represent impossible structures? The present print comes from an apparently unrecorded series. Almost all the Lunar men owned canal shares, and Boulton had a lucrative sideline supplying metal parts, locks, bolts, brass valves for pistons, copper boxes, rasps and rings.

Each horse hung in tackle for six or seven weeks while George and Mary stripped the flesh off layer by layer so that he could draw the fat beneath the skin, the muscles and veins, tendons and ligaments, joints and bones and finally drooping skeleton. You could use frozen blue soft-shell crabs instead. A network of feedback mechanisms kept Earth in the stable state to which we were accustomed. Evidence from inland shelters and caves shows how sheep and goats, and later, the other domesticates were gradually taken up.

Under the care of Gillies, he endured a series of surgical procedures to help rebuild his lower face, using a flap of skin from his neck. There are some hints of coastal specialization. Aviation fuel storage tanks were, if possible, installed underground. Recognized meanings were ordered in a gradation derived from and controlled by Greek social class structure. These prejudices are, to some extent, hard-wired into our brains. Japanese companies, flush with cash, beat a path to Hollywood's door.

This book is not a literary history of the period. The jaws, moreover, of the working ants of the several sizes differed wonderfully in shape, and in the form and number of the teeth. These newly professional actors performed in a variety of venues and styles. Are you listening? A fish trap involves considerable labour, and the trap and its catch will therefore belong to those who constructed it. The first object-oriented language was SIMULA (Khosafian, 1993) that attempted to simulate the way in which organizations carry out their tasks.

As he was running home a policeman on the beat saw him drop his glove. This enzyme-related article is a stub; you can help *Wikipedia* by expanding it. With its solid enlarged features, it's like a classical sculpture. Fingers and toes were covered with protective gold caps and individually wrapped with long, narrow strips of linen. Foraging bumblebees, the authors argue, bring pollen and nectar into the nest, and their peers learn what to search for by the target's scent. They show that greedy routing yields the fastest journey through networks such as the Internet. These are patterned across the mire surfaces, with drier areas of heaths and wetter areas of sphagnum and standing water.

An old employee gives some idea of the output, when he reports that five men made 400 swan-neck hoes in one day, from cutting the steel bar to the polished and varnished final product. Then there are "rain makers", valued for their ability to deliver clients. A crucial design choice was the game's emphasis on cooperation rather than competition. Red deer, elk, roe deer and pig are represented and the site appears to have been a hunting camp from where hunters went in search of these animals on the encounter basis described above.

Male biased births were higher for rural families who were allowed a second child after having a girl. For Display Until (DU) and Best Before (BB), see neck of bottle. This attribution is not specific to fascist discourses. It was designed to allow three horses, three dogs and two men to drink at the same time. Mr. Benjamin Bassett was the first to make gas in Bury, and light up his foundry with it. Danneman, an ice skating instructor turned drug addict, who many people suspected knew more about Hendrix's death than she let on, committed suicide in 1996.

Three cemeteries contain evidence for vertical social differentiation, indicating that the first ranked societies of Europe appeared during the Mesolithic. Referral benefits involve the opposite flow. Absorbed in the rural scenery, the Chinese-speaking actors at a distance mediate the audience's tourist gaze. In 2007 Pfizer laid off 10,000 employees, mostly in sales and marketing, and announced the closure of three R & D facilities in Michigan. The network image of a market is the population ecology image of a niche. Away from the frontier, where people are more homogeneous, contradictory expectations of relations are less frequent. These truisms were collected together in extensive lists and wheat-pasted onto hoardings surrounding SoHo construction sites. What font do you think in?

Reading On

By its very nature, reading says that we are alone. A rich cobalt blue is sometimes introduced into the borders, and overlaid with gold stars. The *P. infestans* genome is the largest so far sequenced, at about 240 megabases, with an extremely high repeat content close to 75%. Like a spinning top, these bits have momentum, and it takes them time to reverse their magnetism from one orientation to another using traditional means. Strong horizontal bonds between surface atoms act as a tough shell that can resist denting by a sharp tip. Michael and Yvonne have four children and five grandchildren. In the past, patent literature has been difficult to search, but this is no longer the case. Substantial payments between businesses were made by bills of exchange. Mark tried farming but preferred Hang Gliding. A special car park has been built, and picnic tables installed.

The families of Grimspound gave up the struggle and joined the steady retreat down into the valleys. Many hands would then be needed to sort the catch. The view lacks hatchings in the water and sky as well as on the buildings, and a three-masted ship that appears in the foreground of the Dutch original has not yet been engraved. These are large wash drawings in sepia and various combinations of Chinese and Indian ink, diluted with water. Please take a moment to check your delivery address, travel details and cost breakdown. That depth of focus and reality, that largeness of context, is as moving as it is beautiful. Drawers can be used for easily lost items such as scissors and string. This phenomenon, called persistence of vision, occurs when frames run between twelve and sixteen per second. I'd like to see the location and familiarize myself.

Two sorts of yellow were used, one transparent, the other opaque or thick, composed of sulphate of antimony, litharge and sand; the flesh tints were usually in this colour. If a fog comes down when approaching the Channel Islands it is safer to return to sea. But the man who bought the clothes was not al-Megrahi, nor was he Libyan. This is a simple, straightforward use of a prominent oblique line. Easter Sunday fell on April Fool's Day in 1934. In an eight-bit

RGB image, each pixel can have one of 256 values for each of the colour channels. Isoprene scavenges OH radicals and suppresses the formation of new aerosols. By now Olive was living with us to help with the four children and this allowed me to have interests outside the home. We had long trenches made, each holding about 60 girls, with pumps to remove the nightly accumulation of water, and dim lighting from car batteries.

The stages from persecution to destruction were visualized by series of a few pictures each. Parachutes are packed in tin-lined cases in order to prevent damage by seawater. Today the site is enclosed on three sides by managed commercial woodland. I was alone in the small screening room, and I was shown a print that still had no credits. The decision made sense in many ways. Tear the paper into small pieces and soak in water to soften and break down the fibres. Sets were built and properties gathered. Temporary accommodation and alternative employment were found, and gradually the village emptied.

The paint on the stakes sometimes becomes faded and weatherworn. You are welcome to offer your own suggestions. Many of the estimated 170 million people infected with hepatitis C virus suffer no serious symptoms, but in about one in four it leads to cirrhosis of the liver. Entrance to the programme has been frozen and further changes are under consideration. By this time the children were scattered. Among my father's papers, I found an old school book with carefully written lists of wild flowers both with their Latin and English names. They were disconnected from the moment and place where they were taken and integrated into a symbolism of simplification. Photographs were used to illustrate, to create a sensation, or to teach.

The largest number of deaths occurred among the newly imported labourers. We have a large bookshelf that my father built during the dictatorship. Glue was applied to the wall, following the design, and then gold leaf. The excavators took internal and external measurements, recording partitions and hearths. Most striking is the painted white edge within which the composition is circumscribed. This extended reach was demonstrated in 2001, when foot-and-mouth disease struck British livestock.

Some of Miturich's spatial posters were based on and illustrated specific transrational *zaum* poems by Khlebnikov. The brain therefore interprets the signals as eye movements. Such high-speed operations could conceivably lead to quantum computing at gigahertz clock speeds. All experiments on great apes would be banned, except during extreme circumstances such as pandemics. Only by applying the drug before the blastula stage could we obtain animals with coiling defects, suggesting that a role in left-right asymmetry might be the earliest function of *nodal* within the embryo (see supplementary table 1). However you paint the larger picture, you are in there; it isn't something you command. When required, the earth was removed from the cellar and again trodden and thoroughly kneaded, until it became suitably malleable.

Most readers of *Photo-Life* are familiar with the Orton technique. Petrol and water are easily obtained. The drops eventually bumped into one another and connected, forming arches. I had the opportunity of working in many departments, including Confectionary, Cocoa, Chocolate-covering machinery, Vegetable drying and Tin soldering. Because measuring endorphins directly would require a spinal tap, the researchers instead used pain tolerance to gauge endorphin release after workouts. A second pulse allowed them to read back the data. In the atmosphere, fewer aerosols would lead to less cloud formation and less of a cooling effect on climate. Neither the colour file nor the monochrome file conveyed the mood I wanted.

The image shows the system of blood vessels in a mouse brain with a tumour at a depth of 2 millimetres. Peer review is hardly perfect but nobody's got a better idea. It was possible to run round the buildings with a handbell between lessons. Civil Law Chamber 143 of the Berlin Supreme Court of Appeals ruled on this case. The receiver is intended for use in Western Europe. This is the visual equivalent of mourning. All the Toshiba cassette bombs that had been seized were found, when tested, to run for 30 minutes after they were set. Range control listens out on channel 8 when firing is taking place.

These signs, composed of rectangular lines, are better adapted for seals or stamps, the lines of the ordinary characters being lengthened and made angular instead of curved to suit the squares or the seal. Long wave might have been fuzzy and unfashionably mono, but its signal was solid as granite. At the same time, a section of the outer wall was also reconstructed. She does not refer to our presence. Sometimes the word NOVE is written in full, accompanied by a star of six or eight points. The holding ground on mud or fine sand is good. The shadow was not part of the film but the effect of a malfunctioning projector. Both amplifiers are provided with separate gain controls. But in the West German image the efficiency of killing was separated from its close relation to industrial exploitation.

Cocoa Essence had a much better flavour than its predecessors and sales rapidly increased. The names Hahnium or Joliotium can no longer be considered for any as-yet unnamed element, because both were once used to name element 105, which is now called Dubnium. When droplets of dissolved or suspended matter dry on a surface, material often spreads to the edges of the droplet forming a "coffee ring" stain. On this pattern of circulation is now being imposed still another element, the new expressway system. Sound waves can also travel easily in both directions along a given path, like electricity does; so acoustic devices could block wrong-way reflections.

The bulk of the music is given to two sopranos and a mezzo, who have to sing into the microphones all the time. I wandered from tent to tent at will. Boulton fired his gun into the darkness. If you go through the door situated at the side of this painting you will enter one of the annexes to the courtyard. Beneath lowering skies, a couple in evening dress dance on a beach while, flanking them, a maid and a butler stand in patient attendance with umbrellas held aloft. While shooting on the edge of a lake, I noticed that the tripod legs had broken through thin ice.

The movement of drops in electrical fields plays a role in processes as diverse as storm cloud formation, ink-jet printing and lab-on-a-chip manipulations. Five quilts of potassium nitrate are provided to assist combustion of documents. The first step would be to mark off, in pencil, a rectangle within which each of the drawings would be made. A small external pocket is fitted to each sleeve, the one on the left for a knife, and on the right a compass. Numerous dotted lines on Long Island show land boundaries that have not as yet been analysed by local historians.

The court did not appear to be persuaded by other documents attesting to how clothing and textiles, and even the hair of victims murdered at Auschwitz, were meticulously gathered for subsequent *Verwertung*. One way to measure quality of life is using a time trade-off method. Rorty shares these concerns, and they will be explored in chapter 3. Recent functional magnetic resonance imaging studies have shown that the brain lights up differently before, during and after writing. This distinction was not new, but competition sharpened in the early 1970s. In the living area, there was a cooking pit of hot ash, as well as a central hearth.

They wanted to be there, in the sunlight, at the picnic. Put on your own mask before helping others. The actual context of persecution and expropriation stood, with astonishing clarity, at the centre of attention in Allied proceedings. The symbolic value of this handful of photographs has to be analysed from a historical perspective, not only with regard to their intrinsic pictorial code, but as essential means for the production of images of the recent past. Suddenly I was attacked by four bears, who sprang out of the water, not once but four times with a marzipan sweet stuffed into my mouth. There is no place called Meryn in Devon today. The Allen Telescope Array has 42 six-metre dishes swiveling in the high desert. Each one was marked with the cathedral and the letter F.

Recognition of the actual word is not enough to constitute reading. The average distance between neighbouring sites is approximately 60km. Being had to be approached differently. Historical examples of fascism are invariably connected to the development of capitalist accumulation and productive relations. Curled as a sentence. Ulysses also discovered that the Sun's magnetic field has a strange asymmetry between its north and south poles. The jump in this analogue is turbulent and dynamic, much as the termination shock is observed to be. On day 14, colony formation was analysed by fluorescences microscopy (representative panels are shown).

Railtrack monitors the impact of a delay to a train in minutes. Closely related to these images are a number of small drawings of single leaves. Packed in bales of ten sheets, wrapped in greaseproof paper to prevent damage by sea water, the whole being enclosed in hessian canvas. It was a "guard book", composed not of full-sized leaves but of narrow stubs, called guards, to which maps or similar materials could be pasted. Common to both types of images were the scenes of people passively arranged in rows by someone in uniform. Born at West Heath House, we soon moved to Adelboden, West Hill Road, Kings Norton and this I shall always remember as home.

We're proud to announce the Expression Analysis GWAS Grant programme. The genome of *Phytopfera infestans*, the pathogen that triggered the Irish Potato Famine in the nineteenth century, had been sequenced. What happens when the intertwined ideals capitalism and liberal democracy are both undermined? The leading marks are rather inconspicuous in daylight. People looked on helplessly as one by one their homes collapsed into the bay. Clusters of researchers and planners filled the spare places. All the windows in the range are modern insertions. Pull off the legs, crack open the top joints and remove the meat from them. There were three or four enlargers and automatic glazers.

Enmer wheat appears to have been the basic mainstay, supplemented by smaller amounts of einkorn and hulled six-row barley, and by peas and lentils. The population ecology framework is a stronger vehicle for pursuing evidence of the survival hypothesis, because it is more articulate about the manner in which survival changes over time. George started abusing children at Little Ted's Nursery in Plymouth after she met mother-of-one Angela Allen and Colin Blanchard, 38, on Facebook in September last year. They would buy bills for cash less a discount. On the surface, the relationship appeared smooth. Some of the unused stubs still show deckle edges. But some part of the lines almost in all the shares in the country are cut away, and these have a need to be new marked.

Map 14 is in the hand of an unidentified Thames School copyist (see introduction). In 1864 they started to produce *Mexican Chocolate*, a vanilla flavoured cake chocolate, which continued in production for over a century. Harnesses of this type are made up to conform to the external dimensions of their respective packages. The first few days we were to stay at a conference centre where the walls were of paper, the floor covered in rice straw (no shoes allowed); tables and desks 12.5 inches high with a prayer recess, flowers and a motto. The occupying army was not required to venture west of the Tamar for any extended period. Here, overexposure directs attention to the delicate grasses, which benefit from the high-key treatment. You may do this on your own, with a friend, or even in a group.

I take it the funny spelling represents both a nerdy joke and a precaution against copyright trouble. The Zodiac inflatable boat tips alarmingly as we skim along the Serrano River, deep in Chilean Patagonia. "Hello Jeff, can you hear me?" Tail-anchored (TA) proteins mediate essential biochemical processes in nearly every membrane. Wildt developed specialized plant chambers to study the types of emissions given off by plants. A paper's authors are not always apparent from the author list. In September 1845 Richard visited Exeter with his daughters Maria and Ann. They realized that the images were not only evocative for purposes of remembrance but also useful as political tools. Many people disappeared due to these reasons.

If a case involved property transfers between private individuals, the "partners to the transaction" confronted one another, in person or through their attorneys. It seems from these words that the form and content of a map were already taking shape in his mind. Four plug-in coil boxes are supplied. The two bears of state 3, however, have been replaced by indications of hills. Officials in the regional finance offices were aided by the law's ambiguity. Large areas of wasteland were taken into cultivation and existing farms were extended, bringing great prosperity to the farmers. Crocodiles and hippos have always lived happily together. This particular shot was taken in the Tarr inlet as we were cruising towards Margerie River. Admiralty Chart no 262a shows the name as "Terrible".

For the timetable you will be using some top-down reading strategies. Baskerville worked for years, challenging a notoriously conservative craft, before he printed his groundbreaking *Virgil* of 1757. The colour is pure and solid, with one brown rectangle superimposed on top of a larger red rectangle, which fills and wraps around the canvas. This, in effect, deletes such objects as stationary helicopters and would also mitigate the effects of a windfarm. Walk now towards the room that gives onto the garden. Use a craft knife to cut along the inside edges of the flower petals. The crucial part of the project is fitting the angled side panel. Yet for most of the time, Tyneham is empty and silent, save for the scurrying wildlife and the persistent crump of the guns.

Since that time, land vertebrates have returned to the sea many times. This was the premise, nine years later, of Arthur C. Clarke and Stanley Kubrick's *2001: A Space Odyssey*. The first thing to disappear is the feeling of effort. D1 Oils has shifted from planting jatropha to focusing on basic research—including starting a breeding programme to develop seeds with high oil yields. The first chamber houses a small mixed stand of different saplings. For that reason, a crime scene must be sealed off until searches are complete.

Provisions were left on the site and payment collected from a receptacle filled with vinegar, thought at the time to be an antiseptic. 170 authors used the consultation web tool in some 4000 visits, providing several hundred informal comments on the assessments. So what is wrong with the current approach to toxicology testing? There are no ambiguities in any of the rune forms. This is coach number 6 of 8. Transporting or encoding information from the short-term to the long-term memory is not an automatic process. The word is written or half-written before the subject knows anything about it, or perhaps he never knows about it.

A factory alone was not enough, even for the Queen's potter, and Britain alone was not enough of a market. Once the painting process was completed, the tape was removed revealing an edge of unpainted paper around the brown upper and the grey lower sections. More or less, the one hundred are obliged to have a shared experience. The photo is the backdrop and the bees the main characters. Chaplin died in 1977 in Switzerland, where he had retreated after McCarthyite investigation, tax problems, and the paternity suit involving Joan Barry. The drawer could either keep the bill and accept payment on the 60th day, or, by endorsing the name of a new payee on the back, could use it to make a payment of his own.

All mention of John Fenwick is omitted from the text. The sheet on which it was engraved has its original wide margins with deckle edges and shows no signs of even having been bound in a book. It was some years before we were given a free Saturday. The array has a wide view of the sky, and within that picture, multiple stars can be analysed simultaneously. It is difficult, now, to recapture the excitement that greeted the first moving images. But a word that can be written with one impulse is not affected by this. Whether or not the Sunshine Act becomes law, the NIH is moving on a parallel track to tighten its own reporting rules for extramural researchers. The Heterodyne Instrument for the Far Infrared (HIFI) performs high-resolution infrared spectroscopy and is intended to detect elements in gas clouds swirling in star-forming regions.

A good agreement with the model is verified. You may not post new threads. The lower third of the Ogilby plate has been cut off completely, thus eliminating the cartouche as well as the list of parishes and plantations. From this context the reader can guess what some of the text will be about. Nonetheless, the court was unable to find any evidence in the documentation submitted that clothing from the Auschwitz extermination camp had gone primarily to Western Germany or Berlin. The last three volumes on the shelf are empty. He found no trace of a hearth in that chamber, but acknowledged that it may have been removed. During this stage, paths that are not yet well worn may be opened up.

Earlier structures created with perishable materials, such as timber and turf or wattle and daub may not have left pronounced profiles on top of the house site and yet their interiors may still show as hollowed depressions in the turf. Farther South, a variant type of glazed ceramic was being made during the Warring States period. If intelligent civilizations were out there, how would they make contact with us? A regenerative second detector enables the set to be used for C.W. Morse reception as well as telephony. All sense of size, dimension, and distance disappeared.

This partly reflected a lack of information: "Knowledge about Africa", Miller admits, "was in fact held hostage by the Slave trade: until the late 18th century almost everyone who went to Africa and wrote about Africans was involved in it". Newspapers and periodicals, radio programmes, regularly published BBC documents, sound archives, official documents, and websites are all cited in full in the endnotes. The deserted village is readily accessible because of its proximity to a minor road. The copy on the poster (shown here) presents a condensed version of this message. There is an English plot to blow up the same cinema. Science targets could include the star-fuelling hydrogen that surrounds galaxies, and the radio afterglow of the g-ray bursts that follow supernovae. The endline was "Not everything in black and white makes sense".

The facility one acquires in rapidly shifting the attention from reading to writing and back, without confusion or effort, is remarkable. Corrections are employed in order to consider the tip-loss, cascade, post-stall, and turbulent wake effects. His proposed remedy was simply to wake the patient in the middle of the night, before the tiny veins in his lungs ruptured. Scripts were therefore written and tapes edited by candlelight; makeshift lines of communication were lashed up. Each space had to contain all of the letters. This summer, the Allen Telescope Array, funded mainly by Microsoft billionaire Paul Allen, has begun to sweep the skies with its 42 dishes in the Californian high country (see page 34).

The standard deviation at 60 minutes is also shown here for comparison. As the airspace is not class D controlled, any aircraft could be flying there at any time, and the pilots are not required to talk to ATC when they operate in such class G airspace. People with dementia forget that they are forgetful. This is a phenomenon we call data mist. Cut out the circle and cover it with clear contact paper. The basin is mainly commercial and sometimes dusty but it is convenient and completely sheltered from all weather. Your transaction has been successful.

The theory given in section 2 suggests that the distribution characteristics are dependent on the diversity among wind farms, and hence the total number of wind farm sites. The images' graphic elements were more important than the historical information they conveyed. John Taylor was a wealthy manufacturer of toys, fancy buttons and buckles; Sampson Lloyd was a member of the iron founders' family. He focuses on designing supramolecules that react to light in a way that would allow them to be used in sensors or solar cells. Neither Mars nor Saturn's moon Titan are likely to have sprites, though both have the right conditions for lightning. The paintings invite the viewer to look more closely, introducing an element of duration and physical self-awareness into the process of perception. Try to imagine what this must be like. Each wave maintains a record of every change.

Children were lifted by their parents into the air. Skin tones were good, though a bit cool and overly pink. Their journey took them through Henan Province, south of Zhenzhou, over the Yellow River near Luoyang then across the Shanzi Province to Shijiazhuang in Hebe Province. Please do not reply to this email. The most noticeable change will come about as a result of the Day 42 refresh. Next, fold the outside scored sections out away from the box. Ayla goes ahead into the world of spirit. A sentence is an imagined masterpiece.

The illusion of real human contact, what young people are searching for, is answered with a feeling of loneliness. Ol Doinyo Lengai is located on the eastern branch of the East African Rift Valley, away from any influence of a deep-mantle plume or subduction zone. In the end, the working group will use complex logic trees based on the full range of expert opinion to reach its conclusions. A big advantage of animals, though, is that the experimenter can decide where in the brains to place the electrodes. The scale of biological language is a measure of how biology has overwhelmed its history. These considerations come together in the concept of structural autonomy.

Indoor space, in particular, provides miniature sites into which the conditions of the two nations are projected. Note the dark silt and clay deposits, which have been developed inside the boat. Most of the solar wind energy is transferred to the pickup ions or other energy particles both upstream of and at the termination shock. It sits above the water level, so fish can swim up into it and look out. 40% of the chemicals that irritated the skin of rabbits were found not to be irritants in the skin patch test in humans. They had been working on the fourth patient for more than two hours. David Hendy studied History at St Andrews and Oxford, before joining the BBC in 1987. The mechanism of these fixed ideas need not concern us. Once a film is done, its script becomes the transcript of the final cut.

Use double-sided tape to stick the pieces in place. Sometimes the horn is impressed and marked in blue on the same piece. A medium shot then reveals that an inverted man is being stuck to the ceiling by two other men. The use of the camera to memorialize lynchings testified to their openness and to the self-righteousness that animated the participants. Common experience with testimony in the law courts or with cases of perceptual illusion reveals how great is the gap between actual facts and the description of an intelligent witness. Their heads are shaved and clothes burned. It was not until October 1960, the deadliest year of the famine, that Mao Zedong fully recognized the need to abandon the policies of the Great Leap Forward. This effect did not disappear immediately when he began to see the printed words. The results were grainy, true-to-life and unpretentious.

The reading becomes unconscious for periods of as much as a page. Richard was able to devote much more time to public work. Step by step, in the laboratory of their experience, Yue potters developed methods that would improve the quality of their wares. Sometimes the materials were new and fresh, but perhaps as often they were out of date. The cases have been camouflaged to represent age and normal wear. Our grandfather, George Cadbury, pioneered pensions, health benefits and sports grounds for his employees and built the first "factory in a garden" surrounded by the first "garden city" to house them.

If the modelled value for each parcel of land-use is higher than the limit for sustainability, that particular land use is considered sustainable. The forge is about 30 foot square and originally occupied the three-story height of the cloth mill. Robert Dudley holds his transitional visa. The region of slower flow beyond the shock is the heliosheath. "Other refinery feedstock" is any other process used for the manufacture of any other petroleum products. Even if she is a miller's daughter, he thought, I shan't find a richer wife in the whole world. "My mind is like a web browser", she writes in one article. Cases were still being reported of dead people found by the roadside, some of them identified but the majority nameless.

An unconnected item of information is retained in working memory, waiting for other information to be attached and thus usurps memory resources needed for the making of inferences. The true and proper lexemes are 60 in number, some of which are used more than once so that the total number of words is 90. Our day's sport, besides the monkey, was confined to sundry small green parrots and a few toucans. We analysed the gene content of the opossum genome and compared it with that of the human genome. The suit consists of a large overall of waterproof material of ample dimensions, terminating in rubber soles. Only in rare cases were victims able to demonstrate precisely where the authorities had shipped their possessions for *Verwertung* (utilization). Many were captured in the interior of Angola, and gangs were driven, often in shackles, down to the coast by slave traders, under conditions of appalling hardship and cruelty. Under the chair there is what looks like a little pile of drawings. Do not make the holes on the fold too large or the layers will be loose. Above these is the Solar (a sunlit upper chamber). The theorist's goal is to understand these observations in a cosmological context. Kändler modelled men and animals of the natural size, as well as peacocks, herons, pelicans and other birds.

As a rule, the best water is found on the outer side of bends in the channels. Barrow wore a handsome red cardboard fez and Dorothy a home made witch's costume complete with a black cat and a crystal ball. In 1953, *Reichskristallnacht* was remembered officially for the first time in many West German towns. This tendency is ordinarily inhibited by the will, but comes out as soon as the attention of the subject is removed. People suffering from mild dementia will sooner or later be unable to solve the simplest of problems. You agree that we may send you notices, including notices of variation of this agreement, with your statement (whether online or paper copy).

The second blade is small and hook-shaped and is specially designed to cut tyre rubber. Acoustic diodes could be useful in improving ultrasound devices such as those used to break up kidney stones. Part of the road and a slipway were destroyed, with one house seriously damaged. At that point, other teams piled in to create pictures of high enough resolution to determine atomic structure. What causes the blood-oxygen boost is unknown: suggested triggers include synaptic transmission and action potentials. The firepot consists of a short cylindrical case of magnesium primed with thermite and gunpowder.

All weekend the lines between Cardiff and Swansea will be closed. Transcriptome analysis and cell-based assays showed defects in neurogenic differentiation and migration behaviour. In 1959 the first non-stop jet passenger plane flew from New York to Los Angeles. Agnes de Mille attended Hollywood School for Girls with Irene Mayer. Though The Four Seasons could accommodate only seven murals, Rothko executed thirty. To the north, and set slightly apart from the ritual landscape, lies an area of settlement that remains visible as a sizeable cluster of 37 stone hut circles.

The mark found underneath these pieces represents the cathedral of Florence painted in blue. Is there a fingerprint for life, in the form of oxygen or methane? How can the miniature arched structures pictured below be created? The lumps were carried some 500 metres away where they were further reduced, used and dropped. This was for the extraction of marrow. All nine people are likely to know about the same opportunities as expected in a cohesive cluster. The earliest occupation, circa 7300BC, is represented by a broad-blade technology and took place in the lake-edge reed swamp during a general expansion of hazel woodland.

Looked at front-on the jaw resembles the prow of a ship. Press as much water as possible out of the sheet of paper, then move it to a smooth surface, such as foam core, glass or Formica to dry. Now we can better understand why the leaf-cutter ant behaves as it does. It was a 2000-year-old spoon made from an alloy of copper and tin, probably used for opening and eating shellfish.

On a cold November morning, I'm looking for sentences that contain the word "reading". The central arrow shows the mean orientation for the birds tested in each group. Men, women and children crowded the area perching on fences, climbing adjacent trees, and scaling buildings for a better view. Sometimes my father drove the delivery van home from work. At least three rockets hit the *Spirit,* one of the most luxurious liners in the world. Before saturating Hose with oil and applying the torch, they cut off his ears, fingers and genitals, and skinned his face. Do not limit yourself to photographs when designing a photo mailer. This card was purchased at a garage sale in Macon, Missouri.

In the commercial a small boy is unable to reach his food on the table. Exploratory brain studies are not yet commonplace. The animals tended to learn faster, remember events longer and solve complex mazes better than ordinary mice. Miss Stein found it sufficient distraction often to simply read what her arm wrote, but following three or four words behind her pencil. Eighteen-year-old Ted Smith was slowly roasted alive on the streets of Greenville, Texas. A Darwinian puzzle is a trait that appears to reduce individual fitness rather than increase it. Skin tries to invent movement for itself.

Extinction was a constant possibility. We can say that we're only going to use these memory drugs for people with demonstrated memory decline. When completed, the machine will heat and compress hydrogen isotopes until they fuse into helium, releasing energy. This design highlights the beauty of handmade paper. Edison's patrons were looking at the light (as we are when we watch television). This created sharper programmes, but spelled political trouble. The floor was grass covered, ivy overhung the window tracery and the kitchen was a shell. If the goal were per-capita equity, Annex 1 countries would have had to stop emitting greenhouse gases entirely in 2007. His own practice was constantly developing, and he continued to experiment with the idea of giving form to syntax.

Translation elongation factors facilitate protein synthesis by the ribosome. Faced with such figures, slow trackers must explain why hunter-gatherer populations increase only very slowly. The 80-

word text, of which only 40 are legible, is written on both sides. There are many kinds of achievement in the study population. Neurodegeneration often has disease connotations. These bison, apart from a few very strange specimens in Texas with white faces, look like bison. A number of special sticks are available, such as: Italic, Adjustable offset, Long line, Self-quadding, Self-centering and the Blank Slug Block (for casting supporting slugs).

The small model consisted of six card cubes each with a different function connected by a wire and plastic umbilical cord. Anthropologists argue about whether carnivory or eating tubers is at the base. Further downstream, turbulence properties recover their upstream values and thus, atmospheric turbulence controls the growth of the wake. Small words would usually be completely written before the subject knew about it, but large words would only get started. Isn't bioluminescence brilliant? This region of the mid-latitudes is associated with strong westerly winds and frequent cyclonic activities resulting from disturbances in the polar front. Individual social amoebae such as K. dictostelium must cooperate to build the fruiting bodies through which they reproduce. Green fluorescent protein and other genetically encodable optical reporters have revolutionized the study of cell function.

By definition, all patients with Alzheimer's have many plaques and tangles; most patients also have Lewy bodies. The mob tended the fire throughout the day. They oriented toward the west at sunset, the direction they would take for an overland flight. This situation can be helped by the use of memory devices; that is, you point to things, or you show what you want to talk about. If the radar service is being provided outside the controlled airspace (ie class G airspace), the problems of clutter and unknown primary returns become more complex. Because of such features, foraging economies typically discourage ambitious production.

When cooling slowed the activity of the pre-motor area HUC in zebra finches, the overall speed of songs produced was reduced, but the acoustic structure of elements within the song was intact. In each of the narrow north and south corridors a line of soldiers faces outwards. The aim is to break the ears from the straw. On the remedial side two issues were critical. In most mammalian cells, densely packed DNA is situated near the perimeter of the nucleus, whereas looser regions containing active genes cluster towards the centre. The same patient will return on the same night each week.

Blight is difficult to control, partly because it adapts so quickly to genetically resistant potato strains. These rings can pile up into ridges that form cups or hollow domes. More oil per seed is the goal. Products such as Robin Starch, Reckitts Blue, Brasso Polish, Silvo and Karpol became household names.

The reading is not entirely lacking in expression, and the pauses are made quite properly. In January 1941 my mother died of a stroke, and thereafter I lived with my father for the rest of his life. The garden scenes and tea parties printed on the Worcester ware are well known. Take three straight pins and gather up ten seed beads onto each pin. I need to explain where "the whole equation" comes from. By daybreak, nineteen people had been killed, fifteen million trees uprooted, and nearly £1 billion worth of damage inflicted on property. Depending on the environment, certain note types are selected and are then reproduced in particular orders to create population-specific dialects—and so it is for language acquisition by humans.

A large ballroom was a warehouse for beds and stoves. The GSK-Pfizer venture reinforces the importance of sharing intellectual property to tackle HIV. These are the players to the far right of the graph in Figure 1.7. It seemed doubtful that Charles Kennedy could retain the Liberal Democrat leadership. Black and yellow hoverflies are often mistaken for wasps. Sex evolved to outwit parasites by shuffling genes. It is hardly necessary to explain why we must have the name of the sentence, and not the sentence itself, on the left hand side of the equivalence. The mass shed from the equator of a spinning body accretes into a satellite if the material consists of particles undergoing energy dissipating collisions.

Hatfill was followed, his phones were tapped, and he lost his job at Louisiana State University in Baton Rouge. The heliosheath ends at the heliopause, beyond which is the interstellar plasma. The main fuels used by final consumers in 2006 were petroleum products (48.5%), natural gas (31.5%) and electricity (17.5%).

Animals not far remote from ordinary forms, prepare the transition from light to darkness. We put the TVs on. What is remarkable is the almost simultaneous appearance of domesticated plants and elite burial. The only subjects we had were ourselves. Normal animals don't learn this association with such a mild shock.

The pencilled inscription on the back refers to the murder of Jim Rush or Bush. Succeeding words may be read before it is written, but their motor impulses do not reach the arm in time to interfere. In 1973 the "boy on the bike" campaign began its 20-year run. The virus was able to spread from infected immune cells to cultured prostate cancer cells. Key evidence for the purported impact was magnetic microspherules discovered in sediments at 25 locations. Most mice require at least six sessions before they can remember the location of the platform in a Morris water maze. An interaction with this conclusion, however, is rarely advantageous for the consumed animal.

The victim's right hand is bandaged and fingers appear to have been amputated. Within one layer of a Middle Saxon pit lay several pieces of structural ironwork. Under these conditions, the benefits of treating each alarm call seriously outweigh the costs, permitting the tanager shrike to take unfair advantage of the relationship from time to time. Gene names and protein structures should be routinely linked to database entries through hyperlinks. The Department of Energy led by Steven Chu (second from right) is trying to accelerate private-sector innovation.

Iraq is still the most dangerous place in the world. Frye, 53, is an environmental activist and surfboard business owner who has served on the city council since 2001. After an operator handles a call, a digital buddy can help by agreeing that it's really upsetting to have to deal with angry people. What does accuracy mean when we talk about memory? Sharing a bed was only found to be a risk factor if the parents had drunk more than two units of alcohol or taken drugs. The remnant core is often described as a tortoise core. It was a flyer printed in the 1980s, depicting a collection of cassette tapes from various artists. Magic lifesavers in the war—Sulfa, Penicillin and Blood—were augmenting surgeons' skill. How does a rock weather away into clay? Not even molecules or atoms were solid or hard.

Add the egg, lemon juice, salt and one third of the cream. On leaving the courtyard, there are two ways you can get to the first floor of the mansion. Polanski believed that Evelyn should die. Like a sentence which trails off in a row of dots, hinting that there might be more to say . . . Another group within the 42 makes use of liquid media. The authors suggest that synaptic transmission may dominate the energy budget of brain tissue. "They are", Andrew said, "Two persons but one artist".

Whereas natural antibodies have two identical binding sites for latching onto their target, artificial antibodies have four different binding sites, minimizing the likelihood that the virus will be able to outwit them. The explosive book is a booby trap, which may be placed on any flat surface, preferably among other books on a tabletop. The Black on Gray paintings were Rothko's final series.

Reading is a mainline train station and is easily accessible from most other places around the UK. The Moss-kings picked up the boat at Trieste. Rembrandt's self-portrait is on the left. As Kean and Easton were escorted around the factory, the analogy with cooking struck them immediately. A wind turbine heat pump system is shown in fig. 1. I remember the night season, how I was among thousands of enemies, and nothing but death before me. Lawrence Beitler, a studio photographer, took this photo. The word "cheese" tastes of cheese. Ian's face is rather colourful after Lee Mason's attack, but he won't press charges for fear of negative publicity. I'm going to read the final section.

The children of working mothers ate less fruit and vegetables, watched more TV and were more likely to be driven to school. Why do so many animals resolve their disputes with highly ritualized, symbolic displays? Under magnification, one can see the girls in this photo clutching ragged swatches of dark cloth. This may be a step towards chemical cell reprogramming that avoids gene transfer altogether. Schneider is by no means the first scientist to feel hoodwinked by filmmakers. Under these names you cannot always recognize your friends. Now the background is white.

The decision to scatter small groups of soldiers across the north of Helmand, in isolation and without any intelligence, was a tactical blunder. The plan forms were almost identical. George Perkins Marsh, in the mid-nineteenth century, was among the first to posit the possibility that cutting down whole woodlands was changing hydrological cycles. The act would require drug and device firms to post any payments to a physician in excess of $100 annually on a public website. This beautiful old house and walled garden with views one way to the Blackdown Hills, the other to the Quantocks, was a family wedding present from Michael's parents.

Most of these pictures were of concentration camps. Three types of tin lined cases are used to ship parachutes. Wind power fluctuations were grouped into forty bins each representing power output changes of magnitude 5% of rated power. This agreement shall be open ended. Acoustic analysis showed that as the pups matured, their calls developed into territorial songs that were similar to those of harem males. During encounters, at least one colony in each pair lost its king or queen and the pairs merged. AB is usually quickly removed from our brains by clearance mechanisms.

The handling time wasted on large impregnable mussels reduces the average payoff for dealing with all mussels. This method cannot be used for vocabulary building and grammatical usage since it is not only time consuming but also a tiring activity. During the recording process, Carey and Houston, who had never previously met, became friends. Here are neither staircases nor passages to keep in order. This continuity of life is now ascertained in the main Etruscan cities by the late Bronze Age. De Kooning, who never learned to drive, found the long stretches and flawless arcs of the freeways, and the enveloping rush of the landscape exhilarating.

Nature Publishing Group has now assembled all of its articles, reports, commentary and news stories on avian flu and the H5N1 virus on one website www.nature.com/reports/avianflu. We have to drop the notion of correspondence for sentences as well as for thoughts, and see sentences as connected with other sentences rather than with the world. A string of coloured shapes across the pram, the favourite for chewing was the red cube. I see it in my mind's eye now. The director came out of his office and asked what Picassos I would put in a show if I had the choice. Liars tended to draw their invented location from an aerial perspective, whereas most truth-tellers drew the scene from shoulder height. The crowd fought over these souvenirs.

Existing data sets reveal neither functional signaling properties of the circuit nor dynamic processes such as synapse plasticity. But this effect is short-lived and does not significantly add to overall star numbers. In the cover graphic, radial glial progenitors in interphase (left) harbour centrosomes of older (red) and younger (yellow) centrioles. He did it with back lighting—a soft glow gave the bottle dimension. Then the naked, mutilated corpse of a black man was pulled up at the end of the rope. We came back through the kitchen of the house. After unification in 221BC the Ch'in coinage was made standard. A variety of materials have been discovered that can boost laser light to frequencies that the lasers alone cannot produce, and each has a set of signature frequencies that it can achieve.

The risk of impact for a mission to the space station is about 1 in 300, but for missions to the higher and more tilted orbit of Hubble the risk is greater. The increase in atmospheric carbon dioxide is effectively fertilizing tropical tree growth. Priestley confessed that he was a materialist. For a given time scale of interest, there exists a corresponding distance over which wind speed is calculated. These relationships are given in equations, (8)—(10) and graphically illustrated in Figure 11.

Would you like to write a review of *Reading by Starlight: Postmodern Science Fiction*: click here for more information. A customer could work the switch or handle that moved the film and turned on illumination. The gang left a trail of receipts for underwear, shoes, dresses and automatic shotguns. Constant advertising helped new products become household names. Before Hose's body had even cooled, his heart and liver were removed and cut into several pieces and his bones were crushed into small particles.

The furs still got to St Louis. I know I need to spend some time searching the forms for topic redundancy, but I need a quick answer. In nature, however, the moths evidently do not perch on tree trunks. Some viewers may find *Triangle* a little too clever, said Derek Malcolm in the *London Evening Standard*. For the most part, brush marks have been smoothed away. A candle burned far more brightly in this new, colourless, tasteless, odourless air. The names at the end are those of the lender, the borrower, a guarantor and two persons pledged as surety. More likely, however, the boy's gesture is directed towards a strange, agitated shape in the lower left of the X-ray. A wide variety of accommodation is available nearby.

The far greater risk was associated with parents feeding babies at night on a sofa, and then falling asleep themselves. Ropes were placed around their necks, and they were hurried into waiting wagons. Writing seems to co-opt brain structures in areas involved in language, visual processing and facilitating movement, and lesions in some of these areas can drastically interfere with writing ability. During a spike, the voltage across a neuron's membrane is reversed when sodium ions flow into the cell and potassium ions move out. Cheating behaviour is limited by various mechanisms, such as kin discrimination and lower fitness of the cheater.

On a few blank pages in the middle he daydreams. Wedgwood was still trying to make an earthenware more like porcelain and was searching for a clay that was truly white, free of the iron that browned it in firing. The phenomenon of disturbed encoding enables us to understand many features of dementia. Nicholson and Towne had talked about *Chinatown*. Make sure you go through all the layers before you remove the tool. Bats learned through imitation. You may not get back the amount invested. Until then houses were seldom divided into such highly specialized areas, and their emergence reflects the growth of a refined sense of privacy.

The dragons seen on the dish (Colour no. 28) have carefully incised scales and twiglike claws. They heard noises coming from a sealed wooden barrel on the deck, and opened it to find two African girls bound inside. Setting them around a table provides a readily grasped framework for their interaction. The shape is outlined in white and filled with a pattern of crosshatched, broken and dotted lines. But once released, it paddled in a wide circle orienting itself by the array of coloured shapes hung above the pool. Both John Thornton and John Seller were makers of maps as well as publishers. At first their projects were directed towards the Cape Fear River and later to regions farther south, closer to danger from the Spaniards in Florida. Over 700 houses had been built over the failing mines. Domestic fowl and goose, and their eggs, were abundant.

Ties of kinship ranged outward from the household into a wider circle of friends and dependents. But the control groups in many of these studies were kept in rather impoverished conditions, which may have exaggerated the benefits of the "enriched" conditions. Windfarms, due to the Doppler Shift that they create in the radar signal, appear as moving targets. It is a trial when at dawn we have to go down into the cabins. The artist painted out at least one figure and cut the composition down from a larger horizontal format.

His phone had become a mobile seismometer. In the Shang cloth no straight weave is visible among the floating threads; but in the twill of the Han period alternate warps are left to interweave normally between the twilled warps, so that some straight weave appears in the midst of the twill. The entire process took just 30 picoseconds—ten times faster than today's technology. The subject was absolutely unable to recall a single word written but nevertheless felt quite certain that he had been writing, and that he had been conscious of every word as he wrote it. A small collapsible aerial is provided which plugs into the front of the set. Terrestrial vegetation releases vast amounts of volatile organic compounds (VOCs) into the atmosphere, mainly isoprene and derivatives such as monoterpenes and sequiterpenes, some familiar as the aroma of pine trees.

Roses never grow in England in the lavish, joyous way they grow here. Each man has just turned away from a design on which he has been working with his compass. The facsimile is in black and white, but the colours of the original include several shades of blue, greenish yellow, yellowish greens, and pinkish purples, with touches of gold and white. A Reading man is under observation after contacting swine flu during a visit to the United States. As he talks his words are transcribed on two sheets of paper affixed to the wall behind him. He has set up a successful business, making, flying and selling Hang Gliders and Micro light Aircraft. Media strategy included teaser ads in the TV listings pages that boosted viewing figures. After long practice this phenomenon disappeared quite suddenly.

The Surge

People cooperated in the various stages of their deportation and eventual annihilation. Volunteers were asked to collect pebbles that were smaller than their fists, i.e. up to 8cm in diameter. Subsequent steps repeat step 3 and bring a correct forecast closer. Jamie walks to the kitchen sink, puts the stopper in the drain, turns on the faucet, and leaves the kitchen. The presence of these two muscles is not a sufficient condition for an enjoyment smile. Consent was not sovereign, but, on the contrary, only valid if in conformity with the norm. We draw upon principles of learning and information theory to adapt processing to the immediate task environment.

He was conscious that he had just written a word, not that he was about to do so. In the eighteenth and nineteenth centuries, Bath stone was mined extensively and used to build the city. You can see that the machine is plugged in. Hospital facilities are still available, but they have been transferred to purpose built units or district general hospitals. Westing ships out of Bristol reached the Labrador coast and dropped down to Newfoundland. The pressure gradient may increase abruptly and outflow from the high may accelerate.

A small cone whose walls lie along the radii is erected at the sphere's surface. We must be able to reason about concurrent events with cumulative or cancelling effects. Measurements were made from colour videotapes, which provided a close-up, head-on view of the subject's face. While uneven reporting remains the fundamental concern, there is also the related problem of the lack of equivalence between landslides. Kfar HaHoresh is located in the upper reaches of a small wadi issuing into the Jezreel valley from the western flanks of the Nazareth hills. Output magnitudes were normalized to unit length and then down sampled by a factor of four.

The system of concepts within which a person conducts life is known as a culture. This does not require any change in relative definitions. Areas with a high frequency of tropical cyclones are stippled. Control thought that Carla might be a suitable candidate. My father disappeared under 60 metres of cold Newfoundland water. If there's a discrepancy, most people go with what the eyes perceive, because the eyes are usually more reliable than the ears. An invention is still valid and enforceable, and remains in public databases, even when the inventor got the science wrong.The blue jay that eats a toxic monarch vomits a short while later. Vector control may be the best antimalarial option currently available. Published research articles are now available to rent, writes Frank Norman on his Nature Network blog, *Trading Knowledge*. Formal taxonomic description is still in the works. Shortly after joining Penniger's lab in 2005, postdoc Reiko Hanada proposed injecting RANKL into the brains of rats, "to see what would happen". *Hanse* means "fellowship" in Middle High German.

Warehouses, meeting halls, and tackle shops are all built out above the shallow water on stilts. Even when using a syntactical truth-definition, a semantical truth definition is not superfluous. Please do not eat in the library. Soapiness depends on all three treatment factors. A box containing 2 buttons, marked "painful" and "intolerable" was located at the subject's left side. This landscape was difficult to traverse during high tide and impossible to cross during spring tide. Reading Recovery is trademarked throughout the world.

An American Black Hawk Helicopter appeared overhead. The painter and his wife stand close together in half-length, suggesting an informal and intimate relationship. Parts of the crater remain in permanent shadow, and so contain a record of the solar system's chemistry and evolution because material that falls in freezes, becoming trapped. The law prohibits removal of vegetation in areas inhabited by endangered species. For the past 30 years or so, tight coupling has been assumed to exist between what people see and hear because of shared experience between the two senses. In addition, more new neurons are activated in rats during memory tasks.

Voltage-gated potassium channels form pores in cell membranes through which potassium ions pass. This does not require a new treaty. Zamecnik grew up in Cleveland, Ohio, and at 16 went to Dartmouth College in Hanover, New Hampshire. The gilded surface reminds physicists that it is the mobility of surface electrons in the metal that accounts for its reflectivity, and the coloration of gold is itself a relativistic effect of the metal's massive nuclei. What stands out is the stark whiteness of the thick flakes of fresh cod.

Wind stress on the ocean surface induces currents, which can lead to profound effects near the shore (section 2.2). When a species is in danger of extinction, it starts reaching sexual maturity earlier. To keep working under the tropical sun, slaves needed salt and protein. We can disregard the mean flow and draw the streamlines of the perturbing flow alone. Terms equally shaped are not counted twice.

After an event occurs, the truth-values of fluents may change. The deception appears to represent a vivid prototype of the genuine display. Some efforts are being made to extend these data in view of wind energy applications. A brand can evoke feelings of trust and be part of a personal relationship. Although the code specified punishment, it provided no real incentives for compliance. Fruitflies and other heavily studied model systems don't have particularly high rates of mutation.

A successor state is not guaranteed to exist, and there may be several successor states. Thus, to reinforce the northern segment of Folly Island, Union troops needed to move artillery and supplies across a flood-tidal delta similar in origin to a low-energy washover fan. Such differences are likely to be significantly reduced as the number of wind farm sites increases. Each of the films was exposed under similar and nearly ideal conditions. The feeling that the writing is not our writing seems to disappear with the motor impulse. We do not know whether Nathan was asleep at timepoint 1.

He found that if he froze greens, they would last through the winter without losing their flavour. In the American South, slaves modified African cooking for white people. We meet these complications by using the results of previous calculations. Several types of commonsense reasoning are not covered by this book. The gouge-auger transect is noted between the two Harris vibra-cores from 1994. Inequalities were less wide for men, but were substantial nonetheless. The marshes around Charleston, South Carolina, lack a distinctive pattern of vertical halophyte distribution.

Anthropogenic additions to the soil include limited amounts of hearth ash but no organic manures. An operator description consists of a precondition, a delete list, and an add list. It has been customary to base the logical calculus upon the primitive idea of the predicate or the propositional function. Extra kinetic energy is furnished by whatever mechanism is deforming the wall. The system remains stationary for two or three days before finally drifting inland over South China or Indochina and weakening (Ramage, 195a). Vorticity disappears by diffusion between the regions of opposite signs.

If the real part is zero, we choose the root with a positive imaginary part. First, we must represent objects in the world and agents such as persons and animals; we must represent Lisa, the newspaper, and the living room. On the other hand you can go back, they will either shoot you or send you to a camp. Most labs cut human brains into blocks before slicing them. Trapped inside pockets along the fibres are bubbles of one or another of two liquid polysiloxane-based healing agents.

There are, of course, an infinite number of lines of force radiating from every point-charge, but in visualizing electrostatic relations it is helpful to arbitrarily set this number equal to the flux of D. Later on, we shall introduce other symbols, namely German (Gothic) letters, Greek letters and Latin miniscules preceding r in the alphabetic order. All of these techniques are vanishing. The men on Leonard's boat are tagging and releasing as many fish as they can catch. The water will start spilling onto the floor. A flow that does not reverse is a flow spoiled by numerical truncations or by defective methods of integration. In general, the digital computer deals strictly with real numbers, and it is necessary to separate each equation into its real and imaginary parts.

Two objects observed at different times and locations in space may or may not be the same object. In the bottom figure a trace of sadness is apparent, caused by the action of the triangularis muscle pulling the lip corners down on the right side of the picture. But the rose he dangles from his fingers leaves open the possibility that some sort of amorously informal mood might have linked their portraits. On a larger scale, the chromosomes are tightly packed into a "fractal globule" (pictured right) that remains unknotted to allow easy access to genes.

There are four different levels at which this book can be read. The table is a central image here, as it is in so many conversation pieces and in much of the writing on marriage from this period. The fusion of data and explanation into a single ideal currency, subordinated to the single aims of explanation and prediction, is essential. During cold stimulation, the subject immerses the right arm in water up to the elbow. The animated character mirrors the facial expression of the user. He recognizes rainfall intensity and slope steepness as controlling factors.

For more information, and examples of this kind of sentence, see the boxed note on "Be" on page 182. The entire landscape is largely capped by eolian sand and covered by forests and steppes. Fine rubified mineral material occurs in all samples, including the natural drift and the buried OH horizon. The data we possess are fragmentary and incomplete. Episodes of a single audible forced expiration accompanied by an AV12 and AV6 formed the lower end of the intensity spectrum of events coded as laughter. In the sphere of value, instrumental rationality does end in contradiction. The event calculus uses an extension of first-order logic called many-sorted first-order logic. The cat jumped onto a chair near the table.

From time to time a great stone lid was levered open and a new family member inserted. The person doing the drawing did not have to be an artist, but the term is used for convenience. Motivation is the willingness of the individual to evaluate a message. Mental health services are one structure within the rehabilitation landscape. East of the valley axis is a reverse west-facing slope of 3–5 degrees that breaks the natural gradient of the surrounding ground. Face detection and tracking software was ported to the *Robovie* robot, developed by H. Ishiguro at ATR.

Each run may cost several thousand dollars because simulated automobile crashes are expensive to conduct. We wanted to test whether a listener would use their tactile sense without being aware of it. On removal of the implants a fatigue fracture was found in the upper right pedicle screw, the side with the lower bending moment in the fixator. An image could be rotated in 3-space under control of the pen. Outlining and shading are in rose ink, another innovation of the last quarter. There's an orange tree behind the house and a footbridge with a willow tree overhanging it in front.

The aspectuality of the sentence is therefore compositionally determined and not simply by the verb. Marsh overwash sediments are typically much coarser in grain size and contain few foraminifers. The smaller the fragment, the harder it is to sustain existing ecosystems, especially those that include animals with large ranges. In their last known refuge, the western continental shelf edge, large skates and rays remain unprotected. Farther south, more cloud and fresher winds counteract greater solar radiation incident at the top of the atmosphere to produce a slight net cooling at the sea surface.

Outside of this sphere, the detailed nature of the interaction becomes immaterial and the net interaction is zero. Action precondition axioms provide an elaboration-tolerant way of expressing qualifications. Several types of reasoning may be performed using the event calculus, such as deduction, abduction, postdiction and model finding. Each target was visible from the chest up sitting at a table; the tester was not visible. Faces were automatically detected and facial expressions classified independently on the four cameras.

The man has not been identified and it is not known how old he is or whether he has any close family in the area. In 1953, Molaison underwent an experimental operation that aimed to treat his severe epilepsy, during which the surgeon removed a part of his brain, including a large chunk of the hippocampus. You cannot consent to a change of identity. The facial coding system we used may have failed to detect differences. His posture is rationalized here by a chunk of earth. I was in Rome at the time, and the coffins were everywhere. All test sentences were grammatical; their appropriateness depended on the context provided by the picture.

Across the foreground of the pattern is the fence or palisade the angry father built to keep the lovers apart. Many cities had a large open area within the walls, where the population from the countryside could take refuge in case of war. Some of the boundary marks were on movable stones, but others were cut on the face of the living rock, and so could not easily be removed. Kolophon was abandoned for some years, though it was eventually populated once again.

For the average couple, 3.6 out of 4.8 children survived to adulthood. Service users were encouraged to develop contacts within community spaces. The maze experience conveyed a unique set of feelings. Often the survival of weaving families was precarious. Participants were asked to indicate which of the two pictures corresponded to the sentence provided. Although both artists used the deeply folded acanthus as an infilling for an initial, the graceful style of the border here is somewhat ahead of the sprays in Arundel 38. Heavy dashed arrows show predominantly tropical cyclone tracks.

The river Alpheus marked the frontier between Tegea and Sparta. According to classical methods, we begin by ignoring the right-hand side. Ion-electron pairs are continuously created by ionization and destroyed by recombination, as we have seen above. Some properties of the world follow other properties in a law like fashion. As a result, we can begin to exploit those minds by feeding them false information in order to deliberately mislead them. We explore methods that merge machine learning and biologically inspired models of human vision. It can be done anywhere in any weather conditions.

Following the telegraph and the railroad came barbed wire. The supergrid would connect the big European nations with sources of green energy. Koong-tse, a rich man's beautiful daughter, lived with her father in the two-storied house at the centre of the pattern. Although cloudiness reduces insolation, the surface of the China Seas gains heat because light moist winds result in only slight evaporation. Each vessel was restricted to 139 days of ground fishing. The warmed surface radiates heat. A conducting sheet can be charged only on the surface, and there is no internal field. In fact, cold advection was greatest ahead of the trough, where the flow pattern was strongly diffluent.

Only three miles from the Green Zone, Mansour is a mixed area filled with diplomats and professionals wealthy enough to hire guards. Drivers switched off their headlights so insurgents could not see us. In satellite pictures, the region looks like silver foil that has been crumpled, and then scorched. About one mile north of the oil seeps I selected my site. Subjects were approached in the waiting room. Twelve to fourteen city-states of the Kotoko have been mentioned above. Records do not name the indigents, nor do they tell us what they did during the rest of the year. If you died today, who would take care of your family?

American and British intelligence think Bin Laden is in North Waziristan because he has good friends there. Weapons transporters and car bombers can't get in or out. "The place of wild goats" would more appropriately refer to all the mountains, which enclosed the Eurotas Valley on north, east and west. Forested peaks are darker than the snow-covered valleys. The International Space Station was located over north-western Romania when this image was taken.

The goal of the surge is not to solve Afghanistan's problems in 18 months. But today, the hesitation is less tactical than emotional. Children began to work in cottage industry around the age of six. We slowly rolled into the market area. A real photographic postcard bearing this image falsely attributes the location and motive for the lynching. Residents close side streets with roadblocks. On weekends and at nights, there may be some delay in comment moderation. We saw Qurban Ali, zookeeper, feeding the vultures their evening meal.

Video cameras could require another set of hands and eyes, and the setting and his appearance could give away minute clues. It doesn't look or feel like a war zone. Snow appears thickest in the upper-right corner of the image, and gradually thins toward the south and west. But, most important, are the large acanthus leaves with spiky lobes outlined in black at the upper and lower ends of the bar. The artist could draw on the adage screen using a data tablet. The system obtained 93% agreement with the emotion category labels assigned in the database.

Commonsense reasoning can be employed to make computers more human-aware, easier to use, and more flexible. The essential difference is that the research context is the real market. The decline in violence isn't necessarily permanent. Table 2 includes only those cities entirely enclosed by walls. Apart from our footsteps, there is complete silence. Many languages use an expulsion of air to change vowel or consonant sounds—in English to distinguish a sound like "da" from the microphone popping "pa".

The last ten messages have been audio only. However, in the following English sentence, *gave* is the verb, *the child* is the indirect object and *a cup* is the direct object. A standard measurement of similar origin is the teaspoon, and with it we come to the story of silverware. Click the sterling flatware button below to check our current inventory. This is an illustration of what the Oort cloud might be like. The Calabrian peninsula appears shortened and distorted due to the extreme sideways viewing angle from the International Space Station.

Vigorous polar anticyclones generally develop beneath and east of upper tropospheric ridges, where convergence is found. In the Northern Hemisphere, solar radiation is least in January. The two regions will subtend the same solid angle but their signs will be opposite, so that the total integral vanishes. A horizontal velocity function could be imposed at the wall, but it should be supplemented by a small vertical velocity to generate the pure vorticity wave. If they are universal quantifiers, we bring the matrix into conjunctive normal form and then contact the scope of the quantifier.

A language L of first-order logic is specified by disjoint sets of predicate symbols, function symbols, constants and variables. The letter is halved rose/blue with crisp indentations and cross-hatching and, below them, a row of dots with a single circle that is also conventional. The vertical scale is greatly expanded. Figure 1-3 shows an arbitrary closed surface surrounding a charge q. Databases are currently being maintained on a hand-to-mouth basis, and the scientists who built them don't know where to turn for maintenance money. The main experiment was recorded with a home video camera.

Enjoyment smiles and enjoyment laughs were combined to form the category of enjoyment displays. Let p and q be such a pair. A fluent represents a time-varying property of the world, such as the location of an object. Roughly 35 miles south of Laverton, Western

Australia, lies the Sunrise Dam gold mine. The jar was found with thirty-four other pieces in a storehouse three metres below ground level.

Have you sold or leased land in the last five years? One way to lessen fearful memories without drugs is through extinction training. A slick of embalming resin is evident between two fingers of an amulet fashioned from obsidian. At the upper left is Thailand, in the centre is Cambodia, and along the right edge is Vietnam. A new gas station in this country is actually a big deal. Priming is the major reason for advertiser choice of product placements. The old *château-fort* no longer existed and there were no seigneurs in the central village.

All three borders have royal arms at the lower mid-point. What has Phaedra to do with the realm of the spirit? Gas lamps flickered. Astronomers also are feeling the pinch. There are few fishermen over fifty. On the property websites, nothing sells. The track makers were still floating in the water while walking on the muddy bottom. The authors brought a sample of their volunteers back to the lab one year later, and gave them a reminder shock. Agricultural fires burned across much of western Africa on 6 December 2009. "I can't see, I can't see", said the driver.

Marie Magdeleine Recher, a spinner, bore fourteen children (none of them twins) during her marriage to Pierre Louis Restencourt, a carpenter. Although the island was covered in pine forest during the civil war, less than 20% is currently wooded. It is hard to say when reality hit. I would seriously consider selling my water if I was offered substantially more than the market price. No salts were added to the samples during tests.

The message and the proposition didn't really change. Gray'at's streets are quiet and safe. The conditioned fear response was virtually eliminated in both groups. The timing of attacks, the authors say, is driven by competition between insurgent groups for media attention. Providers especially value family and family business continuity. They had a melodic language like Italian but did not always write vowels, where vowels were obvious. Over forty percent of known daughters of artisans married artisans. Photographs are on the left, interpretative drawings on the right.

When suspended in solution, repellent faces cluster together, causing particles to clump. They hit upon a strange device, and resolved to conceal him in the building. There is no bar frame and no rationalized support for the separate floral and leaf motifs. Acting in between, but in an opposite direction, was axial spinal load. The batteries suffer irreparable damage if they discharge completely and grow cold. X-ray free-electron lasers, which produce short pulses of coherent x-ray light, may start to assert their superiority over synchrotrons for imaging.

Smaller Kuiper Belt objects are gradually disappearing as they collide with one another. The actuator uses blue-detuned dipole light that pushes the atom towards the area of low light intensity in the centre of the cavity. The concentrate was white, viscous and quite oily. As electronic chips hit conventional manufacturing limits, atomically precise and fault-tolerant biological circuits will replace them. A proton pump from the fungus *Leptosphaeria maculans* enables the neural silencing by blue light.

After several hundred microseconds the contact area begins to increase again. Three humpback whales blast air and water through their blowholes in Tenakee Inlet. The rise is driven by thermal expansion of seawater and by melting land ice. Upstream and middle reaches are primarily forested with Japanese beech and cedar. The gas phase is more ordered than the liquid phase and the material expands as it cools. Water was collected at the inlet of the water treatment plants. The second effluent is spent degreasing rinse. *E. coli* ATCC 25922 (American Type Culture Collection) was used as a representative bacterium and was cultured to seed irrigation water.

Pumped storage hydroelectricity requires mountains, so opportunities are limited by geography. The Colorado River spills, loads the crust, and then there is a rupture. Ben-David et al have studied the evolution of the local contact area between two sliding bodies (PMMA plastic blocks). Tracks were photographed in low-angle light to bring out the details, and were sometimes also highlighted with pigments. The rig construction enabled irrigation of the turf grass to be performed, followed immediately by institution of UV exposure conditions.

Knights and soldiers returning from the crusades brought leprosy with them. A circle of rose marked with a white cross is set into the gold base of the initial ground. The core consists of movements of *corrugator* and *orbicularis oculi*, which lower the eyebrows, narrow the eye opening and raise the cheeks. Conductors permit the free motion of electric charge, whereas insulators or dielectrics do not. Some transfer takes place across the equator into the Southeast Asian heat low.

Three of the four subunits are shown as surface plots in different shades of green, whereas the fourth subunit is shown in cartoon format. Surplus allowances could eliminate any incentive to reduce emissions. My family is fully committed to farming as an occupation and way of life. The southern ocean is the biggest sink, with over 40% of total uptake. Some "deviation actions" will pay for themselves. The throat should be cut as near the gills as possible. The Research Highlight 'Rude Awakening' (*Nature* 462, 544; 2009) incorrectly described the green parts of the image.

Placebo patients improved their depression scores but reported little change in personality. With a small jenny, one woman could produce what it had previously taken twelve to fifteen women to produce. Start reading *The Surge: A Military History* on your Kindle in under a minute. An event flips the truth-value of a fluent. For example, all the money could go into wind power, starving solar and other renewables. The thermal output of a heat pump is much greater than the mechanical power of the rotors at the same wind speed. This energy appears as heat and produces minute changes in temperature and density.

A conducting sphere located in an originally uniform field. The phosphorous level drops markedly in the modern soil. After 2–24 hours incubation with trypan blue (TB), fluorescent or blue latex beads (LB), cultures were washed and fresh medium added. No sludge was created during the anodic oxidation experiments. Human volunteers learned that the appearance of a visual cue (a blue square) predicts a shock to the wrist. A higher level of explanation is required to understand delusions and their persistence.

These are young, highly qualified people. Brand involvement arises because of the individual's knowledge. Johnson exploited the democratic potential of public services and technology such as the photocopying machine. The colour range is still kept to rose and blue, with only the lion's head and one pair of leaves in orange. Bark paintings in this style are unique to Groote Eylandt, and found only during the 1940s and 1950s. The faxes had all been sent just prior to the show's opening.

The chrome paint bucket (as well as the band of glue residue from the label) is conveyed with deft gray washes. The surfaces of Rauschenberg's 1951 monochrome white paintings reflected viewers' shadows and influenced Cage's 1952 Black Mountain proto-happening event. He stood in the Humvee and manned a machine-gun turret sticking out of the top. Violence in Anbar province is down more than 90% over the past two years. In Iraq's case, it looks like the real war will start when we leave. The Curfew is going into effect. A plural state system enabled enterprising minorities to migrate into areas that allowed them to display their energies and talents.

We are asking each service for their data to be published in the future. Climate-sceptic bloggers and mainstream media have been poring over the posted material and discussing its contents. Both observers and merchants thought that carding and spinning were admirable occupations for orphans. The same sentence might be dictated to the subject over and over again; at the end of the series he would not know what it was. Humans who recalled their fear memory 10 minutes before extinction training showed no fear response when tested 24 hours later.

I looked at their darker camouflage and elaborate weapons. Some people become lifestylers by choice, others do so because of circumstances beyond their control. The first occupation was a small reconnaissance force led by Major General John G. Foster on February 8, 1863. Only those who've been to the front line have any idea. We'd been trying to get to Echo Company in a town called Mian Poshteh. This site (an old quarry) has yielded a dozen trackways made by several individuals and numerous isolated footprints found on fragments of scree.Four units produce drinking water from surface water. The lowest site (H3) is located at a fourth-order stream running through an urban area with buildings. A main drawback to structured prediction is that parameter estimation requires repeated inference. Since there are exponentially many possible English sentences, it is highly unlikely to see the same sentence twice. Y-JACK ONE A / WOLFPACK FOUR ZERO / RADIO CHECK OVER.

The girl was wearing an elk-tooth dress. Across the water, two men on a motorcycle rode past, coldly staring at us. Prior knowledge has not received much attention in the context of structured prediction. In one or two instances an expression of pleasure can be detected in a group picture. Isolated rats were more stressed, anxious, fearful and vigilant. Four outcast teenagers acquire mystical powers that allow them to become gods on campus, with deadly consequences. They map the regions where CO_2 is most concentrated, and track the accumulations over time.

This image was taken shortly before the coroner cut the two bodies down. Triplicate samples of turf-grass were collected at each time point. Three French sources used for drinking water production were investigated in August 2004. The ends were covered with tightly stretched rawhide. If we wish to use pieces that are larger than a single factor, then the definition of the node-split graph can be modified accordingly. Most documents contain many crossing skip-edges, so that exact maximum-likelihood training using junction tree is completely infeasible.

Even Blue, the explosives-sniffing dog, jumped out wagging his tail. Irrigators in the Namoi Valley can be clustered into three distinct groups according to the values they hold, and those groups can be useful for predicting and explaining their behaviour. This man is cutting red gum sleepers. A horse tailer fills the cook's packsaddle canteen with water for the camp from the same tank. Malta has no permanent rivers or lakes, but temporary waterways can form after heavy rains. Most of the amoebae present in surface waters have the capacity to form cysts, which are extremely resistant to disinfection.

Extra charcoal is kept in wicker baskets (bottom row). A crowd is assembled at the Log House. Once inside, immune cells initiate inflammation. The people wore tailored skin clothing; two suits of skins with the fur inward, providing an insulating air layer in between. Being involved in farming is more important than owning a particular piece of land. The objective is to treat rinse effluent and discharge in the natural environment. Reader comments are now moderated.

Snow highlights the courses of the Potomac and Susquehanna rivers from the Appalachian Mountains to the Chesapeake Bay. To keep the planet's density that low requires that it contain large amounts of water. The whale brings its tail down hard on the surface. A gill net is a net anchored slightly above the ocean floor. In July 1992, the Canadian government closed Newfoundland waters, the Grand Banks, and most of the Gulf of St Lawrence to ground fishing. Fine weather close ahead and to the right of a slowly moving typhoon can thus be accounted for.

The amount of dimming directly indicates the planet's size relative to the star. Continental subduction can lead to melting of crustal slabs and percolating granitic magma. The Kuiper belt is a remnant of the primordial solar system. As the ion relaxes, it radiates an x-ray characteristic of the wind ion. This has two potential advantages. Shrubs and grasses are patchy, growing in the riparian and the canopy cover was almost open. For the task of noun-phrase chunking (chunking) we use a loopy model, the factorial CRF introduced in Sutton et al (2007).

The chief attraction of this method is that it achieves consistency without requiring inference in the training procedure. Motor task acquisition is followed by the elimination of other spines. Changes in DNA length allow measurement of the rate of helicase action in real time. Art objects moved in both directions. Brackets are inserted only for editorial emendation. The front left tyre was blown about 80 metres into a nearby field, and the bonnet was crumpled. Anderson probably came upon this scene while photographing the Bad Lands.

The woman with braids in line with the doorway is Nancy Blue Eyes. Value preferences associated with family are where the three groups show the clearest differences. Constraints are formulated as a taxonomy of probability ranks and/or ratios based on expert knowledge. Trees and shrubs were drought resistant and had no enemies except fire to hinder their growth. The Sioux evidently stopped using leather thongs as soon as bridles became available. The absence of tetrapods in these deposits may simply be a matter of environmental preference.

It is one of the few places on the lake where the water comes right up to the mainland. In his sketch book notes to the painting *Watchman* (1964) Johns focused on the conceptual and behavioural similarities and differences in spying and looking. He is shown as a much older man in plate 125.

The Street was only ten feet wide in 1819. Meat was pot roasted or boiled. Hundreds of early wrecks must have gone unrecorded or even unremarked. The curfew lasted until at least 1911. There are significant differences between the two drawings. Susannah Wood of Starcross was fined for raking cockles on Fowley. Water instead of fat was used to blend the dry ingredients to keep the biscuits fresh on long voyages. This reproduction is made from a print Mrs Anderson tinted. The community in question had a pastoral background, and was locked in struggle with an agrarian population, whose ritual life was more luxuriant.

Broken middle and high clouds, which are often observed over the eastern Arabian Sea, probably originate in rain systems further east. Distrust of new fishing techniques is endemic. Ten countries are responsible for 87% of global deforestation. The modeller must decide how to split the model into pieces before training. Like modern humans, Ardi could walk upright and didn't use her arms, as chimps do. They were obliged to come close inshore at high tide to throw the limestone overboard, so that it could be collected from the beach at low water.

A further eight boats have followed the second *Victoria*. The style is similar but the lettering of the titles is not. Many shearwaters were seen about the ship. After explaining the origin of H5N1 virus in wild birds and poultry, Sipress describes the first fatal infection in a young boy in Hong Kong in 1997 and the identification of the virus by local and Dutch scientists. As a consequence they started to cook differently, to eat new things. In its new position, the ferry station was more vulnerable. The drift from east to west is quite distinct.

In 1878 the lifeboat was towed on its carriage by horses through country lanes to be launched at Budleigh Salterton. The same hills are visible in the background. Participants gathered in the brush along the creek and decorated their horses with grapevines. This image or video has been moved or deleted. It was a process that was going on all over the world. The inside of the pot was lacquered in the 1800s with a thin layer of gold for use in the Japanese Tea Ceremony. Are you sure you want to turn off your computer now?

The cells were able to incorporate into early mouse embryos. It is difficult to avoid nomenclature that anchors thinking about the complex behaviours encountered within the cluster. The cell-assembly hypothesis assumes that what distinguishes one memory trace from another is the composition of cells that are co-activated within a given network. Orbs more like Earth will be seen as the team shifts attention to smaller planets in longer period orbits. Conditional random fields are one of the most popular structured prediction models. Although these pharmacological manipulations are potentially useful for changing learned fears, their use in humans can be problematic.

We try to manage them with just reassurance. In 1770 John Andrews was transported to the colonies for stealing £12 from Mary Richard's house at Exmouth. The children are sitting on a wooden box. Each mat measured about three feet by six, and the size of a room was determined according to the number of mats it was to contain. Meat from the beef issue has been brought home, and strips are drying on the bows of a spring wagon and on a pole rack arranged for that purpose. A small sandbank called the Fort appears there on 18th century maps.

Sewage floods the backyards of comfortable, spacious homes. In districts like Dora, the strategy of the surge seems simple: to buy off every Iraqi in sight. Even in the initial pilot, which wasn't very accurate, we saw evidence of auditory override. The chief results in this direction are reported below. During the first hour of firing, combustion was high, yielding black smoke. The hotel took hits from rockets at least 20 times. The numbers of the buildings have since been changed. Mark was evacuated by helicopter.

Other parts were played by members of the company. They were allowed to retain their fathers' names as surnames—for example, Dan Hollow Horn Bear. Slicing off the fronts of buildings was a less severe manner of change than that commonly used today. In 1996, only one client had no fixed abode registered in the Trust databases. Pain is commonplace in elderly persons with cognitive impairments, but it is an inadequately studied problem. All three masking smiles show evidence of negative emotions leaking through the smiling appearance produced by the zygomatic major muscle.

If the downstream channel outlet is closed abruptly, a positive surge will develop almost immediately. The initial effect is a continuous flow of objects rushing towards the camera. Media progressively reveal bodily imperfections. According to our model, players prefer to be friends with players that do not need much help. They asked their victims if they wanted to go and see a dead fox. Not all values are so easily captured by markets. A policy requiring explicit, individual consent is not plausible. The movement of stereoscopes and views from child to child was precisely orchestrated.

The visualisation tool uses a red icon to show when two claims conflict and a green icon to show when they're consistent. An inner rigid calcified layer provides structural support and resists bending. The cone was the form of light streaming out into spacetime. If you start to feel nauseous, simply close your eyes. At this stage all friendship relations are possible. Renovation and modelling dominate the evolution of human and chimpanzee Y-chromosomes. Male sex hormones help men but not women to recover from cardiovascular problems.

Because only one amplitude is non-zero, the outcome is deterministic and reveals the mark's location. The wrapping of DNA in the opposite direction around a variant nucleosome introduces a positive superhelical turn. Ring like complexes (pink) hold replicated sister chromatids together. All molecules vibrate in a temperature-dependent manner. *Reflect* automatically recognizes and highlights the names of genes, proteins and small molecules in *Cell* articles. These are sites of intense transcriptional activity.

Many people are intently watching the outcome, because thousands of genes have been patented in the United States. Taking out a second repair pathway should bring them to the floor. Extraction of this information is much harder to automate because computers are notoriously poor at understanding what they are reading. No interiority is needed for successful communication. *Knowledge Dashboard* mines texts and groups them by concept, looking for connections. The player who tries to take the initiative is able to make an offer only when the other player does not.

Language and knowledge as absolute truth was formed by the repetition of the same message across the hermeneutic differences of space and time. The "self" here is both a refuge from and a product of industrial capitalist production. They said that the Imax experience was replacing their own real memories of what it had been like in space. This may be achieved by employing plausible simplifications. Yet it should be clear that it is the entire human being who dies. They are being sentenced in a hearing that is expected to last three days.

The cooperative plan is restrictive as it does not allow for forgiveness, but forgiveness is a standard feature of friendship. An agent's intentions may extend beyond their natural lifespan. The benefit from receiving help is kept constant to make the analysis simpler. These insights don't immediately fall out of data without human ingenuity. Stereographs would reshape what it was to know and perceive reality. When this happens, new alpha males—usually from an outside group—move in, and kill infants from the previous regime.

This occurs within minutes in many cases. The term "brain death" suggests that only the brain dies, not the whole organism. Cells placed in the motor cortex extended to the spinal tract by the same route as native motor cortex neurons. The charge that was eliminated is called the image of the other charge, and the way of using this method of images can be most clearly explained by the examples that follow. Changes of locale occurred abruptly through editing, moving the camera position, or abandoning altogether the perspective from the front or rear of the train.

This is the primal scene of the supercession of presence by programming. Table 2 shows an inventory of the values discussed in the course of this section. There are no unicorns but there have always been plenty of horns and horses. Major areas of conflict are predation on livestock and the transmission of rabies. The case for xenograft use of animals is much stronger than the case in any general use of animals in research labs, for food, or for sport. Nevertheless, energy concepts are useful in discussing certain consequences of the choking process.

The elder boy replied: "No I can't see and I can't move my body". Is it meaningful to speak of a living human who lacks the capacity for social interaction? The return to a third-person point of view occurs with the loss of motion and effects. As a young man he had been one of Red Cloud's warriors in Montana. The camera made our eyes forgetful to past sights.

The last solar cycle peaked at about 120 sunspots. Pore size also affected how much hydrogen could be stored. Metal foundries and blast furnaces have for years captured waste heat in stacks of refractory bricks. A shorter lag would suggest that the peak for cycle 24 will be small. Elevation seems to be a universal feeling. Cybernetics transforms language into an exchange of news. We might be in danger of knowing too much. The film's actual subject is superfluous. Time axis manipulation allows eavesdropping on the speech and song of bees, dogs and other creatures.

Dynamics permeates all three sources of complexity that we have already discussed. The effect must be to slow down the motion of the surge. This is how fantasy works, of course. The subscript 0 indicates initial conditions. Mangroves break up waves and absorb energy. This has freed up the narrow strip of flat land where the mountains stop just before the water's edge. The new wave function has equal amplitudes at each configuration. There is nothing that impels the flow to seek the critical condition. The trailing feather edge will probably be attenuated rather than steepened by bed resistance.

Because of a quantum property called spin, electrons attached to these chains act like tiny bar magnets. Depicted here is an experimental set-up for a two-qubit system that consists of two trapped ions (blue spheres). Researchers found spent shells and canisters containing white phosphorous on Gaza streets, apartment roofs and at a UN-run school. Drugs that block reconsolidation can degrade the original fear memory. These entanglements must be resolved before the chromosomes can be segregated.

A straightforward way to cause membrane bending is to create bilayer asymmetry. The cavity walls rapidly collapse because of water pressure. If a magnetic field were introduced, the particles would self assemble into chains whose lengths depend on the strength of the field. Consider a surge approaching a channel junction, as in Fig. 8-15A. Intuitively it seems that pseudolikelihood attempts to match the model conditional distributions to those of the empirical distribution. All of these objective functions are maximized using limited memory BFGS.

This image shows more than a thousand young stars. Two groups report the observation of mildly relativistic outflows from seemingly ordinary type 1bc and type 1c supernovae. No sooner was my camera placed for this view than a shower of small stones fell around us. The atoms are arranged in parallel chains. This property could be used to build a device that directs light around an object so that it appears as if nothing is there. Writing would make everyone forgetful, worried Socrates in the *Phaedrus*. When we read we visually process about twelve letters at a time.

Annese wants to slice, digitize and disseminate brains, including some from people with memory problems. There was a great deal of variation in the ability to learn movements and write spontaneously. Curtis returned to Seattle with over one thousand negatives. The "near future" may yet be a year or two away for American scientists. Viewers would have the same feelings if they were on a stereoscopic tour or actually present in a country. Label noise is also an important issue in machine learning.

The first step is for the text- or semantic-mining tool to recognize key terms, or entities, such as genes and proteins. Dikpah says that her model has retrospectively predicted the past eight cycles with 96% accuracy. A theme throughout the book is how reading involves a balance between evoking the sound of a word in spoken language and rapidly translating print to meaning. Scientists are struggling to make sense of the expanding scientific literature. *Reflect* obtains this information from its dictionary of millions of proteins and small molecules. A closer look at the knowledge network suggests that these genes were involved in tongue development because the tongue is the largest muscle group in the head.

Prions are needed to maintain the myelin sheath that surrounds nerves and ensures that they function properly. Data are based on hydrodynamic properties, protein number and spatial position of the members of each protein complex. There is also an entropic penalty incurred between the entangled polymers, known as polymer repulsion. We had to find the right detergent: one that could dissolve the membrane surrounding the protein without denaturing the protein. Such entity recognition can be done fairly accurately by many mining tools today. But does a DNA spring function in the force range that is pertinent to protein machines?

Graphics Equaliser

This is the end of the animation. Nineteen Chinese labourers were drowned in rising waters as they picked cockles in Morecambe Bay. Adding one grain of sand to another does not make a heap. Expect images of weird life forms to begin streaming from the end of March. White phosphorous, which is used to lay smokescreens, is legal only on open ground. I would love to hear from any of you about what you're reading or what you think of my reviews. Many photographs of lynchings and burnings reappeared as popular picture postcards and trade cards.

Ofcom censured *The Great Global Warming Swindle* for breaking several rules in its broadcasting code. A treatment is a short document that summarises the main idea of the story. Sticky ends can be reattached by another enzyme called ligase. Certain orientations give stronger highlights than others, depending on axial rotation. The new president probably wouldn't mind some Helium-3 but he does not seek to make his mark in space. Other people find that their condition improves with time. While all of the facts are true, they do not tell the entire story.

I have used this generic label to include relationships to fathers, mothers, wives, sons, daughters, families, clans and in some cases forms interpreted as "slave of". Magrassi immediately prescribed drugs to treat the swelling, which was pressing on surrounding brain areas, and within a couple of days the patient was able to write again. He designed a square house with windows on all four sides, each window having a view to the south. Not that there was any visibility at all on this Saturday afternoon. The computer creates the "in-between" frames, which the animator adjusts as necessary.

There are a number of treatments, which are described below. A slave woman is chained to a weight. Officers used ten rounds of pepper-balls to disperse the crowd and one student was arrested. Simple repeats are common in assembly gaps and therefore cause alleviated read depths. This is a document in which abnormal hieratic and early demotic both appear, side by side. Mr Orendorf's house is somewhat nearer the public road than the limekiln. Two brothers who brutally attacked two young boys witnessed serious domestic violence against their mother and had a toxic home life. I also saw a pair of shoes that were saturated with blood.

The Great Dismal Swamp on the border between Virginia and North Carolina acted as a particularly strong magnet for runaway slaves. Those resisting arrest were stunned with taser guns. Forked branches are synapses (neural junctions). For multiple constraints, the degrees of truth are combined using further logical operations. The hunt was suspended last October after it ran out of money. Because police cars blocked the street, ambulances were temporarily unable to reach those needing assistance. Radiotherapy is sometimes given along with chemotherapy.

Many patients have been falsely determined to have irreversibly lost heart functions. Features of the head tend to be lost before those of the trunk, including the notochord and muscle blocks. Sometimes scratch voices are so good they're not replaced. "Axenor of Naxos made me". It is convenient mathematically to choose the z-axis parallel to E0 and through the centre of the sphere. Bigelow Aerospace already has two inflatable test platforms in orbit, and hopes to build an inflatable space station. This x-ray image shows plumes of hot gas bursting from the galactic disk, in an extensive outflow driven by a burst of star formation.

The Kepler team announced that it had identified five new planets. Over the next 24 hours, four more M-class flares erupted from the same sunspot, each more powerful than the one before. The telescope could monitor the red planet every day and locate methane bursts with a resolution of 10 kilometres. Rendering the deep shadow passes with this shader, gave the attenuation of light through the volume for free. They divide the atmosphere and oceans into thousands of grid cells, and include interactive land-surface and biophysical processes. Sequences not carrying a 100% match in the index read were excluded from all downstream analyses.

An α–decay chain is a sequence of radioactive decays in which elements transform into one another by emitting an α–particle. In the sparsely explored territory of super-heavy elements, an "island of stability" is expected. Earth system models are based on physical climate models, and include additional ecological and chemical processes. Users received feedback to their phones showing stills of stitched-together video with their own contribution highlighted.

The same process explains how we hear our own voices, and why they sound different when recorded and played back. The prisoner's child was about ten months old. In each time period every player has to decide which players in the population they want to help. No one thought it necessary to keep an accurate record of the digging.

Producer price indexes can be used in contract escalation. Those caught or taken prisoner were marched to the coast to await purchase. "Speaking objects" demonstrate a non-rational or magical use of writing. There may have been no standardised letterforms at this time. Challenging expeditions towards the island have so far led to the discovery of elements up to 118. Moving by cross-country skis, hauling gear in dog sleds, Eske Willerslev hunted Moose, set traps and skinned mink and sable. There was a substantial and relatively recent migration across the Bering Strait and over North America to Greenland (see Fig. 3A).

Editorial uses the information to fix the length and other elements of each shot in a sequence. You learn about craters, basins and lunar seas. Assume that no betrayals occurred in the past between any two players. A single egg is shown here. Trace amounts of methane are released from the northern polar cap when its surface melts during summer. High-resolution ice cores have been extracted before. This winter the vortex has weakened and in many places cold air is spilling further south than usual.

It is a healthy sign that a common first response to geoengineering is revulsion. The new schedule calls for 155 orbits around Saturn, 54 fly-bys of the methane-shrouded Titan and 11 fly-bys of the icy moon Encedalus. Masten promises that it will fly any payload into space and back for $250 per kilogram, starting in 2011. Closer integration of scenarios is required to address feedback loops and other issues such as the ecological and economic implications of different sets of adaptation and mitigation policies.

Click on the animation screen to watch it again. In the Sunbelt, migrant labourers still have rights to a plot back in their villages, where land has not yet been privatised. Airships passed over Stoke

Hill towards Thorverton and no harm came. A world cooled by solar radiation management (SRM) will not be the same as one cooled by lowering emissions. Hacinebi is situated in the foothills of the Taurus Mountains in Anatolia, on a key crossing of the Euphrates River. Invasive species have adapted more quickly to temperature changes, shifting their flowering time an average of 11 days earlier than native plants over the past 100 years.

In today's ecosystem, only a small fraction of the energy moves through wild mammals, humans and domestic animals dominate flows. It is not quite correct to assume that the water downstream of the surge is always stationary with a horizontal surface. Maroons resided in the swamp throughout the antebellum era. Please see image 24 and the endpapers for the Jesse Washington torture and lynching on May 16, 1916. There was blood on the walls, and on the floor in the entry. These scenes of the animal world are as cruel and ferocious as the narrative beneath them.

Police issued two numbers in connection with the incident. The body is hidden, as in the Turing test, so that the machine can fool you. One such dangerous moment occurs when Franklin and Ebenezer Kinnersley use large Leyden jars to electrocute chickens and turkeys. The first criterion for irreversible coma will be the absence of brain-mediated reflexes. Local effects of the brink are therefore confined to the region AB; experiment shows this section to be quite short, of the order of three to four times the depth. Have a good look at the photos and drawings.

Paronomasia enabled scribes to record the sounds of all words in the language, not only those that could be represented pictorially. Who is the woman to whom this petition is addressed? Second from the right is Mrs Pawnee, the agency laundress. She wears a double string of pearls and a cluster of golden earrings; her head is adorned with myrtle and some strands of hair fall alongside her cheek. On her feet she wore wooden shoes. Weavers reached their peak between twenty-five and forty. Clusters of wooden, earth-covered houses were scattered along terraces overlooking the sea.

The style of the two illustrations excludes people who were constantly drawing their drinking water from the conduit. They were treated without explicit consent. It seems doubtful that the ability to contract and dilate the pupil and to execute any other reflex arc that happens to pass through the brain stem is in any way a significant sign of human living. The implant would be inserted into the most damaged part of the retina. Woody has one hundred avars in his face alone. It means a person who is related to another by birth rather than by marriage.

Cedric Robinson is known as the Queen's sand pilot in Morecambe Bay, and has been leading walkers across the sands for 25 years. In the model, Player one's belief will be common knowledge throughout the game. This viewpoint also makes clear the bias in the piecewise estimate. Males have just six basic types of call but combine these in context-specific sequences to convey different information. A fur system had to be developed to handle these situations.

The information commissioner has been granted leave to appeal to the House of Lords. Morecambe Bay is a public fishery, so anyone can come and fish. The shader is separate from the surface to which it is attached. Choose a biology animation by name. This futile discourse was taking us closer to the fringe of London plane trees and ash on the south side of the common. I am Nestor's cup, well made for drinking. Below are three couples at a banquet, resting on couches. A destination object encapsulates a provider-specific address.

These interneurons coordinate the output of dopaminergic neurons in the ventral tegmental area (VTA) of the brain. Theory predicts half-lives as long as minutes to hours, a trend that is supported by experiments. Even the smallest tremor cannot be foreseen. The pure despise alliteration. The team hope to implant the device into a live pig soon, before testing it in humans. She had a blue dress on when she came to my house. In practice this is never true. Typically the argument proceeds from water levels that are known upstream and downstream or upstream alone.

The same risk currently exists when family members make decisions to forego life support. Cosmetic surgery is usually not covered. Pupil contraction in response to light is given as the typical case. A leather-bound book gilt with gold lines worked as a kind of luminous lightning rod. This cinema invades the body rather than inviting consciousness to leave the body behind and enter into the movie. Player 1 obtains as many signals as is beneficial to her, and then starts to make offers. All of the mice survived to day 50 after transplantation, then treatment was discontinued.

Most shod runners make initial contact with the ground heel first (rear foot striking, or RFS). The need for some level of manual curation is common to the various literature tools, and limits their scalability. Something is rapidly destroying the methane. There may be value in a "red team / blue team" method. The company has been working to convert sugars into tailored molecules for several years. Bubbles in the ice are a special prize. They indicate a series of ascending and descending jets. Without the mountains, convectively heated air from the Indian Ocean could move northward and counteract the effect of radiative cooling (second term).

Most forests being lost are in tropical countries that have no emissions targets. Small lakes and wetlands are especially vulnerable to the effects of acid rain. A Cormorant helicopter was sent to the area from 19 Wing Comox and rescue officers located the plane's wreckage about three hours after the crash. These are air sacs with walls just one cell thick. The read depth (green) varies along the chromosomes. Fate Therapeutics of San Diego has been granted the first US patent for genetic reprogramming technology to create induced pluripotent stem (iPS) cells.

The courthouse has been densely crowded all day. The sentencing hearing, which is expected to conclude on Friday, was adjourned for a short time after the younger brother became distressed. The mother consented to the xenograft transplant, signing a form that summarised the procedure. Around her neck and over her shoulders she wore a scarf folded into a triangle and tied at the throat. The price is not mentioned. We may also be missing many cases because of incomplete (damaged) inscriptions. On friendship estate, Ann Smith asserted that she was "entitled to sit down" because she was pregnant, and then refused to work.

Certain geological features, most notably mountaintops and cliff tops, amplify earthquake waves. One victim was forced to strip naked and perform a sex act. Plate 153 was photographed at the same site. The boy's throat was cut; his bowels ripped open, and his head mashed. I recall waking in the middle of the night, thinking: we can do the whole genome. Primer trimming was an integrated part of the mapping during the alignment of each read. Trainee scribes copied and memorised thematic lists of nouns related to the accounting practices of Uruk.

The use of Linear A in administration clearly implies literacy by some and this must have had a major social impact. The team used high-throughput sequencing to isolate short fragments of DNA. The most widespread feature is the three-lined arrow-tip shape for the letter alpha. By layering these deformers, artists were able to quickly create, and change, the look of Kong's fur, in a procedural and non-destructive way.

Navigation is the most significant element in web design. On 5 August 1992 we first made our way into the Omarska camp in northern Bosnia. Could you still relax and enjoy the film? The prisoner told me she had used it to cut greens in the morning. They drove 75 metres along a track until they reached a gap between two compounds. The casually dressed men had been posing as tourists, and escaped through a window at Drumlanrig castle carrying the Leonardo under their arms. We have plenty of ambient energy but not on people's roofs.

Smoke filled Concepción as looters burned a supermarket, and several fire-fighters were injured by falling debris. The prosecution destroyed the "fake pictures" argument. The painting is executed on a ground of white slip, the details incised through the black to the white beneath. Another factor was the speed of the ground shaking. Certainly the change makes for a better picture. Both the man whose paintbrush tells us that he was a fellow artist, and his wife sit informally with their right arms thrown over the backs of their chairs. Types of laughter are usually differentiated by the emotion attributed to it but not on a morphological basis.

Works of the late 1970s featured coloured fragments of plastic that were assembled into life-size figurative silhouettes and built up like puzzles reconstituting the human form but creating an image of human excess. The mine was named after its most famous ex-employee, following his death in 1977. Bryan Griffiths is pictured in the gyrocopter he was flying when he struck and killed hunt supporter Trevor Morse. A soldier identified only as "O", who was in another vehicle, gave evidence from behind a screen. The faces that gaze coolly past you from their cases are challenging and formidable in their beauty.

These are mere inscribed objects, and yet they speak. Actors recorded lines in several different ways, and the best reading was eventually animated. They didn't have any safety gear and some of them were naked because they had taken their clothes off to help them swim. A comparison of the tsunamis produced by the two quakes has been added. Excellent water quality is essential. Keep taking action until you have reached the end of the worry strips. Surrogates are already presumed to have authority to terminate all life support on these people. Radovan Karadzić opened his defence behind a bulletproof screen in The Hague.

The temperate zone areas, where we live and where the Great Lakes are located, are comparatively poor in biodiversity. Sulphur dioxide in the air can combine with other pollutants and water to form fine particles that cause serious complications for some people with heart and respiratory disease. Key drivers in mix design development are application requirements, placement, finishing and cost. The banquet is damaged, but the side walls have well-preserved scenes of beautiful dancers. Nearby is a small wooden figure (1539–1075 BC) with a bowed head and severe curvature of the spine.

Some objects assert their own nature, some leave it implicit, and others designate it with the verb whose subject is the proper noun. We found men, some of them skeletal, behind a barbed wire fence in a compound under guard. Livelock is a special case of starvation. The tests were negative, and the surgery was called off. Trevor Morse, 48, was flung aside by the gyrocopter's rotor blades, which ripped out part of his brain. The Land Rover's front wheels had cleared a ditch but an IED was triggered as the back wheels rolled over. Seven does, in a sense, structure the way we encounter the world.

Persimmon builds mainly family homes on private estates. Some people find it helpful to practise French kissing on ice cream. Everybody thinks working in a hospital is like an episode of *House*. That people will disappear from the face of the Earth. The Cormorant is the only State-produced space vehicle whose design has come from a third party. Hazard warning lights should be used whilst unloading on pedestrian areas. Cast iron would have come from the furnaces at Petworth or Pallingham Lock.

The woman at left, holding the tiny baby, is Ella Turkey (Red faced woman), the wife of Henry Turkey. Between 1833 and 1851, eighty-eight children from fifty-nine families received free tuition. Meaningless work can contain all of the best qualities of old art forms such as painting, writing etc. The brackets may be omitted under the same conditions as in W4. A small Kuiper belt object (KBO) crossing the line of sight to a star will partially obscure the stellar light.

Reducing the Earth's absorption of solar energy and thence global warming by somehow reflecting sunlight back where it came from was thought possibly dangerous. Most of what is known about past CO2 levels comes from the dust-free Antarctic ice. Alarmist statements have worked before. Atreya, and Paul Mahaffy from Goddard, propose using a balloon to measure gases in the Martian atmosphere.

Strong winds remove gas from the region of star formation. Here's the scene with a 3D object we want to composite loaded in. I'm in the street; we're all sleeping in the street. If it became available to me I would like to use colour. The leader often has tiny holes in it, with times, numbers and words printed into the film. Any affected text and strokes will appear in red. Hit the stopwatch to start key framing. High fidelity qubit readout schemes are under development. No system is fully free of decoherence, but small amounts may be removed through various techniques gathered under the name of quantum error correction (QEC).

Animals with 10% of mass transmitters gained less weight over a month. Snakes are the warriors of Osun. A fallen stone lies in the background. Young men left to find work in coastal towns and young women followed them to earn a living as prostitutes. Their spots are copper discs and their eyes are mirrors. But time is not on the side of North American bats. My heart was beating fast. Pictorial depth was virtually eliminated. Let me ask you about some specific tapes. A school of fish dives and darts to avoid a predator.

The Responder X is designed to accurately quantify the vertical component of motion associated with the startle reflex. After they left the fMRI scanner, volunteers did a memory test. The path to the spirit world lies across the sea and the souls of those who have died must pass over the water. Virginia Woolf wrote this paragraph. The bats rouse and fly around when they should be conserving energy; having burned their fat, they eventually starve to death. The dislocation line is a mobile line whose presence reduces crystal rigidity. A grain of the mineral apatite shows off rainbow hues under a microscope.

Tiangong—1 or "Heavenly Palace" will first be used for orbital docking practice with three spacecraft; after that, crewed ships will visit the module. A ruler is pivoted at the vanishing point and another at one of the distance points. All the figures have red hair. The Flash video encoder can only read transparency stored in the alpha channel. Resolution is reasonable, but colour accuracy is poor, with an obvious blue shift. I decided to go through the act of painting myself the way a woman paints herself to face the world. Since the earthquake we live in the street.

The Buddha is lit from the inside, so as you approach it, the object turns into its shadow. If one concentrates on the upper target, with its black dot, one is able to transfer a complementary afterimage to the lower target. Leaders allow you to handle the ends of the film without damaging the picture. Measurement is achieved by observing the induced current in a coil surrounding the sample of an ensemble of qubits. The upgraded portal monitors were installed last year and can now be found at every border crossing, port and airport in Georgia.

When Osanobua decided to populate the world, he gathered his three sons and sent them off in a canoe. All the children are gifted, each in a special way. The picture remained unsold when the exhibition closed, and Clausen subsequently added the girl with a hoop on the extreme right. The plane broke up in a dense area known as Forbidden Plateau, which is covered in trees and brush. As Kong progressed through the film, his fur needed to reflect the environment and story. We met Azagar, a former slave who managed to escape his master. "I am the memorial of Glaukos".

The non-native mayweed chamomile now flowers 23 days earlier than it did in 1900. These leaves were printed from copper plates. The carefully drawn objects in the top left hand corner of the sheet are yokes for oxen. You can pump up the luminosity value past 100 percent (255 levels of brightness) to make a super-bright object. The hand reappears in several works on stone, most recently in the Gemini numeral 7, both in black and in colour. I fell from a house —many people have died. In this animation, you should start with a close shot of the face and then pull out from there. Facial marks are notoriously subject to changes in fashion and borrowing. A map of the Hebrides is referred to on page 170. Here the section ends.

A middle ear infection (*otitis media*) is the most common cause of eardrum perforation. Thin metal rods, slipped into a long pocket, can be used to represent the rays. A little extra thickness was left if the stick had to be carved to show a design in relief. In polycrystals, the boundaries (green) between crystal grains of different orientations are regions of atomic thickness where atoms are not ordered, owing to the competing influences of adjacent lattices. James is sitting on the floor busily cutting pictures from an illustrated catalogue.

The left leg and the base of the stool are missing. He slept one night under a tree and in the morning found a leopard above him on the branch. Updates in this release are mainly centred on the ability to render in layers. You'll need to extrude these lines, merge them into one editable mesh and then position the individual elements to intersect the outer wall object. The drawing was executed in midstream in order to clarify the structure of a painting then in progress. If you could manage a little transfer to me it would be good. Write one worry on each strip.

War crimes at all three camps have been the subject of numerous convictions at The Hague. About four out of ten people with anorexia make a full recovery. The mother left the hospital with the baby. In the timeline window, move the red frame slider to frame 80, making sure that the peg is still highlighted. You can remove the hands, arms and head from your character and then animate them individually using pivot points. I would take my eyebrow pencil and go up here (pointing to left eyebrow), and the damned thing would end up over here (pointing to right eyebrow).

Some internalization of these narrative episodes is inevitable. Local voice is constantly getting squeezed out. The mess-room was a large tent, open at one end. Four of the six large plates received additions in aquatint; the other two, Flag and Numbers, were kept transparent and linear with a sparing application of open bite. I lost my sister, a brother and my cousins in the earthquake. My doctor said I should have another child so my depression would go away. I tried to get the man to look like he's walking rather than gliding along. Green lines show optical waveguides; yellow components are metallic contacts.

This splitting is caused by a helical rotation of the crack front (thick black lines in right panel) around the principal direction of crack propagation (grey arrow). Neither Macalister nor McNab is an island name. Cult objects act as intermediaries between man and the life forces, and may be destroyed if not efficacious. Multiple mutation signatures testify to the cocktail of carcinogens in tobacco smoke and their proclivities for particular bases and surrounding sequence context. Blue lines show locations of genomic rearrangements observed in the amplicons, with the thickness of line proportional to the number of reads spanning the break point.

Cusps are predicted from numerical simulations that include only dark matter. There is a close analogy with electrical conductors. The figure is 24 inches high, excluding the plinth, which is buried in the ground. Paste a duplicate and put it on one side. So far you have only added black trash, but a grunge font usually has white in it too. Development had come to California. My aunt gave me a magnifying glass that I still have in my studio. The food the UN is giving did not reach us. The sentence is enclosed in quotation marks, so one would suppose that he really spoke it.

Memory formation is known to occur at the level of synaptic contacts between neurons. Sequences are fragmented into millions of short pieces that require sophisticated software to yield useful information. Squishy nanoparticles can be easily filtered out by the kidneys, so don't need to be degradable by the body. Some of the mass is delocalised and the remainder is localised. But the size of the domain that falls under the synaptic influence of a single astrocyte is not clear. European bats hibernate in small groups, ranging from 1 to rarely more than 100, whereas bats in the United States usually hibernate in groups of thousands or hundreds of thousands. These two are just passing by the window.

Red and brown appear to be colours of individuality and egotism, while blue and green are colours of impersonality. Sacrifice is the focal point of nearly all Benin rituals. The Rota-count rotation monitor measures circling behaviour of up to eight animals in clockwise / counter clockwise directions, as well as partial rotations. Eventually, random processes add or subtract energy from the oscillator, bringing the system to thermal equilibrium on a timescale called T1. Consider improving your code so that it is more reliable and future modifications are simple. It must be possible to extract the computer's entropy to maintain its quantum state. Using your photomontage for reference, start to pull the building apart. It's all I wanted to say, everything is OK.

Turing's original *Imitation Game* was played for the first time ever at Simon's Rock College of Bard in Great Barrington, Massachusetts, on Saturday, April 16, 2005. Is the EEG measuring whole-brain function or something more limited? When players make their frequency of initiative taking dependent on the identity of the latest proposer, the players alternate their offers (possibly with some stochastic delay). First we measured the discount rate for about 200 subjects. Robert Barker of Edinburgh invented the large-scale panorama as a "step-in" spectacle.

Many spangles were used in conjunction with painting, especially where the ground was of silk, which was the favourite material at this period. Eshu is the only deity normally portrayed in Yoruba art. The diagonals provide orientation for objects whose faces lie at 45 degrees to the picture plane. An alpha channel can be either pre-multiplied or taken straight from *After Effects*. Click on the man and not on the red dot that indicates the motion path. As soon as my body hit the wall, it affected my voice. Each print, version, or state has been given its own number.

Garage Sale was shot in Venice, documenting subcultures in seventies LA. I lost my phone in the rubble; it had all the numbers of the people I knew on it. To reproduce ambient light in the area you are working in, use another light set to the colour of real ambient light. When the LUMO is half full, the resulting material is a superconductor. Not only his costume but also his eyes are often painted red. A few heads are approximately life size. Ordinary glue and cement is too stiff and hard, and causes the skin or paper to crack. The scene is contained in a cartouche-shaped space, but there is no actual border.

A model of the structures to be painted was built above a squared mirror and viewed from an appropriate distance and angle (plate 131). Solid wall panels are bolted on and reinforced vinyl fabric with patent zip fastenings covers the roof. If a flat screen intercepts the divergent pattern, a reversed and inverted image will be formed. The rain came last night and there was nothing to cover us, so we had to stand. Mr Lin drove the cocklers to the shoreline in an old van but did not join them on the sands.

The salmon farming industry is highly regulated and the fish have ample room to swim freely, says Scott Landsburgh. An allowance for security should have been made in the budget. Each element is, as the title implies, distinctive, there are no repeats, no two exactly alike. After several months research into lightweight buildings on the market, Pavilions in the Park Advisory Service became convinced that the structure they were looking for did not exist. Not being models in Baudrillard's sense they should not be art. The catalogue contains several articles and also a colour section in which the complete exhibition is illustrated.

I've added a large luminous plane off to the left tinted blue to simulate the window. Try animating the clouds, switching streetlights on and off, or maybe even adding background characters. It isn't the same war now. We're having a tough time; it's not really good for us right now. Many lines later, the warning to stand still is repeated more sharply. Does D-serine release participate in this extra-synaptic activation? One strand of DNA holds the lid shut; a separate DNA "key" springs it open. In both cases, however, the light is otherworldly and mysterious.

Hill's studies often show children engaged in farm labour. Small highlights tend to coalesce and expand as circular globules of light known as circles of confusion. The inclusion of shaded planes also reflects our feeling for geometry as the visual science of actual objects. Production has fallen since Soviet times. The haze that these particles form also contributes to visibility reductions, especially in parts of central and eastern Canada. Inside Orion's main building, workers in Teflon suits and hairnets are busily scrambling around gigantic white scaffolding.

In a superfluid, atoms move coherently because together they form a macroscopic wave of matter. Why this pathway should be more effective in highly transcribed regions is unclear. I shall, however, briefly summarise what the situation is at the beginning of our passage. The author compares Sunbury ancestor-tree enclosures to those in Angola. He worked in a radio station; his car and clothes were contaminated. Decoherence comes in several forms. For the time being, keep the flat, grey material on the object. Shift the camera to view the full clip. This image will be the trash you vectorize.

'Hesitation Blues' is a popular song written by Billy Smythe, Scott Middleton, and Art Gillham. Firefighters placed a guitar, a saxophone and two laptops on the sidewalk and asked family members if they recognised them. *The Vehicles*, differing from one another in colour only, are cast in solid plaster. The results were then transcribed line-by-line onto a similar squared drawing. It was twenty inches wide and twenty feet long, so a lot of strange things happened to anybody who walked into it. Number 41 is completely destroyed.

A map shows peoples and places mentioned in the text. The figures are roughly sketched, and the red of their exposed arms adds to the impression of heat. There are five million labourers in Pakistan bonded to their employers by debt. Mariko is the woman described in chapter 4. Every single person here has lost someone.

Repeat step 8 and paste it again onto the letter. The symbol is at one end of the rectangle, left of the inscription, which runs left to right. A plywood manufacturer is developing a prototype. A chiselled gouge in the frame denotes the top of a chair back, and real chair studs have been hammered along the top edge.

The same optical events are operative here as in *Targets*. Authority's latest challenge "Who are you?" is easily satisfied with a signature or a PIN number. Tamale pie is kind of a strange dish. Any health insurance policy must have some limits on coverage. The SWAN team is working to automate parts of the curatorial process, such as extracting gene names. Gabriel Aeppli has spent decades probing the nanostructure of materials, but today it is financial woes that are on his mind.

Prion proteins are needed to maintain the myelin sheath that surrounds nerves and ensures that they function properly. Adult rat brains contain more young neurons than adult mouse brains, and these cells mature much faster. A high mutation rate in mitochondrial DNA can be adaptive. This is not self-evident. Galton used the new photography to produce composites that might distil the essential appearance of types. The carved head rests on a special plate with designs of kola nuts and sacrificial animals.

Most of the receptors are broadly active, responding to a range of odours, but a few are more specific. The room was dark and people could watch the monitors. Artists were asked to contribute 24 images that were installed in the exhibition hall in one 4 x 6 grid, reminiscent of film sequences. Make sure that the layer you are working on is highlighted in blue, as it can be infuriating to find out later you have been adding to the wrong layer. The computer must operate in a Hilbert space whose dimensions can grow exponentially without exponential cost in resources (such as time, space or energy).

The approach does not explicitly resolve the structure of material at the atomic scale. A complication of quantum computing with single atoms in a vacuum is the need to cool and trap them.

Once you have finished tracing, zoom in to inspect the results. A single qubit could be emulated by a classical oscillator with a randomly timed, single-bit read-out, but quantum mechanics also allows entanglement. This time the power of colour was given full play, creating a field that exists entirely independent of numbers. Areas of human disturbance (such as the Cajun farms) could be counted on to nurture hybrid swarms.

Though graphene is essentially two dimensional, a layer of carbon atoms just one atom thick, it is in fact always slightly crumpled. Use the onion-skinning tool to double check you have created the correct movement from one frame to the next. The hardware was set up to layer these images on top of one another in real time. Hello, everything is OK. No single work in this series is identical with another in size or colour or combinations of elements. The use of interceptions at the vertical through eye point (v), or at the engraving's edge, does not seem to yield such consistent results.

Points at which the rulers cross provide key locations for drawing the object in its projected form. Galaxies are a biased tracer of dark matter, and this bias varies with scale. Ten long-pulse and two short-pulse lasers allow precise control of temperature and pressure in target materials. The question to be answered is whether this paradoxical state of matter really exists.

If it is greyed out, highlight Peg 2 in the Timeline. Film can record detail from the darkest shadows to the brightest glow. This animation does not replace the need for personal advice from a medical practitioner. On the screen of the monitor is the viewer's own face, filmed by a hidden camera. From this an especially thick magnesium photoengraving plate was made; it was etched commercially and used as the female in printing. The crew had their shirts off. Long Beach Museum of Art was just starting to show video.

This intervention seems to decrease the rate of cerebral palsy in children surviving very premature births. A number of *Nomoli* and *Pomtan* specimens have a hole in the top of the head. Both the mouth and the hand will need a hit area to deflect the collision. Even with different aspect ratios, we were able to make them match perfectly. I preferred to work in basements. After beetles had picked the bones clean the skeleton was rebuilt using wire and steel rods for support. Each generation illustrated a different experience of twinship. The figures are quite small beneath the towering and impressive mountain forms.

A needle is pulled up through fabric a short distance ahead of the preceding stitch. This fills in the darkest black to be your ambient colour. The guard sticks are carved wood and fretted ivory, similar in ornament to the inner sticks. Hand quilting is done on a frame using needles called "betweens". Thin silk plain weave was the more usual material for wax-resist dyeing. The four-line initial also has two small roundels of leaves at two corners, with four leaves curling in a vine inside the letter *E*.

One watched his arm with an idle curiosity, wondering whether or not the expected word would be written. We could not use tape recorders because of the sensitivity of the interview subject matter. Yutaka works as an executive for a large textile fibres manufacturing corporation. Tailors and dressmakers capitalised on demand by offering fragments, cuttings and ready-cut patches for use in patchwork and quilting. Too many "on Mondays" can clutter up stories, however, and seem odd if you are actually reading on a Monday. The text ran sideways so that residents of a neighbouring bed could read the news.

Captions have been embroidered over the pictures. On the right, a gunner ignites the powder in the cannon. One twin may command the right arm and the other the left. Toshio is a semi-skilled worker at a large chemical processing plant that hired him after he graduated from high school. The first DNA profile was made in September 1984. If you use the mouse to scroll down the page, there is more information about the origin of your surname. I looked to the south and could not see the end of the mountain range.

Before he died, Old Tom Twining was rich enough to afford a portrait by Hogarth and a fine country home to hang it in. Another way of understanding piecewise training arises from belief propagation. The unidentified woman is decorating a moccasin top with porcupine quills. Looking back, all I could see were blue clouds. In movie-themed films, the referent is not a landscape to which the spectator might in reality have physical access but is a movie instead. Climbing on one mountain, we looked directly across to another. This difficulty was not a serious one, and could readily be dealt with as soon as it was clearly recognised.

The rivet head is jewelled with a white paste set in silver. When the textures are done, apply them on top of the 3D model. The scale will depend on the final dimensions of your game. A friend told me it is possible to make free phone calls, so I came here to call you. Part of the pleasure of viewing older collections comes from not knowing exactly what to expect. Jeremy (left) and Julian (right) pose with a friend on their scooters. Many people have died. The woman was in some sort of white wicker casket with her face made up.

Yang emphasises that the loan will be paid back. The reconstruction of the room permits Vermeer's viewing positions to be deduced for the six paintings. Hence there are no construction lines. A time seems to have dawned in which the object is central to art. Lucie Schwob was born in 1894 into a provincial but prominent intellectual Jewish family in Nantes. The people fled to this mountain.

We took notes in the course of each interview and statements were reconstructed after the end of each session. This gives you a full and comprehensive breakdown of all syntax and code errors in any page submitted. Kazuo is a sculptor. You'll see that the opacity of the clicked instances has started to reduce. Above the Qingke Plateau, deciduous trees could not survive. Cahun and Moore were eventually caught and sentenced to death although the execution was never carried out. The making of new memories can interfere with old memories of similar events.

Any pagan may join the Pagan Federation. Frobenius collected several figures in 1911, but it is doubtful if he actually visited the site. The decoration consists mainly of small paintings on mica insertions. They are backed with red foil, which shows through the interstices. In the painting, Palmer reduced the landscape's openness, adding hills and cottages to the valley, thus obscuring the sea view. Here too images are drawn from the everyday. The shaven head is stretched so that it is seen simultaneously from two vantage points.

Sewing up the incisions must be done carefully, with close stitches, and finally glass eyes and details in oil paint are added. It seems likely that they are binding rather than gleaning. Jeremy has had his hair bleached, while Julian's is cut very short. These are the Daoists descending from the upper reaches of the mountain. Interviews with wives were conducted at their homes. Wang struggled to free himself from existing pictorial vocabularies of mountain forms as well as from established conventions for travel paintings. Early development is a blind process without a notion of self.

The brain has great difficulties with nested recursions a few levels deep. Patients, whether or not they have suffered an adverse event, would generally like to be fully informed. The distinction between errors and violations is not always clear-cut. Cooke's thighbones were allegedly sold for more than $7000 despite their cancerous condition. Shipman killed patients with intravenous injections of diamorphine. The person who talks to you about what happened is likely to be one of the health care team that is looking after you.

A small, tilting screen folds out from the left-hand side and can be swivelled to any angle. Adverse events and patient safety incidents are best thought of as overlapping rather than directly comparable happenings. The sisters believe that time is running out for them. Different approaches are being adopted to deal with the problem. Soon however, the mystic atmosphere of Lourdes begins to take over. Sewing helped me feel more in control of myself. In an otherwise monochrome painting, a pale blue roof and pink walls focus our attention on the shrine.

No grass was growing on the path; however, fallen leaves covered it. Mariko has not worked outside their home since she married. The needle is passed through the wall of the follicle as slowly and carefully as possible in order to prevent fluid leakage or damage to the egg. We can grow skin and cartilage tissues to treat people with severe burns or damaged cartilage. In both cases the heads have been broken off and replaced. The donor is given painkillers or placed under intravenous sedation. In genre scenes such as this one by Alexander Farmer the quilt is used as a symbol of comfort and solace.

Grey washes are complemented with pale blue. It is ideal if the patient's electronic health record can be projected or displayed on a big screen so everybody can follow case presentations. The roof caved in, and water came into the studio when it rained. The image is a commentary of the high death rate of Victorian children from disease. I painted with motor oil; it was black and cheap, I mixed it with oil paint. You couldn't see where one finished and the other started. The areas occupied by foliage could also be drawn in.

We tried staining each leaf with a different tone of green. The transect quadrat was a line of quadrats laid out across a valley or mountain slope. Behind the rugged cliff, large rocky forms are nearly dissolved in mist. Pound's aim in counting samples of vegetation (remarkably no one had done it before) was to create more precise and minutely subdivided categories of abundance. Transplants were kept in isolated spots on rocky hillsides that cows could not get to but seeds and pollen could.

In this position it is steadied by a piece of marble or other weighty substance. The leaf has also been removed from a mount and pasted onto a panel of wood, which has been painted to complete an oval shape. The same method could be used to characterise precisely the vanguard patches of an invading association. The dataset begins as a matrix of zeroes and whenever a report contains one of the key terms the corresponding cell is changed to one.

This apparatus is used to separate DNA fragments of different sizes, and can be used to measure those sizes. For this step, an empty layout has been created for you to follow. Individual identity is asserted to very different degrees. Quadrats can also be made into instruments of active experimentation. Some were purchased from professional centres of production such as Exeter or Canterbury, others were made within the home itself.

Painting This

An object is a model of a single entity in the real world. Knowing that the baby would die without its mother, we shot it. The number of spikes within the encoding window encodes the stimulus, and their timing does not add information. Every year a new principal field was cut out of the forest. During the day the window becomes a screen and the carriage space is more expansive. Later, the event replays itself in your mind. If the animal can be given oxygen it may survive and eventually recover. The task was to press the space bar as quickly as possible with the index finger of the dominant hand. Depiction involves selecting an appropriate letter string to express the text. Objects are distributed without binding people together. A process in which outputs are used as inputs is known as a recursion loop.

This person represents two villages. Paired spirals emerge from a three-state cellular automation. As the needle moves forward, there is a visible gap between each stitch. Subjects are indicated by enclosing the related classes in a box. The 32 images of the United Kingdom in this book are taken from a mosaic produced by the National Remote Sensing Centre. The target object for a scan never appeared as a non-target object in another scan. On the edges, hardly anything is visible. Montgolfier balloons were constructed from sections of paper and cloth (usually linen and silk), often with buttoned seams.

When I was seven we used to have to thread the needles for my mother. The bindings exert pressure on the ventral edge, causing damage to the dorsal edge. None of the objects were red and when the cue was presented, no other objects were present in the field. Determining the encoding time window is problematic is such situations. Bees were trained to discriminate odours while the temporal structure of neural activity in their antennal lobe was manipulated using pharmacological agents. We can distinguish what sentences mean from what speakers mean in using them. Many names have been abbreviated.

The weavers who created the Fulami wedding blanket report that there is spiritual energy woven into the pattern, and that each successive iteration shows an increase in this energy. Mental spaces are small conceptual packets constructed as we think and talk for purposes of local understanding and action. Texts only achieve their communicative functions when they are coherent. Opacity and presupposition projection are classical problems for the logic of language. You should watch the sun and the running water. Spontaneous activity during quiet wakefulness is also bilaterally synchronous. The thickness and volume of the landscape lessens.

At least five percent of the population has reported hearing voices. Subjects pressed a magnetic resonance compatible button when they deflected a target. Each dot is the mean firing rate for an individual neuron. The refractory layer acts as a memory, providing the directed growth (i.e. the breaking of symmetry) needed to create a spiral pattern. The sensor is passive and therefore the data is obtained with the aid of reflected radiation. By increasing or stretching the image contrast and utilizing the shadows cast by oblique illumination, it is possible to exaggerate the natural variations of the terrain.

Under such a regime information is hidden in objects. Property is put to work explicitly to develop symmetrical ties of friendship between people. This continues until all the villages have chosen a representative. Each subject received sixteen scans. The language form prompts for setting up two mental spaces. Repositioning involves moving the text block relative to the surrounding text on the page. Our example had a subordinate space corresponding to "belief". If this precision equals the encoding window, the code becomes equivalent to the spike count. Nerves were gently desheathed but remained unteased, and were cut to about 5–6 cm long.

Negative affect decreased after examinations in both groups, but it was not affected by treatment. Performativity requires no special explanation, much less a special sort of convention. To create noise, a percentage of the target stream locations in each field were randomly coloured, with each pixel displayed in one of five randomly selected hues. The image that is produced by radar is not a normal image as the characteristics are dependent on the sensor look angle and the direction or orbit of the satellite.

The finite state automaton (FSA) has a list of transition rates that tell it how to change from one state to the next, depending on its current state and the symbol it is reading on the input tape. At the top we see three big clusters, like the arms and head of a lumpy snowman. The performance gap between computers and the human brain should disappear sometime between 2020 and 2050.

The asterisk in the Nucleus and Satellite fields indicates to the planner the position at which to include the semantic content that eventually becomes the text. Readers may notice that small areas of woodland have been omitted whilst other areas in close proximity to one another have been combined. Villages could stay on the same site much longer if they made their living by fishing rather than farming. Steep banking was thrown up from the ditch and allowed to spread into the interior. As I had no orders, I thought it would be a good position to hold. The scene contains 2340 scan lines representing a total of 390 scans taking place for each image.

Services could be identified from the functional model. In the switchboard corpus, a very common type of check is the reformulation. To test for short-term memory deficit, we conducted spontaneous Y-maze alterations. The experiments were performed in a darkened and sound attenuated room. Once the corridor was constructed, the courtyard was levelled with bulk clay infill. Volunteers swallowed a concoction of tobacco that rendered them unconscious, at which point relatives lovingly strangled them. There is an absence of felt movement because a free balloon moves with and at the same speed as the wind.

Barbed spears with fire-hardened points, dipped in poison, were used only for hunting. Periods of rest were recorded from each subject. Social memory, spatial working memory and prepulse inhibition were also impaired. Each triangle is an amplifier with two outputs, one normal and the other (black circle) an inverted output. The image was recorded on 20 April 1982. Villagers 3 and 4 move down one edge. The text structure planner has no ability to reason about formatting implications. It's not a transcription of nature. "He landed on a public beach".

Gradient ecology was essentially descriptive, rather like community ecology without the typology and nomenclature. We saw an iron chain hanging down from the cliff top. The node is located near the middle where the axon is constricted. Tracery has been reinstated. Most of the area was still inhabited by nomadic hunters and gatherers. This painting is probably the result of composite memories. People talk about long-dead friends and relatives as if they just walked out the door, as if all time runs together in a perpetual present moment. And, at least from the ground, the experience of balloon ascent became a collective event of spectacular witnessing.

The Great Sun's cabin was burned, and all the fires in the village were extinguished. The spiral structure visible in the photo was mainly due to the carefully maintained sacred forest surrounding each local neighbourhood. A constant growth pattern, shown in high resolution, looks similar to the cross section of an internal organ. Compositional devices impose an internal structure on the affected text body. Data was eliminated from two subjects due to eye movements and from one subject due to movement artefacts. An ordinary Z specification can be type-checked. Assemblages are composed of artefacts that serve particular functions, and thus represent tool kits.

Cases of speaker meaning that outpace (contextualized) expression meaning are very familiar in pragmatics. Early western Bantu speakers believed that the "real" world went beyond the apparent world. Vision is muted by the presence of other passengers that enclose and restrict the visual field. A typical hafting scar is a scalar, almost circular fracture that resembles a balloon. Charms were always perceived as tools. The distal part, originally sharp and pointed, is missing. Although spike rates and phase values overlap, their joint distributions separate in two-dimensional space.

This mimesis does not count as mathematical thinking. Each map is orientated in the same direction as the image and has been drawn at half the scale to allow for the inclusion of text. The transferring controller relays information to the receiving controller in the following order. Box plots depict medians (box centres), inter-quartile ranges (box boundaries) and 10–90th percentiles (whiskers). Data is plotted from a child, a young adult, and an elderly adult. The term "object" is increasingly applied to any encapsulation, but not all encapsulations provide the full benefits of object technology.

To ensure readability, automated text generation programmes must not only plan and generate their texts but be able to format them as well. In our simulation the active line became located towards the centre of the spiral. We turned with some difficulty, and then retraced our steps at a walk, because snow was already drifting in the street. A light retouch of the blade is all that's needed to give the edge the aspect of a finely serrated saw. Since February the *Los Angeles Times* has stopped using "today" and "yesterday" to reference the day of the week, both in the paper and on the web. We're thrilled that the café is popular and we really want to keep it that way.

Trains in Britain are currently run by 24 private companies that each provide services within defined geographical areas. Work on commodity chains is normally concerned to identify the points at which value is added and profit extracted. The incised design on this Etruscan mirror shows two naked women at a basin, framed by foliage. Place a circle round your present age. Eng and Sarah had six sons and five daughters. Cluster analysis can be used to group similar reports together by using the data in the key term matrix. Be open about errors and their frequency.

Matt Curnous spotted this circumzenithal arc overhead as he walked home from work in London on 27th April. Processing occurs at all levels and the net result of all this distributed activity feels to us like the unified beliefs, desires and intentions of a single mind. Simplified advice is covered by the new adviser-charging regime, but no decision has yet been reached regarding minimum levels of qualification. Z is a specification language based on set theory.

The encoding time window is the first important timescale characterising a neural code. Confocal image analysis was performed on single myelinated axons located near the surface of the nerve bundle. Large window embrasures light the hall from all sides. A strip of marshland to the north and west completes the natural enclosure. The type has a broad leaf-shaped blade, with lenticular cross-section. These are the people from the centre of the great salty lake. Seventeen couples were living in nuclear households. Gray washes of ink shade the entire grotto area, while even darker tones indicate the recessed tunnels that separate the rocky pillars.

This is a nodal point for most routes passing into the southwest peninsula and is also the principal market for east Devon. With Landsat 3 the thermal band could be used in the ascending mode. This cline of variation is largely one of roundness, extending from angular to perfectly smooth. Encapsulation is the property of forcing an abstraction. The next section describes our characterisation of text formatting devices. Don't be afraid to use the surroundings to emphasize scale. The mountain was chosen for its clear nights and dry climate.

In the next shot we see a body washed up on a beach. Chimps not only understand the concept of death but also have ways of coping with it. With no ozone layer, Mars cannot screen the lethal amounts of UV emitted by the sun. Bosson corpses were mummified by dry season conditions and carried for 68 and 19 days respectively before they were abandoned. What arrives along the optic nerve is a deeply distorted, non-greyscale, blurred image, and then the brain makes it worse. Surface-mounted chips can be very densely packed. Each point on the sound wave creates a copy of the echo at a different loudness. The writer, a mere machine, is able to declare that it cannot think.

One might expect M1 to receive some kind of proprioceptive input, signals about the present dispositions of the muscles and joints that it controls. Generally speaking, each map has six layers. We need to start with affordable, practical low-power components. All finalists will automatically receive an invitation to the gala dinner, but if you would like to buy a table or an individual place, call Mason Mclean. Direct physical harm is unlikely, but the potential for privacy violation is great. If you're pushed for time, head straight for the eastern side of the palace. With moving vehicles, a bit of blur gives a sense of motion.

The toes at points A and Q will be seen at points B and P for an observer at R, looking through the surface of the water MD. Next, click the Add Shape Area button within the Pathfinder menu and then click on the Expand button. A new cartoon shader enables you to create hand-drawn effects. If you're getting off at Westbury you should move forward from coaches A and B as far as coach C. The sea is warm; the hills carpeted with wild flowers; and with the season just beginning, people will be delighted to see you.

Those who go through this kind of experience generally emerge as fanatical, even manic believers. Documentation is often fragmentary and not always trustworthy. The car ferry looms towards the camera, head-on, lights glittering in the pouring rain. As the trees thin out, the sea gets louder and we emerge at the top of the dunes. Phonolite is a fine-grained igneous rock with a preferred place of cleavage. An automatic two-step linear stretch was applied to all bands to enhance cover type differences and a colour composite was produced using bands 4, 5, and 7. Waste tips with a light growth of vegetation appear a blue/green colour.

Images could only be recorded with a hidden camera. Their faces are doll-like and blank; their bare feet dangle some way off the ground. We need a way of turning volcanic basalt into a plant-supporting structure. Specific terms for farming tools have been identified. Voice hearers lost their prominence and social influence with the rise of agricultural states. Most large villages were located along inland watercourses or the coast. Food is placed in fine red boxes and carried to the pier where they await collection by the boat. Pale blue mountains ringed with clouds loom above them. It was almost certainly Clements, not Pound, who first recognised the quadrat's potential as an ecological tool.

In colour, the left photo would show brown pigment that turns black in the firing. I left my cap, shoes and outer garments at the monastery. Chewing time is noticeably less for cooked meat. Seawater, expelled from the shell by the progressive penetration of the blade, lubricates the sawing. A44, which now means "hoe" in many languages, originally meant "axe" as it is derived from CS1703 "to cut". Towns and villages pass by. Cod like the water this time of year because they think it is warm. A pair of oars valued at 10d washed up to the east of Red Rocke towards Offculme Clyffe, and another was found next to St Andrew's Pool in Littleham.

Cold water stays in the Arctic, cooling it down, while Antarctica does not receive the cold water it normally would, shifting southern temperatures up. The simplest form of this problem arises in the outflow from a lake of known surface level into a long uniform channel of mild slope. Dr Carrick had a map marked with the places where bears had been located. A hole in the highest part of the roof allowed smoke to leave. The Boruca name for this area is Shuintan, a sacred place in ancient times. Lines of postholes represent wattle fencing. There were small scented lamps on the tables, which seemed to collect the smoke and cause it to evaporate.

Biosphere-based greenhouse gardens would be much more manageable. The detail window is fixed in space. We currently pick up only one out of six images for obtaining the clustered textons. Their evolution over time can be seen as a fluid-like system. No parentheses and no braces are allowed, which protects against the case of "?{" getting through. Services want to make efficient use of humans, paying careful attention to the way in which humans interact with the data centre. Deployment of bits is an example of code that needs to be automated. A pause can lengthen into a paralysis of indecision.

What relatives in the village possess is theirs. Newton argued that God acted in order to keep heavenly bodies in their place. Cnut's empire fell apart after his death. Readers are invited to compose their own clues for the word above. Inside a small, square leather book are pages made up to look like miniature chessboards. If the centre and surround are about equally illuminated, this part of the retina must be looking at a continuous surface. We start by viewing a tree network as a system of road segments connecting villages to the capital city (the root). The satellite's path is parallel to the left hand edge of the image.

Once a plane is assumed, the controller can send clearances to this plane. Extracting the white dots as detail, requires aggressive smoothing of gradients, which would also blur single edges that are to be preserved. We wanted to ensure that our language would be sufficiently general to work for interface generators running on a variety of platforms. Bacon is known as rashers, green spring onions are scallions, a pram is a car and potatoes are sold by the stone. Children are sturdy, the product of millions of years trial and error. Each egg would either fall through a hole along the way or slide off the end because it was bigger than any hole.

The scorecard should be shared with all development team leaders. A memory chip next to each processor stores the changing synaptic weights as simple numbers that represent the importance of a given connection at any moment. Sun Life of Canada moved back into the market after a decade of being closed to new business. This is not a retake though; it's an entirely different movie. User interfaces designed for small screens would need every branch in the tree, whereas large-screen interfaces might display some deeper branches together on the same screen. The final boundary between the sky and the buildings is robustly regularised by optimization. The skin is reddened, moist, and deeply creased. Everything already exists, but some things have not yet become manifest.

Beauty quarks take us back to the first moments of the universe. Who knows where we're going to go. When the boat sets out at sunset, two oars move in unison. As the signals move past each other, they are compared to produce a measure of their phase difference. When the echoes are added together, this is the sound that leaves the filter. If the hand is closed and its position is different from the previous one, then the model triggers an event move. Each interface supports the complete set of appliance functions. A CP mesh is a triangle mesh whose incircles (orange) form a packing. A transfer function with high transparency was chosen to avoid early ray termination.

Street side images are captured by a camera mounted on a vehicle moving along the street and facing the building façades. The texture atlas memory is organised into slots of a certain size, depending on the application's needs. This principle makes our language easy to author and easy to process by the interface generator. A schema is a cognitive structure to which experiences are assimilated, and which reorganises in the process. When you have half of them, fasten them together with a rubber band or a piece of string. The SPT wants to thank Ted Morris for allowing us to use his artwork on the cover of this bulletin. After burning, the char was scraped away and new areas were prepared. Living in the present moment, bands and tribes existed largely unfettered by past regrets or future worries.

The prefix means "the children of" or "the people of". The weather in May is fine across Tunisia, but for real heat, you need to head to the far south. All photos in the photo gallery will be fully credited. An object of the class would be an actual BT customer, such as the author of this paper. There is more to building coherent text than the mere generation of single sentences. I took this picture in the Turpan Basin in Xinjiang Province. You have to try to predict what's going to happen. If both ears hear the rising edge of the waveform at exactly the same moment, the sound must be directly in front of us or behind us.

The bass control is called a low-pass filter, because it removes all the high frequency components from a sound. Food is generally available without requiring much effort to grow or catch and is freely shared. If you rely on scale-up, you'll probably get killed. The function is implemented as a white list, which means that only the allowed characters are appended to the returned string. Some examples of design choices influenced by this situation are discussed in what follows. For monkeys the dose is 2–3 darts, and for small birds just one shot will do. Cages containing nightingales hung on the stairs. Suddenly a bright flash and a loud explosion occurred.

When she dies the zalanga is broken and her soul is released to eternity. On these worn pieces remnant flake scars are usually present. An object is usually described by a collection of data called the attributes. From the application programme, the planner accepts one or more communicative goals along with a set of semantic representations of relevant material, which can be used to form the text. The relevant parts of the two sequences are shown in figure 3. Even if enough suitable targets can be found, there are more problems to overcome. The surface is congested with signs competing for attention.

Active waking states are more common before than after feedings. X-rays suggest the blame lies with small-unnoticed pieces of shot. Deep ocean currents are now being monitored for signs of change. A quilt is evidence of much time spent quietly and usefully. If a change is possible an administration fee will be charged. Limestone cliffs jut from the sea, and beneath the surface a blanket of coral is embroidered with marine life. The bias of what is on show is towards intricacy. In real retinas there are two distinct populations of cells, one called on-centre / off surround and the other called off-centre / on surround.

Perhaps your eyes are looking at the wrong spot, but you still see the bird there because that was where it was when the image hit your eye. A person becomes a member of the older, responsible generation. In plain fabric quilts the lines of stitching alone can be complicated. There is an impelling need to be together and to share experiences. The pair-wise matching of line segments is extended to the whole sequence. We extract detail by subtracting a smoothed image that we call the mean, from the input.

The defensive life pattern seeks to avoid the recurrence of an unbearable threat. Control systems can be classified as open loop or closed loop. Nerve impulses from the two ears arrive at the superior olive and are combined before passing on to the cortex and inferior colliculus. Following a post-task fixation period, the scan ended. Small and inconspicuous plants were counted first, decimetre by decimetre, and then easier ones. Both sources transcribe the entire Mount Hua text. Sumie's own education ended when she finished junior high school. Two large stone buildings are present on the south side of the site. To code incident descriptions, a list of key terms that may appear in the free text is needed.

Attributes are documented in the templates. Inside each joint is a separate sensor, which knows where it is actually pointing. Craig Allison travelled to a hill-range slightly north of Burton upon Strather, north Lincolnshire, to watch the sun set on 26th April. We propose joint image-noise filtering for image-noise separation. These leaves and flowers have the perfection of contextual fitness. A different random order was generated for each participant. Thinking is a wave on the surface of great intuition. Table 3 demonstrates cumulative traumatic exposure. In addition to observing public behaviour, it is also possible to identify between public and private opinion by eliciting a statement under circumstances where the person is assured of anonymity.

These authors attempted to plant rumours and to study the extent of their spread in a small private school. Rank of insignia did not exist until 1802 when a complete system of epaulettes was introduced. Role assignment is done through a rigged lottery wherein the participant is always chosen as the advisor. PNS (personal need for structure) is conceptually very close to some other personality constructs, such as authoritarianism, dogmatism, and uncertainty orientation. Each participant plays the game with two partners. The death anxiety buffer serves to protect one from thoughts of death and not negative affect in general.

We should be cautious in stating that truth telling is healing. Myth holds before us the horrors that follow upon unthinkable behaviour. There were three engineers in the room when the engine was fired up. The upper floor has been greatly altered, if not fully reconstructed. Confusion was evident in the mix of different types and quality of registers being maintained. Nurses are more likely to report than other staff groups. Hiroko is a freelance interior designer for homes and restaurants. Claude Cahun published few of her photographs during her lifetime. The sleeping posture became the distinguishing feature of Chen Tuan religious images. The fabric is recycled from blackout curtain.

Thin strips of palm leaf were twisted into cord and rope, and then tied into nets. Population densities there were very low. I disembarked at Brindisi for Paris, and the others continued their passage for Venice. The mutant mice had cognitive symptoms such as deficits in spatial working memory and short-term social memory. The sound of your breath in a quiet room is about 30 db; the hum of a refrigerator averages above 50. Our experience, once again, is a kind of suspension. Little or nothing happens, yet somehow everything is different. The dog's tail whacks the floor. Adviser remuneration must be negotiated with the client.

Assembly Language programming is a must if you need the most efficient code. This troubled me too. The setting sun created a wonderful spectacle over Frodsham Hill in Cheshire on 26th April. Children become capable of using symbols and language. We have now seen most of Dublin that lies along the river axis, and it is time to change direction and move from north to south. We have found that simple thresholds on error counts work well. The segmentation is noisy and needs to be optimized in a coherent manner for the entire reconstructed sequence. Of 135 subjects in 32 different groups, 19 (14 percent) showed forced compliance. All land that is good for agriculture is already in use. Exactly the same communication, as far as content is concerned, was given to all subjects. Do you think that you yourself know anything connected with the war that should not be repeated? It was clear that the Japanese, who were arbitrarily moved to relocation camps, saw this as an act of hostility directed towards them by the United States.

Each one of us believes we saw something that other people did not see. Identities have both cognitive and affective meaning. Actors are motivated to engage in secret negotiations. The payment was 14s for the medium quality. This is a very private village set in lush gardens on the very edge of its own lagoon. The subject was given the second card and asked for his final decision and confidence based on all twenty numbers. We show how triangle meshes can be optimized so as to have the incircle packing property.

Training is also needed to translate observations into a correct and robust task model. Embedded and device developers require tools that are often unique to the target device. Just as he rang the doorbell he lost the vision in his left eye. Let us look at the problem a little more closely. The average baby born at term weighs seven and a quarter pounds and is twenty to twenty one inches long. More of your everyday life depends on finite impulse response filters than you might ever have guessed. Sometimes a representation of a grammatical subject emerges, which triggers a series of associations that continue until we choose one.

Therefore, it is possible that applied fragrances serve as an individual marker, as well as natural odours themselves. The display motif works beyond the vegetation component of the landscape. It is clear that the actual content of the propaganda did not determine whether or not the subjects evaluated its characteristics favourably. Advertising material is a potential source of cognition, which would be consonant with having purchased the product. We make the assumption that agents do not come closer together than a specified distance, say d min.

The motivation is to take the guesswork out of the routine. A Moray eel eases out of a shell in a fish tank, freezes and stares at me for the rest of the interview. Spheroids and battered stones form a class of smooth edged artefacts. The rockhead, as distinct from the silted bottom, is 300m and in some cases 380m below sea level. In the ascending mode (going northwards) the satellite crosses the equator at approximately 22.00 hours when it is dark, so that images will only be collected in the descending mode. When we think of these waveform lengths in terms of memory, we can begin to see a connection to computational power.

The space between enclosure walls, serving as roads and footpaths, creates a branching pattern. The concepts of encoding time window, spike counts and temporal codes are illustrated using simple examples. A spiral stair rises to the third floor. Noko actually meant "intermediary" in some languages. At the intersection, two species of iris came together and hybridized. Incident reports that are not scoped further are still very valuable. The underlying representation for this example consists of a semantic network of 18 instances, defined in terms of 27 air traffic domain concepts and 8 domain relations, implemented as frames in the Loom knowledge representation system.

We believe that our design decision simplifies our language and makes specifications easier to write, even though it gives up some descriptive power. The manipulation of pieces can be done either by using a classic mouse or a combination of data glove and motion capture advice. The solid portions of every curve refer to situations where forced compliance has occurred; the dashed portions refer to situations where forced compliance has not occurred. This reality is the thing's self, its fundamental nature. Higher scores showed greater agreement with the source.

Rumination is incessant, repetitive thinking about past trauma. Both actors are willing to negotiate for some other speech histories. Gerard Pipart, the chief designer at Nina Ricci, selected a green linen fabric in a loose weave. In one of the pictures Mrs Harriet Williams of the Koasati Beaver clan is intent on twining Spanish moss threads on a small vertical loom. Weaving sheds were installed in the upper floor with two high windows to each station, giving excellent light for work. To build intuition, we begin by separately analysing behaviour in all sub games corresponding to the secret negotiations stage.

The majority effect is due to the consensus information provided by the percentages of people supporting each position. A witness is anyone who lived in Rwanda during the genocide and who chooses to give his or her testimony at the *gacaca*. Previous studies have shown that mortality salience effects occur after people have been distracted from death reminders. Copies of the messages can be obtained from the first author. He describes how he was wounded by a strong bullet during the Tibetan expedition. Even the axioms of geometry are based on a kind of intuition.

A person enjoys having a clear structured mode of life and likes to have a fixed place for everything. Endpoints of a response scale may also be considered as anchors that are used for comparison. With a majority source, there was no effect of message quality indicating that heuristic processing had occurred. All survivors had lost a close family member in the genocide. In the model, secret negotiations are always eventually revealed. The section of wool illustrates subtle morphing between colours.

No sampling or tagging programmes are currently underway. All outlines are to the same scale. Nodes shown in bold may be expanded further. Oil and dispersant can coat gills and primitive lungs (which are used to breathe at the surface). We may never be sure that the model we converge on is the right one, rather than one that has merely been tuned to fit previous data. As nuclear burning spreads like wildfire, buoyancy lifts the flame and ash upward like a mushroom cloud. These signals have the greatest amount of power in the lowest frequencies (longest wavelengths).

Deep-water formation may gravitate to open water, where the heat flux out of the ocean is much greater. Peering through the cloud of stellar ash, the observer can quantify the complete stellar distribution of material throughout. Forecasts may converge, but only on the same range of uncertainty, which users will have to live with. Strongly bound inhibitors yield profiles with higher peak forces, whereas the force profiles of weaker inhibitors are flatter. The enamelled crown is low with a small diameter.

Internet services focus on streamlining failure modes and recovery scenarios. When the hut is rotted by termites, the villagers gather and collectively build a new one. All of this happens very quickly. First they taught individuals to expect more food at site A than site B. Entrants had to devise a strategy that their agents would use to decide between these options. Late capitalism was the dawn, not the dusk, of a thoroughgoing capitalism. More and more funds will have missing cumulative performance over one to three years as they switch away from front-end loads. The finding is not necessarily inconsistent with perspective theory.

Since we are dealing with updates of methods, it is useful to define and classify the different types of relationships between them. Chemical analysis of tiny paint samples can be definitive. Logistic regression is chosen when the dependent variable is dichotomous as in the study: depression or no depression, PTSD or no PTSD. The colours of the field sign and the sash were the colours of the royal coat of arms. Subjects are required to draw a line as slowly as possible. If you do not want to learn to write it—which is a nightmare—to talk Tibetan is simple.

Height precedes width followed by depth. We therefore experimented with both low and heavy loads on shared memory. Work on skeletal remains suggests a decline in living standards. If the investigation takes a long time, you will be kept up to date with its progress. The uses of human tissue have expanded to include bone dust in periodontal surgery, transplant of dissected heart valves, cadaver skin grafts for burn victims, and beauty treatments such as facial injections. Some of the feelings of fear, guilt, anger, embarrassment and humiliation were unresolved at the time of the interview, even a year after the incident.

The results of the recall test clearly showed a tendency for subjects to forget those items of information that introduced dissonance. One of the things I didn't bank on was the dreadful noise that all these plastic gearboxes make. The runway of RAF Greenham Common south of Thatcham is clearly visible. The orbit is circular with an inclination of 99 degrees. We had a guideline of what depth levels to reach. This also facilitates failure isolation and prevents negative feedback loops. After the general commentary, reference to specific destinations is made. Banda and several hundred of his followers were brought in chains to Delhi and paraded through the streets.

A partition scheme was then introduced to separate buildings into independent blocks using the major line structures of the scene. The ensemble stands on a sculpted base, perhaps a later replacement, of four female sea creatures with bifurcated serpentile tails. Species richness and evenness can vary independently, so communities can contain the same number species but still differ in evenness. The fossils take the form of three-dimensional sheets with scalloped margins defined by radial slits and an internal radial fabric. Deeper blue shading in the interior indicates a higher concentration of regenerated nutrient and thus excess CO_2.

Dashed lines are guides to the eye. We have used an object model of the database that is more current. Long values cannot be indexed, but they should be available so that we can perform a sequential search on them whenever there is a query on a slot with character values. Agents are more complex entities than particles because they have a goal that they intend to achieve in an optimal way. The animals breathe at the surface and dive deep to feed on squid, exposing the whales to oil and dispersants at a range of depths. The first Orbiting Carbon Observatory (OCO) crashed into the ocean in February 2009 after the clamshell fairing of the Taurus rocket carrying the probe didn't separate. The inferred asymmetry is generally consistent with that expected from off-centre explosions. Grain size and mass of ash fall per area can be used to reconstruct volcanic plumes. The compactness property could be violated if there are redundant rules. A good model must both reproduce life-like behaviour and be as simple as possible.

The viewer has the feeling of looking through a window after rain. Predators and prey move along sites following a simple set of rules. Among the devas can be seen the god Indra, with his many eyes. How can we utilize idle periods to speed up the loading time? You will not find another book on this subject with so many practice questions. Proposition 4 is not supported. Some children think that they are supposed to check the advertised products at stores. Any amendment to an individual's body would be loaded with cultural meaning and typify an act of symbolic consumption.

Things or equipment are at our disposal. A blue filter will darken the foliage and lighten the sky. Very quickly the tents came down and were stacked away. In total, there are four types of abstract question. Complete the series. Each slot name forms the roof of a small tree; its children are individual slot values and facet values. Hatchlings moving out into open water, where they may encounter oil, need to be monitored too. Titania is depicted in a state of trance, intently staring ahead yet obviously taking in the apparitions surrounding her. This is a chair with electrical contacts in the seat and arms. Also, on the screen is a list of the six statements in Table 1.

Responses were not scored, but served to prime thoughts of death or a neutral topic. Mr Ke is a consumer who is aware of and demonstrates this flux in symbolic product meaning. The enhancement of pleasure, luxury, and discovery has wrapped many hotels in botanical splendour. But this data would be more useful if operational in real time. Do not turn over the page until you are ready to begin. The deeper you see into a mass of snow or ice, the bluer becomes its substance, and a strong filter will severely exaggerate the contrast.

In working with Paul, I felt that his wish was that I should join him in grieving over the loss of the past. Priority is not really a core issue. We have not chosen to be in the world. The points, lines, and areas we encounter are all different. Early surveyors used to base land ownership maps on so-called witness trees. The leaf was about four inches wide and varied from one to two feet long. Bits of the non-human world may themselves be the sources of moral obligations. More than 3000 litres of water are used to produce a kilo of American beef. Our grandparents caught a lot of animals because they dreamt with the animal spirits.

This was a low contrast subject in soft light. Two bees and an inscription fill the upper left corner. Product or brand meaning varies across social situations. The assumption is that somewhere inside that grid cell we will find the represented point object. Somewhere off Plymouth a wrong course was given. As it turns out, surface features are composed of an infinite number of possible height values. No border of light defines the frame of these images: only the figures themselves give off light into space. This anxiety doesn't have an object. The process involves matching the primary key (column) in one table to another column in the second table.

If such a line ends without dividing, it represents the species becoming extinct. The input scale may vary from the display scale. Jeff is a full-time, on-site manager in charge of human resources for our manufacturing operations. The teashop interior is suffused with a dim light in which the silhouettes of the two conversing men appear like paper cutouts. Aim to get the balance between speed and accuracy right. This viewer supports a variety of relationship editing operations.

External exposure to oil causes burns and infections. Whale sharks are filter feeders that subsist on fish spawn and plankton blooms—typically off the Mississippi River Delta in the summer. People live and work on these boats. The namazu is an enormous mythical catfish said to live underground in Japan, which wriggles about when it is angry, causing earthquakes. It would make sense for each individual fish to stay in sync with the crowd, turning together to avoid a predator. Nutrient-bearing subsurface water is converted into nutrient-depleted sunlit surface water. On the horizon fishermen are casting their nets.

Stories about their first Guru support Sikhs throughout their lives. Distant clouds were at least twice as luminous as the moon itself. Jack's share of the field is one hectare in area. In the lower part of the figure, triangular faces are marked. A resort carefully anchored in a sensitive environment can preserve its indigenous beauty and promote conservation. In our model, actors decide whether to participate in negotiations. Integrated threat theory proposes anxiety as one of four proximal predictors of intergroup attitudes, and defines contact experiences as distal predictions.

At the moment that its grammatical subject appears in consciousness, the entire sentence is already implicit. Look out for the blue markings on posts, and turn right down a steep lane marked with a "No Through Road" sign. Both approaches offer spectacular views. The horizon sky was very bright and of low blue saturation, hence it appears quite light. As the viewer walks through space, electronic switches are triggered, and figures walk forward until they're approximately life size. Jake, a client, came to see me after his father's sudden death.

Four men were washed overboard close to land, and three drowned. Living, it emerged, was anxious work, and the world a dangerous place. I noticed how my prejudices kept coming up. Let us examine this a bit more closely. One may assert that dissonance is to some degree an inevitable consequence of forced compliance. We selected setups that create a heavy load on shared memory, giving no opportunity for time slicing. Only error messages are printed. If the union of restricted domain of the object is equal to the domain of the object, there is no missing value.

Mostly you're alone with yourself and the projection. You must complete these tasks against a time constraint. Try to measure large areas of single luminance if they exist in the subject. Images often touch but rarely overlap. The locking model of controlling concurrent access may work well for short online transactions, but in a collaborative environment, it prevents users from working together. Line segments denote paths taken by predators and prey. They'll show up looking for food and find oil. Invasive species are held responsible for driving native ones to extinction.

Freud speaks of "those wrecked by success". The four prototypes can be expressed as combinations of two dimensions: anxiety (self model) and avoidance (other model). A witness can therefore be a survivor, an *inyanga-mugayo*, or a neighbour. Each communication consisted of the interviewer's question and Dr Wilson's 150 to 200-word reply. This combination of opposing feedback loops also appears to be at the heart of conditions that sustain self-organising structures. Few texts longer than a paragraph are written without appropriate formatting. In this process only word stems are retained, for example, “injection”, “injecting” and “injected” are all replaced by “inject”.

To obtain scalability, one can use an indexed file that lets us selectively retrieve frames by some key such as the frame name. Two exceptional rules exist in the example workflow. Mainly it’s up to you and those people who get up for you and come forward as if to make contact. Today’s customers are looking to satisfy needs that have both cognitive and emotional dimensions. Apprehensions of moving landscapes are not uniform and can be experienced in different ways, depending on the direction of travel. The sum of all overlapping echoes will give us the waveform of the sound after it has passed through the tunnel.

We use semi-dense structure from motion in our current implementation to automatically compute semi-dense point clouds and recording positions. The required first-order derivatives are computed exactly. Sceptics have made the most of their chances. The Kemp’s Ridley sea turtle nests in Mexico and South Texas, far from the spill. Increased Antarctic density stratifications would, in turn discourage Antarctic deep-water formation. The map is a small, simplified version of the earth itself.

Trays should be level and rest on an open grid frame or rack an inch or two above the bottom of the water jacket so that water can circulate underneath them. Objects observed closely enough to be clearly seen to occupy both length and width are called areas. In May 2007 I spent a day in the park, making three ascents in the Eutelstat balloon. The artefact was lying on the ground in a zone of cliff screes, with no other object of the kind around. Heavily worked pieces such as flaked spheroids fall into the category of multifacial or polyhedral tools. So the focus is on building a platform intended for reuse in products and applications. The default action is to ignore the input character and simply to append a space to the return string.

Global Signals

Downy gentian flowers open one or two at a time during daylight hours and will sometimes remain closed during overcast weather. Cell nuclei are stained blue-violet, and the nucleoli red. We only need an associative link between the two. Emma is subject at the present time to a compulsion: not being able to go into shops alone. Note the massive disruption caused by the entry of gas and shot into the skin. The course of events can now be reconstructed as follows. Each successive streak leads to an increasing dilution of the organism to be identified on the plate. Of course these blacked-in areas are perceptions, which are also remembered. Try not to wonder about the validity of the test.

Self heal is an introduced species. A small amount of crust is collected and smashed in a drop of pure water. The original plate has been heavily retouched with figures added and others erased. White patches imitate the effect made when printing with worn-out blocks. Orange and red filters will lower the diffusion values of green leaves somewhat, and will exaggerate the depth of shadow value. The spread-plate method has not changed significantly since its introduction. Inhaling volatile components can lead to unconsciousness, pneumonia, organ damage and death. The deceased would be replaced by the "offspring" of a different agent. Defensive life patterns are not the same as patterns of ego defence against anxiety.

Another option is to obtain a waiver that usually requires all the data to be anonymised. Taken together these findings suggest that close interpersonal relationships may function as an effective terror management mechanism. Only at first glance is this definition uncomplicated. The helpless were directed to stand or kneel near the edge of a large pit that had been prepared. Rifle bullets are usually longer than those used in handguns and often have a sharp point and stepped waist. The overriding effect of displacement is incongruity. The entry wound may appear smaller than the diameter of the bullet.

Plastic surgery, paid for by the parents, appears to represent another manipulation of the parent-child relationship. There was no executioner in the dream. Anything can happen on the blank picture surface. Through a snowy wilderness, the hero leads his hollow-eyed trackers at last to extinction, and is then inexplicably resurrected from an avalanche to become the new medicine man for his tribe. The Navajo applied a poultice of wedge-leaf frog fruit to spider bites. Hawkmoths, hummingbirds, and bees pollinate the flowers. The leaflets are sensitive to touch and will fold together when disturbed. Shadow values are substantial, and the entire scale is much more informative.

Add a vertical line to the shape at the bottom of the series. The right hand side of the figure presents three input devices. Some implementers configure their systems through files that are stored locally on each node. For real animals, including humans, most activity is like this too. To look natural, they pretend to be fishing. In the Jola funeral ritual four bearers hold a platform aloft and move in response to questions. If the observer is not careful, these prehension traces could be mistaken for use-wear. The group had no anti-venom and minimal first aid supplies. When the trail got steeper, there were freezing streams to cross, and the air was noticeably cooler.

Fog values are lower than might be considered realistic. In *Beacon*, there are two different images projected out through the ends of a tube. The meanings given to shopping were a creative defence against death anxiety. Sensitivity to features is a function of the current state of scientific knowledge. Some lines are squashed and therefore shorter than they were. As you can see, this is really a two-dimensional run-length code. The decrease in function is followed by atrophic degeneration. Where are we falling? Point features are spatial phenomena, each of which occurs at a single location. The bedsit was very tidy and the mother stated that it was completely out of character. Infinity makes its debut at this year's American Film Market with a slate of fifteen titles, most of which are completed projects. Once a print is located and rendered visible, it should be photographed. Exhaust fumes were piped back into the camouflaged van.

A single plant may produce thousands of seeds but many are infertile. The genocide convention is silent on the defence of duress. Bells were struck with small bronze or wooden drumsticks. The reverse side is typically jet-black. Drawings in which the model appears to be cooperating in the removal of his own skin to reveal his innards are not uncommon in early anatomical plates. Don't forget my little shoes. Practitioners at these clinics claim that their treatments are safe and effective. Both fear and reverence are completely meaningless, blind emotions. However, betting on the magnetism of water is not exclusively limited to the fantasy resorts. No couple is completely typical.

Outside the cave was a flat stone like a chessboard. We left Tver at night, in pony-sledges, and drove to a village near which a bear had been located. Performatives are utterances whereby we make explicit what we are doing. The image shows a very well formed low-pressure cyclone south east of Greenland. A regional effect was detected in which the Southern and Eastern provinces had a similar influence on the regression, so these two regions were merged into one. The topmost part of this section consists of an oxidised and stromatolitic hardground surface. A small, low oblong door at the front was the only entry.

Reducers are used to remove density from a developed negative. Lift cards have a smooth surface and are usually transparent. The god Brahma is visible on the right, seated on a lotus. Significant event auditing did not arise in a vacuum. Alistair Cooke died at the age of ninety-four from lung cancer which had spread to his bones. The background of a photograph can provide additional valuable information. All the descriptions dedicated to this illness are summarised in the volumes on which the arm rests. Macrophages smother specialised cells and change the area into connective tissue. They migrate into skin or leave the organism altogether.

The purpose is to gather spiritual powers together to promote the operation of the *dharma* or law. Children of slaves were themselves slaves. The residuals are for commercial sources. Not only is there malleability of product meanings but also with respect to the sources of meaning. At the same time, public transport users have more time to notice and be discerning about their surroundings. Many early passengers were regarded as ballast on empty timber ships returning to Canada. Marriages are listed in the indexes under the names of both parties. Sobibor was not a concentration camp but an extermination centre. Production starts in August on location in Eastern Europe.

Boyer's footsteps, as he moves off camera under the shade, and again as he walks his horse briskly away, are inaudible, and there are no incidental sounds of clothing, sets or props. The standard is tapered down to a semi-circular or swallow-tailed end. Fear spreads when objects and places share common features. You may find that your trail comes to an unexpected and sudden halt. *Heart of Midnight* sets up a similar power struggle, and family melodrama, in another environment with the capacity to make fantasies come to life. Wild plum forms dense thickets. This simple family tree will help to show you the gaps in your knowledge. Occasionally the wife of the householder is mentioned by name. She settled rapidly, and when the cargo of wheat began to swell, the crew took to boats.

Ancestors who were poor, illiterate and unemployed can be the most difficult to trace. William was born into bondage on the Cousins Cove Sugar Plantation in 1832. You might feel unsteady on your feet. Viewers tend to absorb these kinds of powerful images more easily. Below, on the left, is Kon Hsüan Shuai, Assistant Secretary of State in the Ministry of Thunder. The idea is analogical or metaphorical, not literal. During the Great Famine of 1845–51, emigration to Australia increased. The thunderbolt is represented as a cigar-shaped central rod issuing zigzag flashes of lightning between two displayed wings. In general, anxiety may continue to rise for about 15 or 20 minutes. Check for instructions to turn over the page. This was the tortoise spirit, small and often ill, his voice is not clear.

Since Venus is close to the tidal lock radius of the Sun, its rotation is almost locked. Spending months in deep space would increase the crew's chances of being exposed to a deadly blast of radiation from a solar flare. The Russian rover Lunokhod 1, which landed in 1970, has a reflector on its back but could not be targeted, as its exact location was not known. The pattern of sonar emission is shaped closely in the time domain. After reading the first part of this book you should be able to decide whether or not you have an obsessional problem. A small blue and white Chinese jar stands by his side, but otherwise the scribe has no equipment, not even a desk or spare reed pens.

Only when an idea is committed to paper can it be protected. The closing lines on the last page state that it was copied in Lahore. The pigment is fluorescent and therefore easy to detect under ultraviolet light. Colour preferences are the most commonly noted aspect of trade with indigenous peoples. The full range of opacity, from opaque through to transparent, can be useful in system development. Shigeru is well versed in the law relating to sterilization. He may be able to discover new information that favours the decision he took or to get others to agree with his action.

Table 2 confirms our expectation that this program can outperform depth peeling for more complex scenes. It would not be easy, under these circumstances, to discard belief. The group is shown in front of a loom frame used for moss weaving. Appraisal refers to evaluative processes that give person-environment interactions their meaning. A metal stent is sometimes used to bridge the weakened section of blood vessel and keep the coils in place. The symptoms slowly subsided but tended to resurface before every vacation break. So far we proposed data structures to model the semantics of methods. Using stubs is also known as pointer swizzling, a common implementation technique for object-oriented databases.

Try the following 10 examples. He wore a thick necklace of black and red beads, feathers in his hair and metal bangles on his wrists. In humid conditions you may insert packets of silica gel in the negative filing box to absorb moisture (the gel can be dried out in an oven for repeated use). Customers are being served in the background. People have no articulate philosophy of shopping. The company developed an ambient strategy that was successfully targeted and moreover influenced the target. Pick out a country familiar to you. The Seven Stones lie between Land's End and the Scillies.

This link means that all the columns in the second table are now related to the columns in the first table. The property of orientation is found in shelterbelts that are planted at right angles to the prevailing wind. I was left alone in the strange room with its anatomical charts. If you want to change a word, press "*+" repeatedly until the word you want appears. Victims were "given special treatment", "rendered harmless" or "resettled". If the gun is pressed firmly against the flesh it forms a hard contact wound. Wild four-o-clock is related to bougainvillea. The individual feels compelled to collect and store certain objects.

Vocalisation occurs principally with an increase of resistance in the respiratory tract. Appropriate spatial proximity of their elements is a necessary condition in soft systems. Each secondary source acts individually as a spherical transmitter, and so the wave propagates by the net effect. Prey-generated sounds typically have peak spectral energy in the lower end of a bat's audible range. One side is persistently heated, and the other lies in long-lasting or permanent darkness. Experiments were carried out in a heated (28°C), double-walled soundproof chamber lined with convoluted anechoic polyurethane foam. Stippled areas denote regions in which electrical stimulation evokes vocalisation.

You must have had at least four panic attacks in a four-week period. The action in question might have a superstitious quality. Work done in living systems is chemical. Exposed muscle tissue was covered with petroleum jelly to prevent desiccation. All existing objects carry information. This condition is stringent. Thought-control is accomplished by dismissing your obsessional thought, then trying to re-obtain it. The objects were looked at in the privacy of a domestic setting and viewed intimately. We bias ourselves towards keeping failure modes simple so that recovery is simple. Each light switch, tap and door may require up to 300 checks. Remedies available after trial are known as final remedies.

You are already making progress towards a panic-free life by deciding to read this book. Sunlight is an ideal form of illumination. A small number of raw materials must be able to pass through the membrane. *Sarowar* is a pool or lake. Constructed tidal creeks are modelled on nearby natural creeks in their length, width, orders, and drainage density. When more than one fractional portion of a lot is given, the position in the section map is located by reading the sub-portions from left to right. Classified pixels are then optimized across multiple registered views to produce a coherent semantic segmentation. In an internet service, each node needs to know the state of all the other nodes it may communicate with.

This would allow online statistics to be updated on a more regular basis. Piece by piece, the elements of a starter kit for the first Mars colonists are coming together. The SPOT High Resolution Visible (HRV) sensors can operate in either multi spectral or panchromatic modes. Climate variations do not seem to have had an influence on the thickness of valves. Our landfill example shows the interaction of two spatial objects. Township and range lines run through the centre of each township of land. To help reader and printer alike, however, they have been segregated.

Domain 4 is revealed to be in the transmembrane region and domain 3 constitutes the mouth of the channel. Tidal forces are shown solid, gravitational forces dashed, and centrifugal forces dotted. Tyre ruts were loci of higher plant diversity in a New Jersey freshwater wetland mitigation site. The membrane behaves like a solid body. Lateral suppression was only observed at extra-tone frequencies higher than that of the probe. The counterweight is a mixture of clay, beeswax and pinesap, that can easily be shaped when warmed up, but is hard and solid when cooled.

When hands are regularly cleaned during use, little polish will form. A series of reduction steps through repeated flaking can yield a polyhedron from such cores. This is a very flat subject, illuminated in sunlight at about 45 degrees. The pallid bat attends selectively to noise transients produced by prey locomotion. This state of arousal has been called sensitization. Just two inhalations of 35% carbon dioxide was enough to induce an attack. The sensor of a chemical automaton must undergo a change in its chemical properties. Its body is usually covered with multi-coloured spots, the coat being white.

You can have panic attacks without agoraphobia, but if you are agoraphobic you will most probably have panic attacks. There is no evidence to date that the emotional motor system in bats (anterior cingulated cortex, PAG etc) is organised differently than in other mammals. Living systems must contain a subsystem that carries information concerning the total system. The frame-editing viewer allows the user to view and edit the contents of an individual frame. A tiny inscription in gold paint at the bottom of the painting reads "amal-I khanazad Chitarman" (the work of the house-born Chitarman).

An exposure increase of about 50% was required because of the lens extension needed to make this close up. Image has four films already completed with another two in production. Sarah Miles, David Hayman, Derrick O'Connor and Sebastian Rice-Edwardes are the leading actors. Atlantic also has plans to produce a film called *1969*, which focuses on two families in small town America during the Vietnam War. In this example it condenses a series of moments pulled from across a span of twenty years to produce an intense and complex sequence. The crime scene is recorded using a pre-calibrated digital camera and a scale is included with each photograph along with a directional indicator.

After checking the cooker several times, the individual may experience a sense of relief. Two basic methods are used: feature elimination and feature smoothing. With a little practice excellent sections can be cut. Regions lying outside the resolvable plane may not be visible. In the eyes of the honeybee, yellow differs from blue much more than green, and blue differs from violet much less than from yellow. Red areas indicate signal intensity during inspiration and expiration. Whole-body vibration is sometimes abbreviated to WBV. The defining characters are neither clear cut nor well correlated. A dynamic object such as a flying insect not only produces frequency (FM) but also amplitude (AM) modulations in the echo.

Every flight manoeuvre causes motion of the image at the eye. To hold the head stable during recording, an aluminium headpin was attached to the skull using a layer of glass microbeads and dental cement. Projected sounds emerge as a sequence of short duration pulses that propagate into the water directly ahead of the animal. In both numeral systems information concerning the value of higher numbers is coded by the order of signs of different qualities. This noisy interruption sometimes results in the mind clearing. An extraordinary glow suffuses the painting, both as a result of the vivid sunset portrayed behind the lake, and the use of gold paint on Bhim Singh's nimbus and shield.

Sumac thickets provide shelter for wildlife. Insects are sieved by webs from the air streams that pass through them. Flowering takes place in spring as the leaves are emerging. One may wonder whether an implication of agency isn't lurking in the term "selection". If it exactly matches the target combination of numbers or letters, the search is done. A white square containing five black bars has a higher contrast frequency than a square of the same size containing only three bars. Each film has a characteristic sensitivity to light determined during its manufacture. Use bright spots are always integrated within a distinctive use polish.

This tiny offset in the point of ignition is enough to drive a massive imbalance in the explosion. The sky was quite bright and demands some "burning in" on the print. We see the projective as a major issue with many resonances. Much of this is based on scale. The data must first of all be detailed for each location. We stand, by implication, alongside the soldiers who are battering down the door to arrest the Jew and his family. *Einsatz* units issued daily top-secret reports that were consolidated in Berlin. Viewed from the side, the profile of the diaphragm is an inverted "J".

Usually the visual scene contains more than one contrasting object. All compliant systems have a resonance frequency, and complex structures have more than one. Increasing the field of view or increasing image fidelity enhances presence. The excitatory event generated by the emitted pulse must somehow be delayed. Your exposure programme should be as realistic as possible. The elements of soft systems are spatially unrestricted. In general, protein glues seem to be less organised at the molecular level than spun silks. The y-axis is out of the page. It was reputed to be light blue and very thin, with fine crackle lines.

Our Personal Universal Controller (PUC) system has the ability to generate new interfaces that are personally consistent with those that the user has previously interacted. A central control module wouldn't explain why the various motor pathways ran along the same chains as the sensory pathways. Yet this is exactly how the eyes and visual circuits of the brain work. Merely printing with less contrast reduces the impact of the image. If there are two possible directions leading to an increase in the distance between a target and a chaser, one is selected with a probability of 0.5.

When foliage appears against the blue sky it is often difficult to preserve the contrast of green against blue in terms of black-and-white values. The insect's survival crucially depends on its capacity to resolve moving images. They remain in the foreground until the viewer leaves the area. The basic model has one free parameter, which is the initial ratio of chasers to targets. The symbols do not tell us which is which. By preserving area we distort angles. A number of topological data models are in common use. Small scarification wounds healed rapidly and all traces of the procedure disappeared after a few days. Gradually you might begin to feel the impact of this positive change. The motor innervation of the diaphragm is from the phrenic nerve.

Humans are inherently highly damped, although resonances are still clearly observable. During quiet breathing expiration is due to elastic recoil of the lung, and the chest wall aided by gravity, and the expiratory muscles are silent. Our smoothing extracts features based on spatial scale while other methods smooth low-contrast features first. Various commercial platforms applying this principle were developed. Before we talk about the last person you spoke to, please rate your impression of the overall service we are providing. The company can be contacted in Suite 250.

Do you have persistent unwanted thoughts? At the time of this survey, insecurity had been hinted at in only one study. The article was embedded in a full-size A3 page of the University students' newspaper. Thought listing was the same as for experiments 1 and 2. Cognitive structures are relevant to the development of employee attitudes and even health problems. The distinction between harsh and soft tactics is more than a statistical artefact. We examined only three emotional reactions to compromise under mortality salience. The intuition behind these findings is also straightforward. Higher evenness resulted in better control even though the different predator species all attack the same prey.

This is the area that lights up when something unexpected happens. There is no reverse transformer that turns this electrical activity back into light waves or molecules. When I see their teeth I try to remember to smile back. Feedback loops may occur between undermining and depression, triggering a vicious circle in which one amplifies the other. Hydraulic rams push the shield through clay and the spoil is taken out through lift shafts. It requires considerable imagination in three-dimensional space to understand these circumstances. Simple phobics and social phobics tend to avoid situations that are likely to trigger their fears.

Thinking about silk protein structure has changed over the last forty years. People are primarily exposed to either localized vibration or vibration that affects the whole body. Additional muscles are recruited with greater efforts at breathing. The length of arrows corresponds to the amount of pressure. No single character is allowed to dominate the film. Light floods in through a large central atrium. With no steady stream to dispose of, trains could go more deeply beneath the ground. Where spaces were vaulted, the ribs of the vault were sometimes carved with chevrons. The best aggregate was a volcanic sand, *pozzolana*, from north of Naples and around the base of Vesuvius.

External walls are of chunky pink conglomerate from Draycott near Cheddar, with Bath stone dressings. Capitals were carved with a form of stylized foliage called "stiff leaf". Petals drop off early in very hot weather or when disturbed. The pods turn brown and persist through winter. Hornbills eat the seeds of fallen fruits. I resolved to hold hard onto substantial things. We flew until the cloud became porous with light. Theories of risk and uncertainty management emerged. Hayek sees markets as essentially unpredictable. A cool evening greeted us outside. Problems at the end of a process are usually caused further back (see figure 4).

Do you remember the Canadian bank in chapter one? Bombing destroyed the interior. Long takes of cloudscapes (shot from an aeroplane) punctuate the film, and establish its real time base. A Yorkshire girl begins to see and hear things that are apparently unseen by others. Social support is a finite resource and people compete for it in a zero-sum game. Conceptual links to crossover are weak and the causality is ambiguous. A pulse is a pulse is a pulse. Performance information should be used by people who do the work. Even quiet passages require this same approach. True automata are those controlled by a program. The second finger can also hit the string perpendicularly from this position.

Industrial bolts that hold together many members are concealed behind elegant iron flowers. An automaton may also contain some extra memory in the form of a stack in which symbols can be pushed and popped. We find that pieces are hard to come by, and the ones we find do not fit. The great batteries of cooking utensils were spotless and cold. Kidnappers were called "spirits", defined as "one that taketh up men and women and children and sells them on a ship to be conveyed beyond the sea". The slave register will certainly reveal the name of the property owner.

It proved useful to clean and degrease the skull with ether and to place screws in the bone next to the chamber. An enhanced differential image is displayed in real time (video rate) on a monitor, thus providing on-line feedback to the experimenter. Note the extensive local halo around the injection site followed by clear axonal patches further away. The cortex is illuminated with red light. Surface representations of segmented anatomy are constructed from line contours of structure boundaries using wire mesh triangulation. The brain in red shows orange images after interpolation and rigid body rotation to the position required for registration with the blue image set.

Suddenly the monkeys got a salt drink when they saw a blue light. Up and down arrows represent sharp pitch shifts in the following sounds. Withdrawal was sudden and almost total. Through frequent practicing the body acquires a movement memory and manages to store quite precise information on any motor experience. Four single condition maps are shown in colours that add up to white.

In the theory of pure sets, only a set can be a member of a set. Middleware is built to be deployed on mobile devices. Each button is associated with a keyword. In inch size ecosystems the users do not need to move their eyes to read information from one display to another. The red curve shows experimental data; the black curve shows inferred spin state. Only a tall tower can provide detailed measurements of a large area of forest. All activities defined in the process of definition are the basis for the process execution plan. Many deaths occur where there is no attempt to perform vengeance magic.

All that exists is true, not only what exists in nature but also what exists in the mind. Counterfactual claims about sentences and the propositions they express can and do get conflated with their object-language counterparts. This is usually termed a fork of the process execution. A malicious node assumes the identity of another node in the network. Fixed numbers that are already present in the grid are shown with a white background. Black fungus is the immediate problem the board must face. Now go back and start to clean up and polish each frame. Work is a process that goes through functions.

A cover can be further examined by moving into the floor. The notion of a "single-step transition probability" is no longer valid in continuous time since the step does not exist. One way to object to a theory is to claim that it has bad consequences. A perfect system would execute all started processes immediately. Symmetry rituals can occur in the absence of obsessional thoughts. A catalogue record for this book is available from the British Library. If the task is perfectly predictable and the routine is known, there is no need for a leader. The glazier began by drawing his design usually directly on the work table.

This way the pressure relations in the arm do not change. In the case of a success the current execution path is followed. Once its action ends, the agent becomes again an object. By eliminating a large number of focus shifts we were able to greatly improve system performance. No further runtime overhead is necessary. Other ingredients, such as cow hair, could also be added. However, in principle, a specific mediator is needed for every combination of incompatible elements. Abbreviations are allowed but should be spelt out in full when first used. We sometimes refer to the paradigm by its original label if we are examining material that uses that vocabulary.

The diaphragm is the main inspirational muscle and it expands the abdomen and the lower rib cage. The moving observer changed this continuous space. Virtual objects are projected, and real objects such as light switches and loudspeakers are also present. An extension module should be cohesive. Hitting a keyword button will evoke a cloud-like shape on the floor. During recovery, the fingers often turn red, and this can be the most painful component of an attack. I told him how I was feeling. The town where all this takes place is called Hadleyville, presumably lifted from Fred Zinnemann's 1952 classic western *High Noon*.

Movement-based interaction in camera spaces is problematic in the sense that the interaction tool is invisible to the user. Each base sends out a beam of sound in a certain direction pointing to another base. The conceptual ability of the ear can be trained considerably. For speech recognition a Max object called "Listen" was used. Notwithstanding false advertising, the instrument was stuffed with trumpets, flutes and drums. You could keep expanding this animation by adding a shadow under the walking man. A join requires that the peers along all merged execution paths know where to join with which paths.

Automata are set in motion and begin playing with utmost precision. There are three noticeable acoustic pressure clicks; the second one has the highest peak value. Echo-delay step is a measure of the rate of change in echo delay. A semantic location specifies location meaning and usually groups more physical locations. Every node that receives this request responds with a neighbour discovery reply. The pulley on the right hand wall denotes the eye-point. Places where one strip met another were carefully soldered together.

The hook of a live mussel is embedded in compact clay to hold it vertical. Worn as jewellery and as a display of power, strings of shells were also currency. New cognitive attitudes occurred first in fishing settlements. There were a lot of artists living and working in that part of Pasadena. The brightest reds relate to early sown cereals and grassland. In a wormhole attack, two or more malicious nodes may collaborate to encapsulate and exchange messages between them along existing data routes. Any disadvantage that might have befallen them was trivial when compared to the suffering of the inmates they abused.

Provoked famines were part of the European conquest and settlement of the Americas. This is the tallest verbena in Kansas. Images of discovery crop up time and again in subsequent chapters. Teams are invited to bid for blue or red counters. Harrison identified and classified four cultures using self-reports of organisational actors. The process screens out rather than selecting in. In many cameras a mechanical shutter is closed during the readout time. Re-engineering is in trouble. At the heart of systematic analysis was the scimitar box, a three-dimensional cube, constructed from clear plastic sheets and struts.

The use of threshold cryptography makes impersonation attacks more difficult. In some systems, many people can interact with the same public screens simultaneously. Figure five shows how a camera space can be scaled to cover from small objects to several users depending on the distance from camera to tracked objects. Integers of ten and below are to be spelled out. Death in itself therefore called for no special explanation, and need not have been followed by an attribution of sorcery. Function signatures can be automatically generated from the function code. The service invocation module is responsible to execute one activity of a process.

Most real measurements introduce perturbations that destroy the system's fragile quantum states before they can be reliably determined. The main ATTO tower will measure CO_2, methane and other atmospheric constituents; a series of four smaller satellite towers will be used to track local air currents. In this position the disadvantages mentioned above will be avoided. A large number of ideas are generated systematically within a domain identified by participants from the client company. Now is the time to connect all the elements into an application graph. The first oxide layer, which is purplish or red in colour, is called cuprite. Notice how our newly acquired vocabulary assists us in defining the geographic nature of the placement problem.

Red packet money, called "hong bau" is the largest money gift. Advertising on sites that permit free streaming may be used to generate royalties for media companies. The concept of feedback describes how digital events are visualized for users. These alerts take twenty to thirty minutes to arrive. I used small areas of bounce to raise the values of the ceiling and walls on either side of the window. These observations would provide timely "ground truth" to calibrate and complement remote-sensing techniques that rely on radar, lidar (light detection and ranging) and satellite data.

Our smoothing extracts features based on spatial scale while other methods smooth low-contrast features first. The major Linux distributors, Red Hat and Novell SUSE, have based their developer tools solutions on Eclipse. Elements already provided all required application logic. Figures are to be sequentially numbered in Arabic numerals. The pavilion design competition winner is an octagonal stressed plywood dome. The Hausa live on the grassy plain south of the Sahara and east of the River Niger. Tall fescue could well be the plant that makes a lawn near you.

Such a spirit was linked to a village domain or to the lands of a district. When Moka founded the kingdom, the population was falling as the result of new epidemics such as smallpox. All chiefs and most warriors were aristocrats. Relative overpopulation began in these systems when all the land was in use. These concepts cannot simply be put together since major parts are incompatible. The landscape is used to split disparate image spaces along a rough horizontal line through the centre of the projected image. At the front, the iron frame is once more hidden beneath stone. Its keynote is the use of rectilinear patterns that cover the entire interior. They appear to be carefully prepared mathematical exercises rather than genuine Surveyors' records. The additional line is horizontal and crosses the intersection of the diagonal bars. These could be made of stone and then painted or, for an even more authentic look, real glass windows were installed over black-painted stone. Original India ink drawings or glossy prints are preferred.

The snow comes early and melts late. These pixel-by-pixel changes in reflected light intensity are called global signals. Early detection of debris produced by asteroid collisions may be helpful in many ways. Some of the migrating photons reach the surface, exit the medium, and do not re-enter. Alternative paths in process definition allow for sophisticated failure handling. Structures possessing simple geometry, such as the brain stem, are mapped using landmark-based affine transformations and require no local deformations. Blood flow measurements were made both at rest and with and with the presentation of auditory stimulation with repeated bursts of white noise.

If no reverse route, then create one. Select the Symbol Screen Tool and randomly click on the instances. In application three, input feedback is visually overlaid the application feedback in a very limited area. A set of element types provides support for specific target systems. Roy can recall feeling happier when wearing gloves. At the landscape scale, a channel would be excavated with a meander that mimics a natural river. All that is known is the current production level. Plants wither in total darkness.

Cognitive subtraction is conceptually simple and is a very effective device in mapping functional anatomy. When Jennifer was at her most depressed she thought she was dead. Interviews were initially transcribed to a conventional orthographic level, emphasizing readability and conserving resources. The new material changed the vocabulary of architectural space. Mosaic artists often made mistakes or cut corners. Diagonal bracing timbers connect the posts with other timbers to give the structure extra strength and rigidity. The seismic source was a 7.26 kg manual jackhammer with a flat plate and four hammer blows recorded at each station.

Where space is enclosed the perpendiculars slope inwards, making the space broader at the top than at the bottom. Entangling each bit with two extra bits makes it possible to check two of those bits for errors while allowing the calculation to go forwards in the third. Aerosol particles carried in a stream of air are charged and then sequentially separated on the basis of size-dependent aerodynamic properties. Emotional reactions to instrumentation from scientists are rare. Figure 3 shows that there are pores of varying sizes from a few microns up to around a millimetre, visible from within the geopolymer binder when using a pixel size of several microns.

The horizontal band in the lower part of the image is an artefact of the detector. For each successive position, a hinged board is swung across the frame, and the point of intersection marked by a spot on its surface. This arrangement correlated with an asymmetrical distribution of DNA (pictured in green below) during cell division. The infrastructure for process execution must be able to distribute the load over all providers in a transparent and optimal way. It is notoriously hard to know if a system is close to a tipping point. At 25% humidity, the material appears blue-green, but at 98% it changes to red.

Two lifeboats went out, but could do nothing to save the ship. A darker ocean absorbs more sunlight, raising sea surface temperatures. We are projecting a three-dimensional object onto a flat medium. Primary aerosol is emitted in particulate form and consists of soil dust, sea spray, plant material and soot. At the Climate Code Foundation we encourage scientists to publish their software. We do not perform any form of data buffering which can introduce delays into the timeliness of data. The copy should be evenly printed on a high-resolution printer (300 dots per inch or higher). Each sensor is therefore required to have a uniform packet length and structure.

Our people do not live in the present. Time domain signals are presented with linear axes. Several neurotransmitters are involved in the generation of respiratory rhythm. The membrane-forming molecules produced by the system are spontaneously incorporated into the membrane, thus increasing its surface area. During inspiration, the left motor cortex, the right prefrontal cortex, and both inferolateral sensory cortices are activated. The smaller the radius, the longer the duration of the click and the smaller its peak value. The middle trace represents a sustained onset-evoked inhibitory input to the neuron, followed by a rebound at sound offset.

A neighbour discovery phase involves the mutual authentication of neighbour nodes. This means that strain builds up quickly, and the long straight plate boundary, which follows the coastline, enables big blocks of the fault to slip simultaneously, releasing a lot of energy in a single lurch. The house is completely destroyed, we have nowhere to sleep. But going into the midterm elections, a different narrative is emerging. See page 752 for more. A region associated with empathy called the *anterior insula* was activated. This was true regardless of the sound's duration.

The orientation of images is north up, east left. You should identify a quality that the two shapes have in common. That they are made from plaster is crucial. Shadow values are the three colour values of the darkest part in an image where detail still exists. The slot maker is of type Nation. The object organises the system of relations on which the names of the living, the gods, and the deceased all depend. You could see the fire glowing inside. Any pagan may join the Pagan Federation. A replenisher is a chemical formulation designed to restore the developer to full activity so that it can be reused, up to a certain limit.

Metchnikoff fed rabbits and guinea pigs with small doses of indol and scatol for a period of several months. Twenty-five years have elapsed since then. The farmhouse was a farmhouse only on the outside. Broca's area and the left temporal pole are structures that are known to be important for understanding stories. The brain does not need to duplicate the motor expertise stored in motor areas in order to permit imagination and social perceptive processes: it employs the very hardware of our own actions. The bell calls children to school. The enormous cost of reactors makes learning very expensive.

Galileo maintained a workshop for making mathematical instruments and assembling eyeglasses for sale. Service interaction was thus reduced to a single phase. Helmholtz's sirens and resonators collapsed the distance that had separated listeners from the inaccessible aura of tone. None of the sign groups, however, overlap with those on stone vessels. You can believe my claim that a given cherry tree is tall without believing anything about me. The total biomass of the system has increased significantly, and the vegetation has grown taller. It becomes a path bordered with boxwood hedges. Keep straight on until you join a road. Virtually all systems are permanently subject to natural perturbations.

Mangrove forest, in turn, protects the reef from sediment and extensive algal blooms. Temperatures have risen and the growing season has lengthened. It was on this land that maroons constructed buildings and planted vegetables and corn. Jesup with either symbiont is preferable to monoculture. The leaf is covered by a waxy cuticle, which keeps moisture outside and restricts evaporative water loss from the plant. Thin ends of branches were bent over and lashed together with strips of bark or Spanish moss, forming a domed roof. In this wet world, marshes and swamps blend into lakes or feed a network of creeks.

The next step was to scale the process up and adapt it to cellulose, which is the bulk of plant material. These aroids mainly have a flattened centre but there are also two worm-like centres as in the Oxford border of 1435. The pen work in the sprays and on the gold balls is black, and no lobes are drawn on the feathering nor green tint used, as in later manuscripts. The red border highlights high surface temperatures associated with an active fire. All the monotes species are good bee trees, producing fine honey. *Fire and Ice* moves away from fiction and enters the world of sport.

The red colour is from iron oxide but scientists are more worried about dissolved heavy metals such as arsenic and chromium entering the groundwater. To reduce habituation, we intermixed trials of positive emotions in all three scanning experiments. A Greenland artist made this fine woodcut over a century ago. Returning to the cottage, he finds it all boarded up. As the film develops, however, stereotypes shed their obviousness and the audience has to review their actions in a new light. The location can be seen distinctly with the eye. Small rocky planets lie in the pleasantly warm region close to the Sun. The second pathway is a systemic pathway.

At the ocean surface, the entire food chain was disrupted. Statements are given as a guide under certain numbers. There is more about confidence in chapter nine. In some unions, registers survive that list the births and deaths that took place within the workhouse. The regularities are abstracted from models that assume some kind of closure or boundedness from unanticipated influences for change. Real value has to be estimated and distinguished from nominal value. Increases of connectivity with the hippocampus could finally reflect autobiographic memories triggered by the scripts. A cross-check against catalogues of astronomical objects tells you that no known body in the Solar System should have these coordinates and drift.

Sources

Abbott, Alison. 'The Plague Plan'. *Nature*, 456 (13 November 2008): 161.

—. 'Opening up Brain Surgery'. *Nature*, 461 (15 October 2009): 866–868.

Ackerman, W. *Solvable Cases of the Decision Problem*. Amsterdam: North-Holland Publishing, 1954.

Adam, David. 'Bigger Trees Helping Fight against Climate Change'. *Guardian* (19 February 2009): 13.

Adams, Ansel. *The Negative*. Boston, MA: Little, Brown, 1981.

Aldhous, Peter and Jim Giles. 'Pfizer's Payments to Censured Doctors'. *New Scientist* (1 May 2010): 8.

Allen, James. *Without Sanctuary: Lynching Photography in America*. Santa Fe, NM: Twin Palms, 2000.

Allison, Philip. *African Stone Sculpture*. London: Lund Humphreys, 1968.

Amarante Mesquita, André L. and Alex S.G. Alves. 'An Improved Approach for Performance Prediction of HAWT using Strip Theory'. *Wind Engineering*, 24 (2000): 417–430.

Anderson, Perry. 'Sinomania'. *London Review of Books* (28 January 2010): 3–6.

Anonymous. *Flight out of Fancy*. London: Bodley Head, 1948.

Appleyard, Donald, Kevin Lynch and John R. Meyer. *The View from the Road*. Cambridge, MA: Massachusetts Institute of Technology, 1964.

Arnett, Bill. *Nine Planets*. Online: www.nineplanets.org. Accessed 21 June 2007.

Ascherton, Neil. 'Raging Towards Utopia'. *London Review of Books* (22 April 2010): 3–8.

Asma, Stephen T. *Stuffed Animals and Pickled Heads: The Culture and Evolution of Natural History Museums*. Oxford: Oxford University Press, 2001.

Ayala, Hana. 'Resort Hotel Landscape as an International Megatrend'. *Annals of Tourism Research*, 18 (1991): 568–587.

Aybeck, Ali, Selcuk Arslan, Enver Yildiz and Kamal Atik. 'A Comparison of the Heat and Mechanical Energy of a Heat-Pump Wind Turbine'. *Wind Engineering*, 24 (2000): 437–442.

Babbitts, Judith. 'Stereographs and the Construction of a Visual Culture in the United States'. In Lauren Rabinovitz and Adam Geil, eds. *Memory Bytes: History, Technology and Digital Culture*. Durham, NC: Duke University Press, 2004, 126–149.

Baker, Adrienne, ed. *Serious Shopping: Essays in Psychotherapy and Consumerism*. London: Free Association Books, 2000.

Baker, Philip J., Luigi Boitani, Stephen Harris et al. 'Terrestrial Carnivores and Human Food Production: Impact and Management'. *Mammal Review*, 38 (2008): 123–166.

Baird, Ljiljana. *Quilts*. London: Museum Quilts, 1994.

Balibar, Sebastien. 'The Enigma of Supersolidity'. *Nature*, 464 (11 March 2010): 176–182.

Barbier, Jean Paul and Douglas Newton, eds. *Islands and Ancestors: Indigenous Styles of Southeast Asia.* Munich, Germany: Prestel Verlag, 1988.

Barkham, Patrick. 'Creatures of the Night'. *Guardian*, international edition (27 August 2007).

Barley, Shanta. 'Jungle Funerals: How Chimps Mourn their Dead'. *New Scientist* (1 May 2010): 9.

Barnes, Nick. 'Publish Your Computer Code: It is Good Enough'. *Nature*, 467 (14 October 2010): 753.

Barske, Lindsey A. and Blanche Capel. 'An Avian Sexual Revolution'. *Nature*, 464 (11 March 2010): 171–172.

Barthels, Monika, Ralf Bröer, Johannes Büttner et al. *Senses, Sensors and Systems.* Basel, Switzerland: Editions Roche, 2004.

Barton, B.T. *History of the Borough of Bury and Neighbourhood in the County of Lancaster* (2nd edition). Didsbury, UK: Morten, 1973.

Bate, Jonathan. 'The Ode "To Autumn" as Ecosystem'. In Laurence Coupe, ed. *The Green Studies Reader: From Romanticism to Ecocriticism.* London: Routledge, 2000, 256–261.

Batuman, Elif. 'On Complaining'. *London Review of Books* (20 November 2008): 6–12.

BBC News, 6 February 2004. 'Tide Kills 18 Cockle Pickers'. Online: news.bbc.co.uk/1/hi/england/lancashire/3464203.stm. Accessed 25 February 2010.

—. 26 March 2009. 'Israel Phosphorus Use Criticised'. Online: news.bbc.co.uk/1/hi/world/middle_east/7964057.stm. Accessed 3 February 2010.

—. 20 January 2010. 'Brother Tortured Edlington Attack Victims'. Online: news.bbc.co.uk/1/hi/england/south_yorkshire/8469424.stm. Accessed 3 February 2010.

—. 21 January 2010. 'Edlington Attack Boys had "Toxic" Upbringing'. Online: news.bbc.co.uk/1/hi/england/south_yorkshire/8473112.stm. Accessed 3 February 2010.

Beacham, Peter, ed. *Devon Building: An Introduction to Local Traditions.* Tiverton: Devon Books, 1990.

Beeby, Alan and Anne-Maria Brennan. *First Ecology.* London: Chapman and Hall, 1997.

Beinart, Peter. 'Admit It: The Surge Worked'. *Washington Post* (18 January 2009). Online: www.washingtonpost.com. Accessed 11 January 2010.

Belforte, Juan E., Veronika Zsiros, Elyse R. Sklar et al. 'Postnatal NMDA Receptor Ablation in Corticolimbic Interneurons Confers Schizophrenia-Like Phenotypes'. *Nature Neuroscience*, 13 (2010): 76–83.

Ben-Amos, Paula Girshick. *The Art of Benin*. London: British Museum Press, 1995.

Bereiter, Carl and Marlene Scardamalia. *The Psychology of Written Composition*. Hillsdale, NJ: Erlbaum, 1987.

Berger, Molly W. 'Manon of Second Life: Teaching in the Virtual World'. *Technology and Culture*, 49 (2008): 430–441.

Besredka, A. *The Story of an Idea: E. Metchnikoff's Work*. Translated by Abraham Rivenson and Rolf Oestreicher. Bend, OR: Maverick Publications, 1979.

Betchov, Robert. *Stability of Parallel Flows*. New York: Academic Press, 1967.

Beuys, Joseph. *Actions, Vitrines, Environments*. Exhibition guide edited by Sean Rainbird. London: Tate Modern, 2005.

Bigelow, Ron. *Transcript for Highlight and Shadow Values by Channel*. Ron Bigelow Photography, online: http://www.ronbigelow.com. Accessed 28 October 2010.

Biemann, Ursula. *Mission Reports: Artistic Practice in the Field, Video Works 1998–2008*. Bristol: Arnolfini / Bildmuseet, 2007.

Bird, Alexander. 'Lowe on A Posteriori Essentialism'. *Analysis*, 68 (2008): 336–44.

Bishop, Elizabeth. *Exchanging Hats: Paintings*. Edited with an introduction by William Benton. Manchester, UK: Carcanet, 1997.

Bissell, David. 'Visualising Everyday Geographies: Practices of Vision through Travel-Time'. *Transactions of the Institute of British Geographers*, 34 (2008): 42–60.

Black, Jeanette D. *The Blathwayt Atlas* (volume 2 commentary). Providence, RI: Brown University Press, 1975.

Black, Jeremy. *A History of The British Isles*. New York: St Martin's Press, 1996.

Bloch, Raymond. *Etruscan Art*. London: Thames & Hudson, 1959.

Bloom, Kerry and Ajit Joglekar. 'Towards Building a Chromosome Segregation Machine'. *Nature*, 463 (28 January 2010): 446–455.

Blouin Jr., Francis X., ed. *Vatican Archives: an Inventory and Guide to Historical Documents of the Holy See*. Oxford: Oxford University Press, 1998.

Bollen, Georg. 'Weighing up the Superheavies'. *Nature*, 463 (11 February 2010): 740–741.

Bolton, Charles F., Robert Chen, Eeelco F.M. Wijdicks, Udo A. Zifko and Michael H. Silber. *Neurology of Breathing*. Philadelphia, PA: Butterworth Heinemann, 2004.

Bordahl, Vibeke. 'A Drum Tale on "Wu Song Fights the Tiger"'. *Chinoperl Papers*, 27 (2007): 61–106.

Borger, Julian and Declan Walsh. 'Eight Years and Counting'. *Guardian* (25 June 2009). Online: www.guardian.co.uk. Accessed 11 January 2010.

Bowker, Geoffrey C. *Memory Practices in the Sciences*. Cambridge, MA: MIT Press, 2005.

Bradley, Pat. 'Animation Made Easy'. *Computer Arts*, 115 (2009): 71–73.

Bremner, Rory, presenter. *Speak on the Dotted Line*. BBC Radio 4, broadcast 10.30–11 am,16 June 2007.

British Museum. *Crafting Beauty in Modern Japan*. Display texts, exhibition guide. London, 19 July–21 October 2007.

Broglio, Ron. 'Heidegger's Shepherd of Being and Nietzsche's Satyr'. *New Formations*, 64 (2008): 124–136.

Brounéus, Karen. 'The Trauma of Truth Telling: Effects of Witnessing in the Rwandan Gacaca Courts on Psychological Health'. *Journal of Conflict Resolution*, 54, 3 (2010): 408–437.

Brown, Guy. *The Living End: the Future of Death, Ageing and Immortality*. London: Macmillan, 2008.

Brown, Robin C. 'Tropical Prehistoric Florida'. *Bulletin of Primitive Technology*, 38 (2009): 10–16.

Browne, Julie, and Eric S. Dickson. '"We Don't Talk to Terrorists": On the Rhetoric and Practice of Secret Negotiations'. *Journal of Conflict Resolution*, 54, 3 (2010): 379–407.

Bryon, Mike. *How to Pass Diagrammatic Reasoning Tests*. London: Kogan Page, 2008.

Buchen, Lizzie. 'Disease Epidemic Killing Only US Bats'. *Nature*, 463 (14 January 2010): 144.

—. 'What will the Next Solar Cycle Bring'. *Nature*, 463 (28 January 2010): 414–415.

—. 'Famous Brain set to go Under the Knife'. *Nature*, 462 (26 November 2009): 403.

Buckley, Steven, ed. 'American Film Market'. *Stills*, 30 (1987): 40–75.

Buijsen, Huub. *The Simplicity of Dementia: A Guide for Family and Carers*. London: Jessica Kingsley, 2005.

Bullard, R.K. and R.W. Dixon Gough. *Britain from Space: an Atlas of Landsat Images*. London: Taylor & Francis, 1985.

Bullock, Alan and Stephen Trombley. *The New Fontana Dictionary of Modern Thought*. London: Harper Collins, 1999.

Bunyard, Peter and Edward Goldsmith, eds. *Gaia: the Thesis, the Mechanisms and the Implications*. Camelford, UK: Wadebridge Ecological Centre, 1988.

Bure, Kristjan, ed. *Greenland*. Translated by Reginald Spink. Copenhagen, Denmark: The Royal Danish Ministry for Foreign Affairs, 1961.

Burt, Ronald S. *Structural Holes: The Social Structure of Competition*. Cambridge, MA: Harvard University Press, 1992.

Buruma, Ian. 'Desire in Berlin'. *New York Review of Books* (4 December 2008).

Bury, Stephen, ed. *Breaking the Rules: The Printed Face of the European Avant Garde 1900–1937*. London: The British Library, 2007.

Bush, Robin. *The Book of Exmouth*. Buckingham, UK: Barracuda Books, 1978.

Cage, John. *A Year from Monday: Lectures and Writings*. London: Marion Boyars, 1968.

—. *Silence: Lectures and Writings*. London: Marion Boyars, 1968.

Campbell, Peter. 'At the V&A'. *London Review of Books* (22 April 2010): 21.

Carocci, Max. 'Clad with the "Hair of Trees": A History of Native American Spanish Moss Textile Industries'. *Textile History*, 41, 1, (2010): 3–27.

Carrell, Severin. 'Pay £4m or the Leonardo Gets it: Lawyer Accused of Extortion over Stolen Painting'. *Guardian* (2 March 2010): 3.

Carter, Rita. *Mapping the Mind*. London: Weidenfeld and Nicolson, 1998.

Cave, Damien, Steven Farrell, Ahmad Fadam et al. 'Assessing the Surge: A Survey of Baghdad Neighbourhoods'. New York Times (6 September 2007). Online: www.nytimes.com. Accessed 11 January 2010.

Chaffers, William. *The Keramic Gallery: Containing Several Hundred Illustrations of Rare Curious and Choice Examples of Pottery and Porcelain from the Earliest Times to the Beginnings of the XIXth Century, with Historical Notices and Descriptions*. London: Gibbings, 1907.

Chan, Kara and James U. McNeal. *Advertising to Children in China*. Hong Kong: The Chinese University of Hong Kong, 2004.

Chambers, John. 'More Giants in Focus'. *Nature*, 467 (23 September 2010): 386–7.

Chekhov, Michael. *The Path of the Actor*. Edited by Andrei Kirilov and Bella Merlin. London: Routledge, 2005.

Chivers, Sam. 'Fair Ground Graphics'. *Computer Arts*, 115 (2005): 57–61.

Clark, T.J. 'Living Death'. *London Review of Books* (7 January 2010): 10–12.

Cohen, Bruce E. 'Beyond Fluorescence'. *Nature*, 467 (23 September 2010): 407–8.

Cohen, Josh. *How to Read Freud*. London: Granta, 2005.

Coleman, Samuel. *Family Planning in Japanese Society*. Princeton, NJ: Princeton University Press, 1991.

Coles, K. Adlard. *Channel Harbours and Anchorages*. London: Macmillan, 1982.

Collins, Jeff. *Heidegger and the Nazis*. Cambridge, UK: Icon Books, 2000.

Collings, Matthew. 'High and Lowe'. *Modern Painters*, 68 (2007): 44–47.

Combs, Richard. 'Heart of Midnight'. *Monthly Film Bulletin*, 661 (1989): 50–51.

Conrad, Peter. 'The Many Faces of Pablo Picasso'. *Observer Review* (8 February 2009): 4.

Conte, Joseph M. *Unending Design: The Forms of Postmodern Poetry*. Ithaca, NY: Cornell University Press, 1991.

Cook, Christopher. *Recent Experimental Graphites*. Yokohama, Japan: Yokohama Museum of Art, 2005.

Cook, Pam. 'The Accused'. *Monthly Film Bulletin*, 661 (1989): 35–36.

Cooper, David E. and Joy A. Palmer, eds. *Just Environments: Intergenerational, International and Interspecies Issues*. London: Routledge, 1995.

Corbett, Stephen. *The Space Saver Book*. Leicester, UK: Abbeydale, 1999.

Cordingley, E.S. and H. Dai. 'Encapsulation – an Issue for Legacy Systems'. *BT Technology Journal*, 11 (1993): 52–64.

Coronato, Antonio, Massimo Esposito and Giuseppe De Pietro. 'A Multimodal Semantic Location Service for Intelligent Environments: an Application for Smart Hospitals'. *Personal and Ubiquitous Computing*, 13 (2009): 527–538.

Cotterell, Arthur. *The First Emperor of China*. London: Macmillan, 1981.

Coupe, Lawrence, ed. *The Green Studies Reader: from Romanticism to Ecocriticism*. London: Routledge, 2000.

Craig, Catherine L. *Spiderwebs and Silk: Tracing Evolution from Molecules to Genes to Phenotypes*. Oxford: Oxford University Press, 2003.

Craig, James. *Designing with Type: the Essential Guide to Typography* (1971). New York: Watson Guptill, 2006.

Cressey, Daniel. 'Masterly Deceptions Brought to Light'. *Nature*, 466 (1 July 2010): 34.

Crill, Rosemary and Kapil Jariwala, eds. *The Indian Portrait 1560–1860*. London: National Portrait Gallery, 2010.

Crocker, Jan. *Drake's Place, Reservoir and Gardens: A Brief History*. Plymouth, UK: Greenbank Community Association, 2006.

Crooks, Paul. *A Tree Without Roots: the Guide to Tracing British, African and Asian Caribbean Ancestry*. London: Arcadia, 2008.

Crosfield, John F. *A History of the Cadbury Family.* Cambridge, UK: privately printed, 1985.

Crouch, Colin and David Marquand, eds. *Ethics and Markets: Cooperation and Competition within Capitalist Economies.* Oxford: Blackwell, 1993.

Cubitt, Sean. 'The Sound of Sunlight'. *Screen*, 57 (2010): 118–128.

Cumming, W.P., R.A. Skelton and D.B. Quinn. *The Discovery of North America.* London: Elek, 1971.

Cunnliffe, Barry. *The Oxford Illustrated Prehistory of Europe.* Oxford: Oxford University Press, 1994.

Curtis, Edward S. *In a Sacred Manner We Live: Photographs of the North American Indian.* Introduction and commentary by Don B. Fowler. Barre, MA: Barre Publishing, 1972.

Cyranoski, David. 'China's Crystal Cache'. *Nature*, 457 (19 February 2009): 953–955.

Dalton, Rex. 'Icy Resolve'. *Nature*, 463 (11 February 2010): 724–725.

Darwin, Charles. *The Voyage of the Beagle* (1845). Vercelli, Italy: White Star, 2006.

—. *The Origin of Species by Means of Natural Selection or The Preservation of Favoured Races in the Struggle for Life* (1859, revd 6th ed 1872).London: Senate, 1994.

Davis, Nick, presenter and Eve Streeter, producer. *Haiti: Phoning Home.* BBC Radio 4, broadcast 11am, 26 March 2010.

Day, Ronald E. 'The Erasure and Construction of History for the Information Age: Positivism and its Critics'. In Lauren Rabinovitz and Adam Geil, eds. *Memory Bytes: History, Technology and Digital Culture.* Durham, NC: Duke University Press, 2004, 76–96.

Dear, Peter. *The Intelligibility of Nature: How Science Makes Sense of the World.* Chicago, IL: University of Chicago Press, 2006.

Demers, Michael N. *Fundamentals of Geographic Information Systems.* Hoboken, NJ: Wiley, 2009.

Derrida, Jacques. *Writing and Difference.* Translated by Alan Bass. London: Routledge, 2001.

Dewey, John. 'The Existential Matrix of Inquiry: Cultural'. In Andrea Nye, ed. *Philosophy of Language: The Big Questions.* Oxford: Blackwell, 1998.

Dickenson, Donna. *Body Shopping: the Economy Fuelled by Flesh and Blood.* Oxford: Oneworld, 2008.

Dolan, Emily I. 'The Origins of the *Orchestra Machine*'. *Current Musicology*, 76 (2003): 7–23.

Donnelly, James S. *The Great Irish Potato Famine.* Stroud, UK: Sutton, 2001.

Doucet, Lyse. *Crossing Continents: Afghanistan.* BBC Radio 4, broadcast 10am, 20 August 2009. Accessed online 14 January 2010.

Driver, Leigh. *The Lost Villages of England.* London: New Holland, 2006.

Dudia, Yadin. *Memory from A to Z: Keywords, Concepts and Beyond.* Oxford: Oxford University Press, 2002.

Dyson, Freeman J. *The Sun, the Genome, the Internet: Tools of Scientific Revolutions*. New York: Oxford University Press, 1999.

Eagleton, Terry. 'Determinacy Kills'. Review of *Theodor Adorno: One Last Genius* by Detlev Claussen. *London Review of Books* (19 June 2008): 9–10.

Eckmann, Paul and Erika L. Rosenberg. *What the Face Reveals: Basic and Applied Studies of Spontaneous Expression Using the Facial Action Coding System* (FACS). Oxford: Oxford University Press, 2005.

Edwards, Brent Hayes. 'Inside the Barrel'. *London Review of Books* (10 September 2009): 23–24.

Eglash, Ron. *African Fractals: Modern Computing and Indigenous Design.* New Brunswick, NJ: Rutgers University Press, 2002.

Elger, Dietmar, ed. Gerhard Richter: *Landscapes*. Ostfildern-Ruit, Germany: Cantz Verlag, 1998.

Elliott, Doug. 'Coconut Frond Basket'. *Bulletin of Primitive Technology*, 38 (2009): 27–29.

Elliott, Katharine J. and Wayne T. Swank. 'Long-Term Changes in Forest Composition and Diversity following early Logging (1919–1923) and the Decline of American Chestnut (Castanea dentata)'. *Plant Ecology*, 197 (2008): 155–172.

Ellis, John, ed. *British Film Institute Productions 1951–1976*. London: British Film Institute, 1977.

Elpel, Thomas J. 'Cultural Evolution: Technology, Population and Social-Political Organisation'. *Bulletin of Primitive Technology*, 38 (2009): 61–68.

Emery, Anthony. *Dartington Hall.* Oxford: Clarendon, 1970.

Enright, Anne. 'Sinking by Inches'. *London Review of Books* (7 January 2010): 21–22.

Epstein, A.L. 'Tolai Sorcery and Change'. *Ethnology*, 34 (1999): 273–95.

Epstein, Richard A. 'Unilateral Practices and the Dominant Firm: The European Community and the United States'. In Stephen F. Copp, ed. *The Legal Foundations of Free Markets*. London, Institute of Economic Affairs, 2005.

Eriksson, Eva, Thomas Riisgard Hansen and Andreas Lykke-Olesen. 'Movement-Based Interaction in Camera Spaces: A Conceptual Framework'. *Personal and Ubiquitous Computing*, 11 (2007): 621–632.

European Space Agency. 'Satellite Eye on Earth, December 2009'. 16 pictures. *Guardian Online*: www.guardian.co.uk/environmentgallery/2010/jan/04/satellite-eye-on-earth/. Accessed 11 January 2010.

Evans, John G. *Land and Archeology: Histories of Human Environment in the British Isles*. Stroud, UK: Tempus, 1999.

Evans, Robin. *A Rational Plan for Softening the Mind: Prison Architecture in the 18th and 19th Centuries*. PhD Thesis, University of Essex, 1975.

Falk, Donald A. Margaret A. Palmer and Joy B. Zedler, eds. *Foundations of Restoration Ecology*. Washington, DC: Island Press, 2006.

Fara, Delia Graff. 'Profiling Interest Relativity'. *Analysis*, 68 (2008): 326–35.

Festinger, Leon. *A Theory of Cognitive Dissonance*. Stanford, CA: Stanford University Press, 1957.

Fink, Torsten and Otto Kasten. 'An Extensible Architecture-Based Framework for Coordination Languages'. *International Journal of Cooperative Information Systems*, 13 (2004): 37–61.

Finlay, Ian Hamilton. *Works in Europe 1972–1995*. Edited by Felix Herausgegeben von Zdenek and Pia Simik. Ostfildern-Ruit, Germany: Cantz Verlag, 1995.

Firestone, Chaz. 'Icy Hunt for Old Air: Antarctic Drilling Project Aims for a Definitive Record of Climate'. *Nature*, 463 (28 January 2010): 408.

Fisher, Richard. 'A Recipe for Stardom'. *New Scientist* (19–26 December 2009 and 2 January 2010): 74–75.

Fowles, John. *Shipwreck*. London: Cape, 1974.

Foyle, Andrew. *Bristol*. New Haven, CT: Yale University Press, 2004.

Fried, Ben. 'A Conversation with Phil Smoot'. *ACM Queue*, 3 (2005): 16–24.

Fuller, Graham. 'Reel to Real'. *Stills*, 30 (1987): 76–82.

Ganti, Tibor. *The Principles of Life*. Commentary by James Griesemer and Eörs Szathmáry. Oxford: Oxford University Press, 2003.

Gaskill, Melissa. 'What Will Get Sick from the Slick'. *Nature*, 466 (1 July 2010): 14–15.

Gaustad, Edwin S, ed. *Memoirs of the Spirit: American Religious Autobiography from Jonathan Edwards to Maya Angelou*. Grand Rapids, MI: Eermans, 1999.

Geiger, Roger L. 'The Riddle of the Valley'. *Minerva*, 46 (2008): 127–132.

Gellately, Robert. *Backing Hitler: Consent and Coercion in Nazi Germany*. Oxford: Oxford University Press, 2001.

Gellner, Ernest. *Plough, Sword and Book: The Structure of Human History*. London: Collins Harvill, 1988.

Gigliotti, Simon and Berel Lang, eds. *The Holocaust: A Reader*. Oxford: Blackwell, 2005.

Gillet-Chanlet, Fabien and Gaël Durand. 'Ice-Sheet Advance in Antarctica'. *Nature*, 467 (14 October 2010): 794–795.

Gilman, Victoria. 'Photo in the News: Female Android Debuts in South Korea'. *National Geographic News*. Online: news.nationalgeographic. com/ news/2006/05/android-korea-1.html. Accessed 5 September 2007.

Glass, Jesse. *The Witness: Slavery in Nineteenth-Century Carroll County, Maryland.* Shin-Urayasu, Japan: Meikai University Press, 2004.

Gompertz, Godfrey St. George Montagne. *Chinese Celadon Wares.* London: Faber, 1958.

Goren, Y. and A.N. Goring-Morris. 'Early Pyrotechnology in the Near East: Experimental Lime-Plaster Production at the Pre-Pottery Neolithic B Site of Kfar HaHoresh, Israel'. *Geoarchaeology: An International Journal*, 23 (2008): 779–798.

Grand, Steve. *Growing Up with Lucy: How to Build an Android in Twenty Easy Steps.* London: Weidenfeld & Nicholson, 2003.

Gray, Todd, ed. *Exeter Engraved: The Secular City.* Exeter, UK: Mint Press, 2000.

—. *Lost Exeter: Five Centuries of Change.* Exeter, UK: Mint Press, 2002.

Grebanier, Joseph. *Chinese Stoneware Glazes.* London: Pitman, 1975.

Greenberg, Michael. 'Just Remember This'. *New York Review of Books* (4 December 2008).

Grunenberg, Christoph, and Laurence Sillars, eds. *Peter Blake: A Retrospective.* Liverpool, UK: Tate Liverpool, 2007.

Gullickson, Gay L. *Spinners and Weavers of Auffay: Rural Industry and the Sexual Division of Labour in a French Village, 1750–1850.* Cambridge, UK: Cambridge University Press, 1986.

Gunn, Alan. *Essential Forensic Biology.* Chichester, UK: Wiley Blackwell, 2009.

Guy, Neil, Kevin O'Brien, Brian Hodkinson, Kenneth Wiggins et al. 'Castles of North Munster, Limerick, April 2009'. *Castle Studies Group Journal*, 23 (2009–10): 4–116.

Haddock, Michael John: *Wildflowers and Grasses of Kansas: A Field Guide.* Lawrence, KS: University Press of Kansas, 2005.

Hall, Michael. *Leaving Home: A Conducted Tour of Twentieth-Century Music with Simon Rattle.* London: Faber, 1996.

Hamilton, Henry W. and Jean Tyree Hamilton. *The Sioux of the Rosebud: A History in Pictures.* Photographs by John A. Anderson. Norman, OK: University of Oklahoma Press, 1971.

Hann, C. M., ed. *Property Relations: Renewing the Anthropological Tradition.* Cambridge, UK: Cambridge University Press, 1998.

Hansen, Mogens Herman. *Polis: An Introduction to the Ancient Greek City-State.* Oxford: Oxford University Press, 2006.

Harper, Joel T., John H. Bradford, Neil F. Humphrey and Toby W. Meierbachtol. 'Vertical Extension of the Subglacial Drainage System into Basal Crevasses'. *Nature*, 467 (30 September 2010): 579–582.

Hauser, Marc D. 'The Possibility of Impossible Cultures'. *Nature*, 460 (9 September 2009): 190–196.

Hayden, Erika Check. 'The Most Vulnerable Brains'. *Nature*, 463 (14 January 2010): 154–156.

Henderson, F.M. *Open Channel Flow*. New York: Macmillan, 1966.

Hendy, David. *Life on Air: A History of Radio Four.* Oxford: Oxford University Press, 2007.

Hepburn, Alexa and Steven D. Brown. 'Teacher Stress and the Management of Accountability'. *Human Relations*, 54 (2001): 691–715.

Herman, S., D. Grange, Y. Pelet et al. 'Zero Liquid Discharge Approach in Plating Industry: Treatment of Degreasing Effluents by Electrocoagulation and Anodic Oxidation'. *Water Science and Technology*, 58, 3 (2008): 519–527.

Hippensteel, Scott P. 'Reconstruction of a Civil War Landscape: Little Folly Island, South Carolina'. *Geoarchaelogy: An International Journal*, 23 (2008): 824–841.

Hirakawa, Makiko. 'L2 Acquisition of Japanese Unaccusative Verbs'. *Studies in Second Language Acquisition*, 23, 2 (2001): 221–246.

Hirschberger, Gilad, Victor Florian and Mario Mikulincer. 'The Anxiety Buffering Function of Close Relationships: Mortality Salience Effects on the Readiness to Compromise Mate Selection Standards'. *European Journal of Social Psychology*, 32 (2002): 609–625.

Hochman, Jhan. 'The "Lambs" in The Silence of the Lambs'. In Laurence Coupe, ed. *The Green Studies Reader: From Romanticism to Ecocriticism.* London: Routledge, 2000, 299–301.

Hooper, Rowan. 'Greenhouses on the Red Planet'. *New Scientist* (1 May 2010): 6–7.

Horn, Laurence R. and Gregory Ward. *The Handbook of Pragmatics.* Oxford: Blackwell, 2004.

Horsefield, Thomas. *Essay on the Cultivation and Manufacture of Tea, in Java.* Translated from the Dutch by Thomas Horsefield. London: J.L. Cox, 1841.

Hovy, Eduard H. and Yigal Arens, 'Automatic Generation of Formatted Text'. *AAAI-91 Proceedings*. Online: http://www.aaai.org/Papers/AAAI/1991/AAAI91-015.pdf. Accessed 22 April 2010.

Howell, Thomas. *The Avant-Garde Flute: A Handbook for Composers and Flautists.* Berkeley, CA: University of California Press, 1974.

Hunter, Caroline and Siobham McGrath. *Homeless Persons: Arden's Guide to the Housing Act 1985 Part III* (fourth edition). London: Legal Action Group, 1992.

Hurwitz, Brian and Aziz Sheik, eds. *Health Care Errors and Patient Safety.* Oxford: Blackwell, 2009.

Inagaki, Shunji. 'Motion Verbs with Goal PPs in the L2 Acquisition of English and Japanese'. *Studies in Second Language Acquisition*, 23, 2 (2001): 153–170.

Ingham, Christine. *Panic Attacks.* London: Thorsons, 2000.

Ingold, Tim, David Riches and James Woodburn, eds. *Hunters and Gatherers 1: History, Evolution and Social Change.* Oxford: Berg, 1988.

Ives, Rob. *Using Tiling Generators in School.* Derby, UK: Association of Teachers of Mathematics, 1994.

Jabbi, Mhemba, Jojanneke Bastiaansen and Christian Keysers. 'A Common Anterior Insula Representation of Disgust Observation'. *Plosone*, 3, 8 (2008). Online: www.plosone.org/article/info%3Adoi%2F10.1371%2F journal.pone.0002939. Accessed 22 October 2010.

Jacobs, Harriet. *Incidents in the Life of a Slave Girl.* Edited by Nellie Mckay and Frances Smith Foster. New York: Norton, 2001.

Jenkins, Russell. 'Boss Left His Cockle Pickers to Die in Sea, Jury is Told'. *Times Online*, 20 September 2005. www.timesonline.co.uk/tol/news/uk/article668606.ece. Accessed 25 February 2010.

Jones, David K.C. 'Landsliding in the Midlands: A Critical Evaluation of the Contribution of the National Landslide Survey'. *East Midlands Geographer*, 21/22 (1998): 106–125.

Joyce, James. *Anna Livia Plurabelle* (1930). London: Faber, 1997.

Kafetsios, Konstantinos and John B. Nezlek. 'Attachment Styles in Everyday Social Interaction'. *European Journal of Social Psychology*, 32 (2002): 719–735.

Kambe, Sinsuke. 'Emergence and Non-Emergence of Alternating Offers in Bilateral Bargaining'. *International Journal of Game Theory*, 38 (2009): 499–520.

Karp, Peter D., Vinay K. Chaudri and Suzanne M. Paley. 'A Collaborative Environment for Authoring Large Knowledge Bases'. *Journal of Intelligent Information Systems*, 13, 3 (1999): 155–194.

Kasen, Daniel. 'The Supernova has Two Faces'. *Nature*, 466 (1 July 2010): 37–38.

Kemp, Martin. *The Science of Art: Optical Themes in Western Art from Brunelleschi to Seurat.* New Haven, CT: Yale University Press, 1990.

Kenworthy, Chris. 'Super 8 to Video'. *Computer Arts*, 105 (2005): 65–67.

Kerridge, Richard. 'Ecothrillers: Environmental Cliffhangers'. In Laurence Coupe, ed. *The Green Studies Reader: From Romanticism to Ecocriticism.* London: Routledge, 2000, 242–249.

—. 'Climate Change and Contemporary Modernist Poetry'. In Tony Lopez and Anthony Caleshu. *Poetry and Public Language.* Exeter, UK: Shearsman, 2007, 131–148.

Keynes, R.D., ed. *The Beagle Record: Selections from the Original Pictorial Records and Written Accounts of the Voyage of H.M.S. Beagle.* Cambridge, UK: Cambridge University Press, 1979.

Kidder, Norm. 'It all Depends: Being Where You Live'. *Bulletin of Primitive Technology*, 38 (2009): 8.

Kinealy, Christine. *The Great Irish Famine: Impact, Ideology and Rebellion.* Basingstoke, UK: Palgrave, 2002.

—. *Tracing Your Irish Roots.* Belfast, UK: Appletree Press, 1999.

Knill, Emanuel. 'Quantum Computing'. *Nature*, 463 (28 January 2010): 441–443.

Knoch, Habbo. 'The Return of the Images: Photographs of Nazi Crimes and the West German Public in the "Long 1960s"'. In Philip Gassert and Alan E. Steinweis, eds. *Coping with the Nazi Past: West German Debates on Nazism and Generational Conflict, 1955–1975.* Oxford: Berghahn Books, 2006, 31–49.

Kohler, Robert E. *Landscapes and Labscapes: Exploring the Lab-Field Border in Biology.* Chicago, IL: University of Chicago Press, 2002.

Koslowsky, Meni, Joseph Schwarzwald and Shira Keshet. 'Moderators of Social Power Use for In-Group/Out-Group Targets: An Experimental Paradigm'. *Journal of Applied Social Psychology*, 38, 12 (2008): 3036–3052.

Kotz, Liz. 'Poetry from Object to Action'. *Roland*, 2 (2009): 35.

Kubanek, A., M. Koch, C. Sames et al. 'Photon by Photon Feedback Control of a Single Atom Trajectory'. *Nature*, 462 (17 December 2009): 898.

Kuehne, G., H. Bjornland and B. Cheers. 'Identifying Common Traits among Australian Irrigators using Cluster Analysis'. *Water Science and Technology*, 58, 3 (2008): 587–595.

Kurlansky, Mark. *Cod: A Biography of the Fish that Changed the World.* London: Vintage, 1999.

Kuzay, Stephan. 'The Wopao Zhuan and other dramas in Shan'ge and Shidiao Songs from Lake Qing China'. *Chinoperl Papers*, 27 (2007): 141–172.

Ladd, T.D., F. Jelezko and R. Laflamme. 'Quantum Computers'. *Nature*, 464 (4 March 2010): 45–53.

Lambert, David M. and Leon Huynen. 'Face of the Past Reconstructed'. *Nature*, 463 (11 February 2010): 739–740.

Lambert, Olivier, Giovanni Bianucci, Klaas Post, Christian die Muizon, Rodolfo Salas-Gismondi, Mario Urbina and Jelle Reumer. 'The Giant Bite of a New Raptorial Sperm Whale from the Miocene Epoch of Peru'. *Nature*, 466 (1 July 2010): 105–108.

Lane, Nick. 'On the Origin of Bar Code'. *Nature*, 462 (19 November 2009): 272–274.

Laws, Eric. *Tourist Destination Management: Issues, Analysis and Policies.* London: Routledge, 1995.

Leach, Melissa and James Fairhead. *Vaccine Anxieties: Global Science, Child Health and Society.* London: Earthscan, 2007.

Leary, Jim with Gary Brown, James Rackham, Chris Pickard and Richard Hughes. *Tatberht's Lundenwik Archeological Excavations in Middle Saxon London.* London: Pre-Construct Archeology Limited Monograph, 2004.

Lehrer, Jonah. 'Small, Furry … and Smart'. *Nature*, 461 (15 October 2009): 862–864.

Leslie, Thomas. '"As Large as the Situation of the Columns Would Allow:" Building Cladding and Plate Glass in the Chicago Skyscraper 1885–1905'. *Technology and Culture*, 49 (2008): 399–419.

Lester, Anthony. 'Building Blocks'. *Computer Arts*, 105 (2005): 105–107.

Lewty, Simon. *Writing Silence: The Art of Susan Michie.* Corfe Castle, UK: Lacerta, 2008.

Lidz, Theodore. *The Person: His and Her Development Throughout the Life Cycle.* New York: Basic Books, 1983.

Liebregts, Peter. 'Between Alexandria and Rome: Ezra Pound, St. Augustine and the Notion of Amor'. Paper given at the 23rd Ezra Pound International Conference, Rome, 4 July 2009.

Lillteicher, Jürgen. 'West Germany and Compensation for National Socialist Expropriation: The Restitution of Jewish Property, 1947–64'. In Philip Gassert and Alan E. Steinweis, eds. *Coping with the Nazi Past: West German Debates on Nazism and Generational Conflict, 1955–1975.* Oxford: Berghahn Books, 2006, 79–95.

Lincoln, Tim. 'Grass and the X Factor'. *Nature*, 464 (11 March 2010): 172.

Liscomb, Kathlyn Maureen. *Learning from Mount Hua: A Chinese Physician's Illustrated Travel Record and Painting Theory.* Cambridge: Cambridge University Press, 1993.

Lok, Corie. 'Speed Reading'. *Nature*, 463 (28 January 2010): 416–418.

Lollar, Sam A. and Carlton Van Doren. 'US Tourist Destinations: A History of Desirability'. *Annals of Tourism Research*, 18 (1991): 622–638.

Lomas, Kathryn, Ruth D. Whitehouse and John B. Wilkins, eds. *Literacy and the State in the Ancient Mediterranean.* London: Accordia Research Institute, University of London, 2007.

Long, Pamela O. *Openness, Secrecy, Authorship.* Baltimore, MD: The Johns Hopkins University Press, 2001.

Lopez, Tony and Anthony Caleshu, eds. *Poetry and Public Language.* Exeter, UK: Shearsman, 2007.

Loret, J.F., M. Jousset, S. Robert et al. 'Amoebae-Resisting Bacteria in Drinking Water: Risk Assessment and Management'. *Water Science and Technology*, 58, 3 (2008): 571–577.

Lovelock, James. *The Ages of Gaia: a Biography of our Living Earth*. Oxford: Oxford University Press, 1988.

Lovett, Richard A. 'Why Chile Fared Better than Haiti'. *Nature* (1 March 2010). Online: 10.1038/news.2010.100. Accessed 5 March 2010.

Lucas, Gavin. *Guerrilla Advertising: Unconventional Brand Communication.* London: Laurence King, 2006.

Lyotard, Jean-François. 'Ecology as Discourse of the Secluded'. In Laurence Coupe, ed. *The Green Studies Reader: From Romanticism to Ecocriticism.* London: Routledge, 2000, 135–138.

MacDonald, Neil. 'Party Rivalries Test Strength of Ohrid Peace Deal'. *Financial Times* (5 July 2007).

Macmillan, D.C. and S. Phillip. 'Consumptive and Non-Consumptive Values of Wild Mammals in Britain'. *Mammal Review*, 38 (2008): 189–204.

McCarthy, John. 'What is Artificial Intelligence'. Online: www-formal.stanford.edu/jmc/whatisai/whatisai.html (revised 1 September 2007). Accessed 5 September 2007.

McCollum, Allan (exhibition catalogue). Stedelijk Van Abbemuseum, Eindhoven, 16.9–12.11. 1989; Serpentine Gallery, London, 21.3–29.4.1990; IVAM Centre del Carme, Valencia, 22.5–29.7.1990.

McCormack, Derek P. 'Aerostatic Spacing: on Things Becoming Lighter than Air'. *Transactions of the Institute of British Geographers*, 34 (2008): 25–41.

Mckibben, Bill. 'The Challenge to Environmentalism'. *Daedelus: Journal of the American Academy of Arts and Sciences*, 137, 2 (2008): 5–7.

Major, J. Kenneth. *Finch Brothers' Foundry, Sticklepath, Okehampton.* Newton Abbot, UK: David & Charles, 1967.

Mansfield, Neil J. *Human Response to Vibration.* Boca Raton, FL: CRC Press, 2005.

Mantel, Gerhard. *Cello Technique: Principles and Forms of Movement.* Translated by Barbara Haimberger Thiem. Bloomington, IN: Indiana University Press, 1975.

Mantel, Hilary. 'Someone to Disturb: a Memoir'. *London Review of Books* (1 January 2009): 13–17.

Markham, Adam. *A Brief History of Pollution*. London: Earthscan, 1994.

Marsh, David. 'Mind Your Language'. *Guardian* (5 April 2010): 29.

Marriott, David. 'Spooks/Postmortem TV'. *Journal of Visual Culture,* 4, 3 (2005): 307–327.

Marris, Emma. 'The Genome of the American West'. *Nature* (19 February 2009): 950.

Maschler, Michael, Joss Potters and Hans Reijnierse. 'The Nucleolus of a Standard Tree Game Revisited'. *International Journal of Game Theory*, 39 (2010): 89–104.

Matthews, James. *Histogram Equalization*. Online: www.generation5org/content/2004/histogramEqualisation.asp. Accessed 16 May 2007.

Matthiopoulos, J., S. Smout, A.J. Winship et al. 'Getting Beneath the Surface of Marine Mammal – Fisheries Competition'. *Mammal Review*, 38 (2008): 163–188.

Maxted, Ian. *In Pursuit of Devon's History: A Guide for Local Historians in Devon*. Tiverton, UK: Devon Books, 1997.

Mazullo, Mark. 'Remembering Pop: David Lynch and the Sound of the 60s'. *American Music*, 23 (2005): 493–511.

McCarthy, John. 'What is Artificial Intelligence'. Online: www-formal.stanford.edu/jmc/whatisai/whatisai.html (revised 1 September 2007). Accessed 5 September 2007.

Medley, Margaret. *A Handbook of Chinese Art for Collectors and Students*. London: Bell and Hyman, 1977.

Meehan, Bernard. *The Book of Kells: An Illustrated Introduction to the Manuscript in Trinity College Dublin*. London: Thames and Hudson, 1994.

Meisner, Maurice. *Mao Zedong: A Political and Intellectual Portrait*. Cambridge, UK: Polity: 2007.

Meteorological Service of Canada. *Acid Rain Factsheet*. Online: www.msc-smc.ec.gc.ca/cd/factsheets/acidrain/index_e.cfm. Accessed 5 March 2010.

Middleton, Peter. *Distant Reading: Performance, Readership and Consumption in Contemporary Poetry*. Tuscaloosa, AL: University of Alabama Press, 2005.

Miller, Lawrence W., ed. *Probes and Tags to Study Biomolecular Function*. Weinheim, Germany: Wiley-VCH, 2008.

Milliken, George A. and Dallas E. Johnson. *Analysis of Messy Data, Volume 2: Non-Replicated Experiments*. New York: Van Nostrand Reinhold, 1989.

Moss, Hilary. 'Arrests on Fountain: Students Attacked while Celebrating Last Day'. *Wesleyan Argus* (16 May 2008).

Mueller, Erik T. *Commonsense Reasoning*. San Francisco, CA: Morgan Kaufmann Elsevier, 2006.

Murrell, Duncan. 'Humpback Whales Feeding in Alaska'. 5 Pictures. *Guardian Online*: www.guardian.co.uk/environment/gallery/2010/jan/05/humpback-whales-feeding. Accessed 11 January 2010.

Nagayama, Chikako. 'The Flux of Domesticity and the Exotic in a Wartime Melodrama'. *Signs: Journal of Women in Culture and Society*, 34 (2009): 369–395.

Needham, Joseph. *Science and Civilisation in China. Volume 1, Introductory Orientations*. Cambridge, UK: Cambridge University Press, 1975.

Nesvorny, David. 'Accidental Investigation'. *Nature*, 467 (14 October 2010): 792.

Nichols, J. and B. A. Myers. 'Creating a Lightweight User Interface Description Language'. *Transactions on Computer-Human Interaction*, 16, 4 (2009): 17–37

Nicholls, Peter. *Ezra Pound: Politics, Economics and Writing, A Study of The Cantos*. Atlantic Highlands, NJ: Humanities Press, 1984.

Norfolk, Simon. *Bleed*. Stockport: Dewi Lewis: 2006

Nussbaum, Allen. *Field Theory*. Columbus, OH: Charles E. Merrill, 1966.

Nyamadzawo, C., M.K. Shukla and R. Lal. 'Spatial Variability of Total Soil Carbon and Nitrogen Stocks for some Reclaimed Minesoils of Southeastern Ohio'. *Land Degradation and Development*, 19 (2008): 275–278.

Nye, Andrea. *Philosophy of Language: The Big Questions*. Oxford: Blackwell, 1998.

O'Crohan, Tomás. *The Islandman*. Translated from the Irish by Robin Flower. Oxford: Oxford University Press, 1951.

O'Hagan, Andrew. 'Goodbye Moon'. *London Review of Books* (25 February 2010): 13–14.

O'Toole, J., M. Sinclair, C. Diaper and K. Leder. 'Comparative Survival of Enteric Indicators, E. Coli and Somatic FRNA Bacteriophages on Turf-Grass Irrigated with Recycled Water'. *Water Science and Technology*, 58, 3 (2008): 513–518.

Orians, Gordon H. 'Nature and Human Nature'. *Daedelus: Journal of the American Academy of Arts and Sciences*, 137, 2 (2008): 39–48.

Paluden, Charlotte. '"The Gold House": Military Broadcloth Manufacture in Copenhagen in the Eighteenth Century'. *Textile History and the Military*, 41, 1, Supplement (2010): 31–48.

Panter-Brick, Catherine, Robert H. Layton and Peter Rowley-Conwy, eds. *Hunter-gatherers: an Interdisciplinary Perspective*. Cambridge, UK: Cambridge University Press, 2001.

Panzeri, Stefano, Nicholas Brunel, Nikos K. Logothetis and Christoph Kayser. 'Sensory Neural Codes using Multiplexed Temporal Scales'. *Trends in Neuroscience*, 33 (2010): 111–120.

Parmesan, Camille. 'Where the Wild Things Were'. *Daedelus: Journal of the American Academy of Arts and Sciences*, 137, 2 (2008): 31–38.

Parry, Bruce. *Tribe*. London: Penguin/Michael Joseph, 2007.

Paterno, Fabio, Carmen Santoro and Lucio Davide Spano. 'MARIA: A Universal, Declarative, Multiple Abstraction-Level Language for Service-Oriented Applications in Ubiquitous Environments'. *Transactions on Computer-Human Interaction*, 16, 4 (2009): 19–30 pages.

Paton, Diana. 'Enslaved Women and Slavery before and after 1807'. *History in Focus*, 12 (2007) Slavery. Online: www.history.ac.uk/ihr/Focus/Slavery/articles/Paton.html. Accessed 3 February 2010.

Patterson, Simon. *Black List.* Catalogue essay by David Campany. London: Haunch of Venison, 2006.

Pavilions in the Parks Advisory Service. *Pavilions in the Parks: A Handbook.* London: no date, circa 1966.

Pearce, Fred. *The New Copenhagen Climate Deal.* Gland, Switzerland: World Wide Fund for Nature, 2009.

—. 'Stand and Deliver your Climate Data'. *New Scientist* (19–26 December 2009 and 2 January 2010): 4–5.

Peirce, Gareth. 'The Framing of al-Megrahi'. *London Review of Books* (24 September 2009): 3–8.

Penrose, Antony, ed. *Lee Miller's War: Photographer and Correspondent with the Allies in Europe 1944–45.* London: Thames and Hudson, 1992.

Peppiatt, Michael and Alice Bellony-Rewald. *Imagination's Chamber: Artists and Their Studios.* London: Gordon Fraser, 1983.

Percival, MacIver. *The Fan Book.* London: T. Fisher Unwin, 1920.

Persaud, Shashi, Brendan Fox and Damian Flynn. 'Modelling the Impact of Wind Power Fluctuations on the Load following Capability of an Isolated Thermal Power System'. *Wind Engineering.* 24 (2000): 399–416.

Phillips, Glen, ed. *California Video: Artists and Histories.* Los Angeles, CA: Getty Research Institute, 2008.

Pixar Website. 'How We Do It'. Online: www.pixar.com/howwedoit/index.html. Accessed 23 February 2010.

Pixar Renderman Showcase. 'King Kong: Shading Fur'. Online: renderman.pixar.com/products/whats_renderman/showcase_KingKong.html. Accessed 23 February 2010.

Pleasance, Erin D., Philip J. Stephens, Sarah O'Meara et al. 'A Small-Cell Lung Cancer Genome with Complex Signature of Tobacco Exposure'. *Nature,* 463 (14 January 2010): 184–190.

Porter, Mark, presenter. *Memory Experience: The Results.* BBC Radio 4, broadcast 24 January 07.

Portland, The Duke of. *Men, Women and Things.* London: Faber, 1937.

Pratt, James Norwood. *The Tea Lover's Treasury.* San Ramon, CA: 101 Productions, 1988.

Price, T. Douglas and Gary M. Feinman. *Foundations of Social Inequality.* New York: Plenum Press, 1995.

Prynne, J.H. *Field Notes: 'The Solitary Reaper' and Others.* Cambridge, UK: privately printed, 2007.

—. *To Pollen.* London: Barque Press, 2006.

Quasha, George and Charles Stein. *Tall Ships: Gary Hill's Projective Installations—number 2.* Barrytown, NY: Station Hill Arts, 1997.

Quinn, Anthony. *Jack Vettriano*. London: Pavilion, 2004.

Quirk, Gregory J. and Mohammed R. Milad. 'Editing Out Fear'. *Nature*, 463 (7 January 2010): 36.

Rabinovitz, Lauren. 'More than the Movies'. In Lauren Rabinovitz and Adam Geil, eds. *Memory Bytes: History, Technology and Digital Culture*. Durham, NC: Duke University Press, 2004, 99–125.

Rail Passengers Committee. *What's Happening to Brunel's Railway: The Findings of the Investigation into the Provision of the Great Western Service*. Bristol, UK: Rail Passengers Committee, 2002.

Ramage, C.S. *Monsoon Meteorology*. New York: Academic Press, 1971.

Ramsbotham, David. *Prison-gate: The Shocking State of Britain's Prisons and the Need for Visionary Change*. London: Free Press, 2003.

Rand, N., S.F. Juliao, J.M. Dawson, Y. Floman and D.M. Spengler. 'Cultured Nucleus Polposus Cellsave Capable of Performing Phagocytosis'. *Journal of Bone and Joint Surgery*, 80 (1998): 246.

Rasmussen, Morten, Yingrui Li, Stinus Lindgreen et al. 'Ancient Human Genome Sequence of an Extinct Paleo-Eskimo'. *Nature*, 463 (11 February 2010): 757–762.

Redman, Tim. 'Ezra Pound and Roman Catholicism'. Paper given at the 23rd Ezra Pound International Conference, Rome, 4 July 2009.

Rhoods, Ann Fowler and Timothy A. Block. *Trees of Pennsylvania: A Complete Reference Guide*. Philadelphia, PA: University of Pennsylvania Press, 2005.

Rice, Trevor. *Mathematical Games and Puzzles*. London: Batsford, 1973.

Rickards, Tudor. *Creativity and the Management of Change*. Oxford: Blackwell, 1999.

Riegel, Arthur C. and Peter Kalivas. 'Lack of Inhibition Leads to Abuse'. *Nature* 463 (11 February 2010): 743.

Ritro, Harriet. 'Beasts in the Jungle (or Wherever)'. *Daedelus: Journal of the American Academy of Arts and Sciences*, 137, 2 (2008): 22–30.

Rivas, Javier. 'Friendship Selection'. *International Journal of Game Theory*, 38 (2009): 521–538.

Roberts, Jim. Strutter's *Complete Guide to Clown Makeup*. Colorado Springs, CO: Piccadilly Books, 1991.

Robinson, Andrew. *The Story of Writing*. London: Thames and Hudson, 1995.

Roediger, Virginia More. *Ceremonial Costumes of the Pueblo Indians: their Evolution, Fabrication, and Significance in the Prayer Drama* (1949). Berkeley, CA: University of California Press, 1991.

Rodrigue, Alain. 'Note on an Aterian Flint Projectile Head'. *Lithic Technology*, 29 (2004): 87–88.

Rogers, Daniel. 'Lessons from the Floor'. *ACM Queue*, 3 (2005): 27–37.

Rogers, J. M. *Islamic Art and Design 1500–1700*. London: British Museum, 1983.

Rohlmann, A., G. Bergmann, F. Graichen and H.M. Mayer. 'More Posterior Bone Graft Placement May Reduce the Risk of Pedicle Screw Breakage'. *Journal of Bone and Joint Surgery*, 80 (1998): 239.

Rots, Veerle. 'Prehensile Wear on Flint Tools'. *Lithic Technology*, 29 (2004): 7–32.

Rudkin, Steve. 'Templates, Types and Classes in Open Distributed Processing'. *BT Technology Journal*, 11 (1993): 32–40.

Russell, Edmund and Jennifer Kane. 'The Missing Link: Assessing the Reliability of Internet Citations in History Journals'. *Technology and Culture*, 49 (2008): 420–429.

Russo, Gene. 'Biodiversity's Bright Spot'. *Nature*, 462 (19 November 2009): 266–269.

Sanders, Herbert H. *The World of Japanese Ceramics*. Tokyo: Kodansha, 1967.

Sanderson, Katharine. 'A Whiff of Mystery on Mars'. *Nature*, 463 (28 January 2010): 420–421.

—. 'What to Make with DNA Origami'. *Nature*, 464 (1 March 2010): 158–159.

Saunders, Dave. *Twentieth-Century Advertising*. London: Carlton, 1999.

Scheffler, Israel. *Four Pragmatists: A Critical Introduction to Pierce, James, Mead and Dewey*. London: Routledge, 1974.

Schifter, Alexander, Mathias Höbinger, Johannes Wallner and Helmut Pottmann. 'Packing Circles and Spheres on Surfaces'. *Transactions on Graphics*, 28, 5 (2009): 139 – 8 pages.

Schuler, Christopher, Heiko Schuldt, Can Türker, Roger Weber and Hans-J. Schek. 'Peer-to-Peer Execution of (Transactional) Processes'. International *Journal of Cooperative Information Systems*, 14 (2005): 377–405.

Scott, John. *Who Rules Britain?* Cambridge, UK: Polity Press, 1991.

Scott, Kathleen L. *Dated and Datable English Manuscript Borders circa 1395–1499*. London: The Bibliographical Society and the British Library, 2002.

Seaman, Mark. 'Introduction'. *Secret Agent's Handbook of Special Devices*. Richmond, UK: Public Record Office, 2000.

Seddon, John. *I Want You to Cheat: the Unreasonable Guide to Service and Quality in Organisations*. Buckingham, UK: Vanguard Press, 1992.

Segall, Robert. 'Fertility and Scientific Realism'. *British Journal for the Philosophy of Science*, 59 (2008): 237–246.

Segun, Mabel. *Reader. Theatre: Twelve Plays for Young People*. Lagos, Nigeria: Mabelline Publications, 2006.

Selerie, Gavin. *Le Fanu's Ghost*. Hereford: Five Seasons, 2006.

Self, Will. 'Diary'. *London Review of Books* (25 February 2010): 34–35.

Service d'Exploitation des Sites Touristiques de l'Ariège. *Niaux Cave*. Tarascon sur Ariège, France: Apapoux, 2005.

Shelton, Dinah L. ed. *Encyclopedia of Genocide and Crimes Against Humanity* (3 vols). Detroit, MI: Thomson Gale, 2005.

Sherwood, Marika. 'Britain, Slavery and the Trade in Enslaved Africans'. *History in Focus*, 12 (2007) *Slavery*. Online: www.history.ac.uk/ihr/focus/slavery/articles/sherwood.html. Accessed 3 February 2010.

Shiga, David. 'Wanted: Attractive Asteroid for Visit'. *New Scientist* (1 May 2010): 12.

Shulton, Charles. *Journey into Space: The Host* (radio play). BBC Radio 4, broadcast 27 June 2009.

Shulman, Gordon L., Daniel L.W. Pope, Serguei V. Astafiev et al. 'Right Hemisphere Dominance During Spatial Selective Attention and Target Detection Occurs Outside the Dorsal Frontoparietal Network'. *Journal of Neuroscience*, 30 (2010): 3640–3651.

Sigmundsson, Freysteinn. 'Develop Instruments to Monitor Volcanic Ash Fallou'. (letters), *Nature*, 46 (1 July 2010): 28.

Silliman, Ron. *Paradise*. Providence, RI: Burning Deck, 1985.

Simon, Steven. 'The Price of the Surge'. Online: www.foreignaffairs.com/articles/63398/steve-simon/the-price-of-the-surge. June 2008. Accessed 11 January 2010.

Skerrett, Ian. 'The Pillars of Eclipse'. *ACM Queue*, 4 (2006): 47–49.

Sladen, Mark. 'Poor. Old. Tired. Horse. / Gallery Guide'. *Roland*, 2 (2009): 4–17.

Smit, Tim. *The Lost Gardens of Heligan*. London: Gollancz, 1997.

Smith, A.J.E. *The Moss Flora of Britain and Ireland*. Cambridge, UK: Cambridge University Press, 2004.

Smith, David R. *Masks of Wedlock: Seventeenth-Century Dutch Marriage Portraiture*. Ann Arbor, MI: University of Michigan Research Press, 1982.

Smith, Graham. *Devon and Cornwall Airfields in the Second World War*. Newbury, UK: Countryside Books, 2000.

Smith, Neil and Ianthi-Maria Tsimpli. *The Mind of a Savant: Language Learning and Modularity*. Oxford: Blackwell, 1995.

Smith, Paul and Quentin Allen. *Field Guide to the Trees and Shrubs of the Miombo Woodlands*. Richmond, UK: Kew Royal Botanic Gardens, 2004.

Snell, Reginald. *Dartington: A Short Guide to the Buildings and Architecture of Dartington Hall*. Dartington, UK: The Dartington Hall Trust, 2008.

Snodgrass, Colin, Cecilia Tubiana, Jean-Baptistse Vincent et al. 'A Collision in 2009 as the Origin of the Debris Trail of Asteroid P/2010 AZ'. *Nature*, 467 (14 October 2010): 814–816.

Solomons, Leon M. and Gertrude Stein. 'Normal Motor Automatism'. *Psychological Review*, 3 (1896): 492–512.

Spurrier, Peter. *The Heraldic Art Source Book*. London: Blandford, 1997.

Stein, Gertrude. 'Cultivated Motor Automatism: A Study of Character in its Relation to Attention'. *Psychological Review*, 5 (1898): 295–306.

—. *Look at Me Now and Here I am: Writings and Lectures 1909–45*. Edited by Patricia Meyerowitz. Harmondsworth: Penguin, 1971.

—. *How To Write* (1931). New York: Dover, 1975.

—. *The Autobiography of Alice B. Toklas* (1933). New York: Vintage, 1990.

Stein, Rick. *Taste of the Sea*. London: BBC Books, 1995.

Steiner, Rudolf. *Angels: Selected Lectures by Rudolf Steiner.* Translated by Anna Meuss. London: Rudolf Steiner Press, 1996.

Stiles, Kristine and Peter Selz. *Theories and Documents of Contemporary Art.* Berkeley, CA: University of California Press, 1996.

Stoctman, Mark I. 'Dark-Hot Resonances'. *Nature*, 467 (30 September 2010): 541.

Storr, Robert. *Gerhard Richter: Forty Years of Painting.* New York: Museum of Modern Art, 2002.

Strick, Philip. 'Slipstream', *Monthly Film Bulletin*, 661 (1989): 36–37.

—. 'Future States', *Monthly Film Bulletin*, 661 (1989): 37–40.

Stronge, Susan, ed. *The Arts of the Sikh Kingdoms.* London: V&A Publications, 1999.

Subr, Kartic, Cyril Soler and Fredo Durand. 'Edge-Preserving Multiscale Image Decomposition Based on Local Extrema'. *Transactions on Graphics,* 28, 5 (2009): 147 – 9 pages.

Summers, Elliott. 'Operational Effects of Wind Farm Developments on Air Traffic Control (ATC) Radar Procedures for Glasgow Prestwick International Airport'. *Wind Engineering*, 24 (2000): 431–436.

Sun-Ok Choi, Claire. *The Art of Card Making.* Hove, UK: Apple, 2005.

Sutton, Charles and Andrew McCallum. 'Piecewise Training for Structured Prediction'. *Machine Learning*, 77 (2009): 165–194.

Tallis, Frank. *Understanding Obsessions and Compulsions.* London: Sheldon Press, 1992.

Tanner, Carmen. 'Context Effects in Environmental Judgements'. *Journal of Applied Social Psychology*, 38, 12 (2008): 2759–2786.

Tate Gallery. *Marcel Broodthaers*. London: Tate Gallery, 1980.

Tate Modern. *Rothko: The Late Series*. Exhibition booklet, curated by Achim Borchardt-Hume. London: Tate, 2008.

Taylor, Helen. 'Bernat Klein: An Eye for Colour'. *Textile History*, 41, 1, (2010): 50–69.

Tennant, Adrian. 'Reading Matters: What is Reading'. Online: www.onestopenglish.com/section.asp?docid=154842. Accessed 15 October 2009.

Thomas, Jeanette A., Cynthia F. Moss and Mariane Vater. *Echolocation in Bats and Dolphins*. Chicago, IL: University of Chicago Press, 2004.

Thomson, David. *The Whole Equation: A History of Hollywood.* London: Little, Brown, 2005.

Toga, Arthur W. and John C. Mazziotta. *Brain Mapping: The Methods.* San Diego, CA: Academic Press, 1996.

Tollefson, Jeff. 'Developing Nations Tackle Climate'. *Nature*, 460, (9 July 2009): 158–159.

—. 'A Towering Experiment'. *Nature*, 467 (23 September 2010): 386–387.

—. 'Altered Microbe Makes Biofuel'. *Nature*, 463 (28 January 2010): 409.

Torelli, Mario. *The Etruscans.* London: Thames and Hudson, 2001.

Totten, Michael J. 'In the Wake of the Surge'. *Michael J. Totten's Middle East Journal*, 24 July 2007. Online: www.michaeltotten.com/archives.001497.html. Accessed 11 January 2010.

Treneman, Ann. 'Political Sketch'. *Times* (13 January 2009): 7.

Triscott, Nicola and Rob La Frenais. *Zero Gravity: A Cultural User's Guide.* London: Arts Catalyst, 2005.

Tsuyuzaki, S. and M. Haruki. 'Effects of Microtopography and Erosion on Seedling Colonisation and Survival in the Volcano Usu, Northern Japan, After the 1977–78 Eruptions'. *Land Degradation and Development*, 19 (2008): 233–241.

Ulmschneider, Peter. *Intelligent Life in the Universe*. Heidelberg, Germany: Springer, 2003.

Underwood, Geoffrey and Vivienne Batt. *Reading and Understanding: An Introduction to the Psychology of Reading.* Oxford: Blackwell, 1996.

Vaidya, Binod, Sang-Soo Yeo, Dong-You Choi, Seung Jo Jan. 'Robust and Secure Routing Scheme for Wireless Multihop Network'. *Personal and Ubiquitous Computing*, 13 (2009): 457–469.

Vainker, S.J. *Chinese Pottery and Porcelain from Prehistory to the Present.* London: British Museum, 1991.

Valenstein, Suzanne G. *A Handbook of Chinese Ceramics.* London: Weidenfeld and Nicolson, 1989.

Van Boerdonk, Koen, Rob Tieben, Sietske Klooster and Elise van den Hoven. 'Contact Through Canvas: an Entertaining Encounter'. *Personal and Ubiquitous Computing*, 13 (2009): 551–567.

Vance, Erik. 'The Field Medic'. *Nature*, 466 (1 July 2010): 22–23.

Van Meter, Trevor. 'Pixel Art Animation'. *Computer Arts*, 118 (2006): 58–59.

Vansina, Jan. *Paths in the Rainforests*. London: James Currey, 1990.

Veach, Robert M. *Transplantation Ethics*. Washington, DC: Georgetown University Press, 2000.

Vickery, Amanda. *A History of Private Life, 28, Exporting the Home*. BBC Radio 4, broadcast 3.45pm, 4 November 2009.

Vicious, Kode. 'Vicious XSS'. *ACM Queue*, 3 (2005): 12–15

Vicsek, Tamas. 'Closing in on Evaders'. *Nature*, 466 (1 July 2010): 43–44.

Victoria and Albert Museum. *Quilts 1700–2010* (exhibition notes). London, 20 March to 4 July 2010.

Virtue, John. *London Paintings*. Essays by Simon Schama, Paul Moorhouse and Colin Wiggins. London: National Gallery, 2005.

—. *Last Paintings of London*. Plymouth, UK: University of Plymouth Press, 2007.

Vogler, Thomas A., ed. *Twentieth Century Interpretations of To The Lighthouse: A Collection of Critical Essays*. Englewood Cliffs, NJ: Spectrum Books, 1970.

Vulliamy, Ed. 'The Horror of 1992'. *Guardian* (2 March 2010): 17.

Wallace, Emily Mitchell. 'The Last Diplomatic train from Rome in 1942: Ezra Pound's Passport and his Kafkaesque Nostos'. Paper given at the 23rd Ezra Pound International Conference, Rome, 4 July 2009.

Watanabe, Kozo and Tatsuo Omura. 'Trophic Structure of Stream Macroinvertebrate Communities Revealed by Static Isotope Analysis', *Water Science and Technology*. 58, 3 (2008): 503–512.

Watson, William. *The Genius of China: an Exhibition of Archaeological Finds of the People's Republic of China held at the Royal Academy London, 29 September 1973 to 23 January 1974*. London: Times Newspapers, 1973.

Wellcome Trust. *War and Medicine*. Exhibition text. London: Wellcome Trust, 2008.

—. *Medicine Now*. Exhibition text. London: Wellcome Trust, 2008.

Wenham, Peter. *Watermills*. London: Robert Hale, 1989.

Weseloh, D.V. and B. Collier. 'The Rise of the Double-Crested Cormorant on the Great Lakes'. *Environment Canada*, online: www.on.ec.gc.ca/wildlife/factsheets/fs-cormorants-e.html. Accessed 5 March 2010.

Westman, Mina. 'Stress and Strain Crossover'. *Human Relations*, 54 (2001): 717–751.

Wheeler, Wendy. 'Postscript on Biosemiotics: Reading Beyond Words—and Ecocriticism'. *New Formations*, 64 (2008): 137–154.

Wilkinson, Keith and Chris Stevens. *Environmental Archaeology: Approaches, Techniques and Applications.* Stroud, UK: Tempus, 2003.

Wilkinson, Philip. *The Shock of the Old.* London: Channel 4 Books, 2000.

Willoughby, Pamela R. *Spheroids and Battered Stones in the African Early and Middle Stone Age.* Oxford: British Archaeological Reports, 1987.

Williams, Fred. 'The Ludlow Letter Press Type Caster (from Type and Press, 1984)'. *Eden Workshops: A Bookbinders Resource.* Online: www.edenworkshops.com/type_caster.html. Accessed 29 January 2009.

Wilmer, Valerie. *As Serious as Your Life: John Coltrane and Beyond.* London: Serpent's Tail, 1992.

Wilson, J.C.R. 'Formal Methods in Object Oriented Analysis'. *BT Technology Journal*, 11 (1993): 18–31.

Wittgenstein, Ludwig. *Lectures and Conversations on Aesthetics, Psychology and Religious Belief, compiled from his notes.* Edited by Cyril Barrett. Oxford: Blackwell, 1970.

Wood, Gaby. *Living Dolls: A Magical History of the Quest for Mechanical Life.* London: Faber, 2002.

Wood, Michael. 'At the Movies'. *London Review of Books* (5 June 2008): 23.

—. 'At the Movies'. *London Review of Books* (10 September 2009): 18.

—. 'At the Movies'. *London Review of Books* (28 January 2010): 17.

—. 'At the Movies'. *London Review of Books* (22 April 2010): 29.

World Nuclear Association. *Chernobyl Accident Information.* Online: www.world-nuclear.org/info/chernobyl/inf007print.htm. Accessed 29 August 2006.

Xiao, Jianxiong, Tian Fang, Peng Zhao, Maxime Lhuillier, Long Quan. 'Image-Based Street-Side City Modelling'. *Proceedings of ACM SIGGRAPH Asia 2009, Yokohama, Japan.* New York: ACM, 2009.

Yard, Sally. *Willem de Kooning.* Barcelona, Spain: Ediciones Polígrafa, 1997.

Yuan, Boping and Sally K. Church. *Oxford Starter Chinese Dictionary.* Oxford: Oxford University Press, 2000.

Ziemann, Paul J. 'Phase Matter for Aerosols'. *Nature*, 467 (14 October 2010): 797.

Zhang, Chuan Li, Po Lai Ho, Douglas B. Kintner, Dandan Sun and Shing Yan Chiu. 'Activity-Dependent Regulation of Mitochondrial Motility by Calcium and Na/K-ATPase at Nodes of Ranvier of Myelinated Nerves'. *Journal of Neuroscience*, 30 (2010): 3555–3566.

Index

www.ingramcontent.com/pod-product-compliance
Lightning Source LLC
Chambersburg PA
CBHW022004160426
43197CB00007B/268
9781848611887